"Why another book on the problem of evil? Judging by the volume of scholarly and popular work on this subject in recent decades, this perennial and vexing human question remains very much on our hearts and minds. Every now and again, though, there are truly new treatments that move the ball down the field. This is such a volume. Simultaneously rigorous and sympathetic in its engagement with contemporary defenders of libertarian free will, Williams also contributes fresh insights of his own to a debate in which 'nothing new under the sun' is often the rule. Especially among those of us who think we've already made up their minds on this question, *God Reforms Hearts* not only deserves but demands a serious reading and evaluation."

—Michael Horton, J. Gresham Machen Professor of Systematic Theology and Apologetics, Westminster Seminary California

"The analytical rigor of his exposition, the way in which the argumentation has been structured to progressively sharpen and deepen the focus of the critique, the compelling clarity of his thought and the almost blistering style of his writing, his ingenious ability to invigorate the discussion with metaphor, thought experiments, and examples from ʾʾ ʾary life, and his evident mastery of the rel   e outstanding features of what can right

—   llenbosch University

"The manuscript provides a well-written, critical analysis of the Relational Free Will Defense and is a significant and original contribution to current scholarship in philosophical theology. Even those scholars who (like myself) do not agree with the author's preferred solutions cannot merely dismiss his arguments, but will be necessitated to provide adequate counterarguments in order to uphold their alternative views. In this way the manuscript is a worthy contribution to the current debate. Even his opponents can learn much from his argument."

—Vincent Brümmer, professor, Utrecht University

"Thaddeus Williams has written a sharp, concise, and original study in the fields of biblical studies and theology. His study is on one of the most central issues of Christian theology: how Christians come to love God. It combines the methods of analytical philosophy with thorough biblical exegesis. He has an exceptional mastery of the relevant literature and has proven to be able to integrate discussions of important authors in his own exposition and argumentation."

—Hendrik Vroom, professor, Vrije Universiteit Amsterdam

God Reforms Hearts

Rethinking Free Will and
the Problem of Evil

God
Reforms
Hearts

Rethinking Free Will and
the Problem of Evil

Thaddeus Williams

LEXHAM
ACADEMIC

God Reforms Hearts: Rethinking Free Will and the Problem of Evil

Copyright 2021 Thaddeus Williams

Lexham Academic, an imprint of Lexham Press
1313 Commercial St., Bellingham, WA 98225
LexhamPress.com

Print ISBN 9781683594970
Digital ISBN 9781683594987
Library of Congress Control Number 2021935525

Lexham Editorial: Todd Hains, Abby Salinger, Abigail Stocker, Jim Weaver,
    Mandi Newell
Cover Design: Lydia Dahl
Typesetting: ProjectLuz.com

For Hendrik

Contents

PART I

Evil and the Autonomous Heart

Rethinking Free Will as a Condition of Authentic Love

1.1

The Relational Free Will Defense

Don't let us make imaginary evils, when you know we have so many real ones to encounter.

—*Oliver Goldsmith,* The Good-Natured Man

THE PROBLEMS OF EVIL

A survey conducted by the Barna Research Group revealed that the number one question posed about God by a cross section of American adults is, "Why is there so much pain and suffering in the world?"[1] In my years of teaching philosophy and theology, students have raised no other question with more frequency and urgency. As Proclus stated the question in the fifth century AD, "*Si Deus est, unde malum?*" ("If God exists, whence comes evil?").[2]

---

1. The Omnipoll (Barna Research Group, Ltd., January 1999). Cited in Lee Strobel, *The Case for Faith* (Grand Rapids: Zondervan, 2000), 29.

2. In *Consolation of Philosophy* (I.4.31), Boethius credits this question to an unnamed Greek thinker. According to H. Chadwick, these words "can be securely identified as a

We need neither modern surveys nor ancient sayings to inform us that reconciling the existence of evil with that of a supremely good and powerful Being constitutes an excruciatingly troublesome problem. Evidencing the magnitude of the problem of evil is Barry Whitney's published bibliography entitled *Theodicy*, which cites over 4,200 philosophical and theological works on the topic in the three-decade span between 1960 and 1990.[3] That factors to a new scholarly publication on the problem of evil every 62.4 hours (in English alone), and the trend shows no signs of abating in the new millennium.

Solving the enduring problem of evil in its multiple and mind-bending forms is well beyond the scope of both this work and author. Rather than arriving at definitive answers to the problem(s), *God Reforms Hearts* enters the mass sojourn to encourage progress, however small, in the right direction toward answers.

This work seeks progress by focusing on one of today's dominant strategies for answering evil—the "Relational Free Will Defense." The defining premise of this Defense is the claim that authentic love requires free will. Many scholars, including Gregory Boyd and Vincent Brümmer, champion this claim.[4] Best-selling books, such as Rob Bell's *Love Wins*, echo that love "can't be forced, manipulated, or coerced. It always leaves room for the other to decide."[5] The claim

---

verbatim quotation from Proclus *in Parm* 1056.10–16" (*Boethius* [Oxford: Oxford University Press, 1981], 129).

3. Barry Whitney, *Theodicy* (New York: Garland, 1993).

4. See Gregory Boyd, *Satan and the Problem of Evil* (Downers Grove, IL: InterVarsity, 2001), 29–30; Vincent Brümmer, *The Model of Love: A Study in Philosophical Theology* (Cambridge: Cambridge University Press, 1993), 162–63; and *Atonement, Christology, and the Trinity: Making Sense of Christian Doctrines* (Farnham: Ashgate Publishing, 2005), 29–31. See also Zachary Hayes, *Vision of a Future: A Study of Christian Eschatology* (Collegeville, MN: The Liturgical Press, 1989), 187–88.

5. Rob Bell, *Love Wins: A Book About Heaven, Hell, and the Fate of Every Person Who Ever Lived* (New York: HarperCollins e-books, 2011), 104. The notion that love requires free will is a guiding axiom throughout Bell's work, the underlying and untested presupposition that leads to his controversial conclusions about the nature of hell. Just a few of the many popular books promoting free will as a condition of love include: Lee Strobel, *The Case for Faith*; Philip Yancey, *Reaching for the Invisible God* (Grand Rapids: Zondervan, 2000); Dave Hunt, *What Love Is This?* (Sisters, OR: Loyal Publishing, 2002); and Gregory Boyd, *God of the Possible* (Grand Rapids:: Baker Books, 2000).

that love requires free will has even found expression in mainstream Hollywood films, including *Frailty* (David Kirschner Productions, 2002), *Bruce Almighty* (Universal, 2003), and *The Adjustment Bureau* (Universal, 2011).

Is this pervasive claim of the Relational Free Will Defense philosophically credible? Does it stray from biblical insights into the nature of love, freedom, and evil? Does the claim that love requires free will clash with a robust relational response to evil in its concrete (rather than abstract) forms? These questions, often unasked in the contemporary literature, form the cornerstone around which I have built this work.

Before clarifying the Relational Free Will Defense and developing the questions above, we must first debunk the idea that there is *a* problem of evil. In reality, the theist faces a plurality of problems with evil. First, we may discern diverse problems in the abstract realm.

(1) *Abstract Problems of Evil in Logical Form.* J. L. Mackie has famously argued that the claims "evil exists" and "an all-good, all-powerful God exists" are logically incompatible.[6] In the famous words of David Hume, "Is he willing to prevent evil, but not able? Then he is impotent. Is he able but not willing? Then he is malevolent. Is he both willing and able? Whence then is evil?"[7] Here the theist faces what is known as the "deductive problem of evil." How should the theist respond to the philosophical claim that it is logically *impossible* for both God and evil to exist?

(2) *Abstract Problems of Evil in Evidential Form.* William Rowe argues that evil's existence in the world, along with its

---

6. According to Mackie, it can be demonstrated that "religious beliefs ... are positively irrational, that the several parts of essential theological doctrine are inconsistent with one another" ("Evil and Omnipotence," *Mind* 64 [1955]: 200–12, 200). The "parts of theological doctrine [that] are inconsistent with one another" in Mackie's argument are God's omnipotence, His omnibenevolence, and evil's existence.

7. David Hume, *Dialogues Concerning Natural Religion*, ed. Norman Kemp Smith (Indianapolis: Bobbs-Merril, 1980), 198.

heinousness and apparent senselessness, render God's existence not logically impossible but highly improbable.[8] This is known as the "inductive problem of evil," which takes diverse shapes and forms.[9] How should the theist respond to philosophical claims that God's existence is *improbable*, given evil as we encounter it in the world?

(3) *Abstract Problems of Evil in Natural Form.* A philosopher could draw a distinction between what Hitler has done and what a hurricane has done, evils caused by persons in contrast to those caused by impersonal forces of nature. There are not only problems of moral evil but also problems of what philosophers often call "natural evil" (e.g., earthquakes, tsunamis, hurricanes, droughts, and Sudden Infant Death Syndrome). Natural evil arguments can also take either deductive or inductive forms.

Moreover, the abstract philosophical problems outlined above are not identical to the personal problems faced in the wake of a bleak medical diagnosis, a broken relationship, an extended season of God's hiddenness, or any other personal encounter with the effects of the fall in a post-Genesis 3 world. Here is "the question mark turned like a fishhook in the human heart,"[10] to quote novelist Peter De Vries.

---

8. See William Rowe, "The Problem of Evil and Some Varieties of Atheism," in *The Evidential Argument from Evil*, ed. Daniel Howard-Snyder (Bloomington: Indiana University Press, 1996), 1–11.

9. Rowe says,

> It is as misleading to speak of *the* evidential argument from evil as it is to speak of *the* cosmological argument. Just as there are distinct arguments that qualify as cosmological arguments, there are distinct arguments that qualify as evidential arguments from evil." ("The Evidential Argument from Evil: A Second Look," in *The Evidential Argument from Evil*, 262)

Paul Draper distinguishes between the kind of evidential arguments forwarded by Rowe and what he calls "Humean" evidential arguments. These arguments "do not rely, either explicitly or implicitly, on a premise asserting that an omnipotent and omniscient being would probably not have a morally sufficient reason to permit certain facts about good and evil" ("The Skeptical Theist," in *The Evidential Argument from Evil*, 178).

10. Peter De Vries, *The Blood of the Lamb* (Chicago: University of Chicago Press, 2005), 243.

Such problems are not a matter of neat logical syllogisms arranged in black and white in a philosopher's text. They are messier, often logic-defying problems that persist in a dizzying array of dark shades in a sufferer's heart. We may add to the abstract problems the following concrete problems of evil.

(4) *Concrete Problems of Evil in Intra-Fide Emotional Form.* The sufferer may be a believer suffering from *inside* the pale of faith (*intra-fide*). In this case, the concrete problem is a distinct problem of *continuing* to trust the God in whom one has a positive belief and prior relational commitment. It is the form that C. S. Lewis articulated with such vulnerable honesty in *A Grief Observed* shortly after cancer claimed his beloved wife.[11] Long before Lewis, David and the Hebrew prophets wrestled with the concrete problems of evil in their *intra-fide* emotional form (Pss 10; 13; 35; 88; Lam 3; Hab 1).

(5) *Concrete Problems of Evil in Extra-Fide Emotional Form.* Conversely, the sufferer may suffer from *outside* the pale of faith (*extra-fide*). In this case, the concrete problem forms more of a subjective blockade to *initiating* trust towards God in whom one lacks any positive belief or prior relational commitment. It is a rejection of God motivated by emotional encounters with evil, independent of abstract philosophical considerations. As Dostoyevsky's tortured character, Ivan Karamazov, responds to a case for God's existence, "I would rather remain with my unavenged suffering and unsatisfied indignation, even if I am wrong."[12]

---

11. Other valuable works on the *intra-fide* emotional form of concrete problems of evil include Joni Eareckson-Tada, *When God Weeps: Why Our Suffering Matters to the Almighty* (Grand Rapids: Zondervan, 2000), and D. A. Carson, *How Long, Oh Lord? Reflections on Suffering and Evil*, 2nd ed. (Grand Rapids: Baker Books, 2006).

12. Fyodor Dostoyevsky, *The Brothers Karamazov*, tr. Constance Garnett (Lawrence, KS: Digireads.com Publishing, 2009), 167.

Here we are confronted with the emotional problems of evil, which multiply with virtually every experience of human heartache and may vary significantly in their intensity, effects, and implicit conclusions from heart to heart.[13] The failure to distinguish these concrete problems from the less personal and more abstract philosophical problems of evil can lead to a wearying assault of misguided and irrelevant counsel. Imagine, for example, expounding Augustinian privationism (the notion that evil is not a real thing but lacks positive ontological status) in an effort to console parents who have lost a child at the hands of a drunk driver. For them, evil is a very real, concrete thing.

We may add to the domain of concrete problems the following existential problems of how to answer the evils in our own lives, cultural contexts, and the invisible world at large.

(6) *Concrete Problems of Evil in Personal Existential Form.* How do we make moral progress against the lingering, potent, self-destructive, internal bent toward moral evil, or in the Pauline ethical vocabulary, "the old man" (Eph 4:22–24, Col 3:9–10) or "the flesh" (Rom 8:12–13; Gal 5:16–24)?[14] Without ongoing engagement with this question, we ourselves become part of the problems rather than part of the solutions.

(7) *Concrete Problems of Evil in Cultural Existential Form.* Within cultural contexts, how do we confront the forceful and multi-fronted *blitzkrieg* of social injustices across the contemporary world? This includes large-scale problems like human trafficking, genocide, environmental exploitation, terrorism, the dehumanizing effects of consumerism, governmental and

---

13. On whether emotional problems of evil serve as "defeaters" for theistic belief see Alvin Plantinga, *Warranted Christian Belief* (Oxford: Oxford University Press, 2000), 483.

14. For a classic treatment of this problem, see John Owen, *The Mortification of Sin* (Edinburgh: Banner of Truth, 2004).

religious corruption, and any other problems we can all too easily enumerate.[15]

(8) Concrete Problems of Evil in Spiritual Existential Form. Add to all the above the problem of the invisible world within a biblical view of reality. Paul says in Ephesians 6:12:

> For we do not wrestle against flesh and blood, but against the rulers, against the authorities, against the cosmic powers over this present darkness, against the spiritual forces of evil in the heavenly places.

To borrow Paul's vivid competitive combat term, how should believers "wrestle" (πάλη) against spiritual evil?[16]

A portrait emerges in which evil represents not a singular problem but a complex web of problems that entangles the heart and the hands as well as the head. For the head, how do we understand God's supreme goodness and power in the many faces of evil? For the heart, how do we foster relational trust in God's supreme goodness and power in the many faces of evil? For the hands, how do we engage in actions that align with God's supreme goodness and power in the many faces of evil? What kind of thinking, feeling, and acting can match the combined force of abstract and concrete problems of evil?

---

15. Honesty would compel many of us to acknowledge that we have been more a part of the problems of existential evils than we have been part of their solutions. The more we listen to thoughtful critics outside the circles of belief, the clearer it becomes that the failure of people within the circles to answer these existential problems generates an equally (if not more) powerful dissuasion from belief than the abstract problems of evil. In this way, our failure to seek answers to the existential problems of evil lends force to both the abstract and emotional forms of the problem.

16. For a philosophical call to reconsider the "profoundly unfashionable" premodern notion of spiritual agencies playing a significant role in the world, a topic beyond the scope of this work, see Gordon Graham, *Evil and Christian Ethics* (Cambridge: Cambridge University Press, 2001), particularly chapters 4–6.

THREE CRITERIA OF THEODICY

Given the sheer magnitude of the God whom the problems of evil involve, there is no room for simplistic or cavalier answers. These problems revolve around a Being perceived "in a mirror dimly" (1 Cor 13:12), a Mind whose judgments are "unsearchable" (Rom 11:33), and whose "foolishness … is wiser than men" (1 Cor 1:25). God is too vast to fit into neatly wrapped philosophical boxes. It may turn out that we err on the side of hubris in the quest for "answers" to some problems of evil. Perhaps meeting the problems is less like breaking through a victory ribbon at the end of a sprint and more like trudging through a marathon, less about answers and more about slow and steady progress.

Progress has often been sought in over-compartmentalized strategies. Forward strides against abstract problems of evil are often formulated and fine-tuned in intellectual isolation. There is a lack of broader concern for how such ideas may impact, positively or negatively, the quest for progress in the concrete realms. We must ask: If we consistently integrated our philosophical theodicies into how we both existentially combat and emotionally cope with evil, would we be better or worse for it?

I am not implying that a given intellectual response to abstract problems of evil must simultaneously meet the challenges posed by concrete evil. Rather, our intellectual responses, at a minimum, ought to comport with how we meet the concrete problems. Hendrik Vroom, a philosopher, theologian, and former hospital chaplain, stated, "Whatever cannot be said in a hospital should not be said in a philosophy or theology text attempting to deal with evil and suffering."[17] Epicurus echoes, "Vain is the word of a philosopher which does not heal any suffering of man."[18] *There should be nothing in the theist's responses to the problems that evil poses to the head that conflicts*

---

17. Hendrik Vroom in a personal interview conducted on December 29, 2009.

18. Epicurus, *Fragments*, no. 54, in *Epicurus: The Extant Remains*, tr. Cyril Bailey (Oxford: Clarendon Press, 1926).

with how we ought to confront the evils present in our hearts and per-
formed with our hands.

Imagine a theist, attempting to answer abstract problems of evil, who imports into his theodicy the following fatalistic ideas of the first-century Stoic, Epictetus:

> Things beyond our will are nothing to us. ... When death appears as an evil, we ought immediately to remember, that evils are things to be avoided, but death is inevitable. ... When you see anyone weeping for grief, either that his son has gone abroad, or that he has suffered in his affairs; take care not to be overcome by the apparent evil. ... As far as the conversation goes, however, do not disdain to accommodate yourself to him, and if need be, to groan with him. Take heed, however, not to groan inwardly too.[19]

Are these ideas compatible with how we ought to address concrete problems of evil?

Even if we lack exhaustive answers to concrete problems of evil, one important normative feature of progress against such problems is that we ought to "weep with those who weep" (Rom 12:15). We should take people's pain, grief, and questions seriously, feeling the weight of loss with them to remove the sting of isolation from their angst. Epictetus advises us not to "groan inwardly." Encountering grief, death, and doubt at Lazarus' tomb, Jesus "was deeply moved in spirit and greatly troubled," and even "wept" (John 11:33b, 35). The Greek phrase—"deeply moved in spirit" (ἐνεβριμήσατο τῷ πνεύματι)—captures an outrage that occurred not merely for outward social show, but with inwardness and sincerity.[20] John portrays an anything but Stoic Jesus.

---

19. Epictetus, *The Discourses*, I.IV, XXVII, and *Enchiridion*, XVI, in *The Works of Epictetus*, tr. T. W. Higginson (Boston: Little and Brown, 1866).

20. On outrage and grief as Jesus' reaction in John 11:33–35 see D. A. Carson, *The Gospel According to John* (Grand Rapids: Eerdmans, 1991), 415–17.

Elsewhere, Jesus confronts concrete evil by expressing a deep internal and action-motivating "compassion" (σπλαγχνίζομαι). Jesus expresses this compassion at people's despair and moral lostness (Matt 9:36; cf. Mark 6:34), sickness (Matt 14:14; cf. Mark 1:40–41), hunger (Matt 15:32; cf. Mark 8:2), blindness (Matt 20:34), and death (Luke 7:13). The New Testament envisions this compassion as a crucial step toward progress against concrete evils.[21] Therefore, a theodicy in which "things beyond our will are nothing to us," mere "apparent evil" for which we should not "groan inwardly," is inconsistent with how we ought to address concrete problems of evil.

From this analysis, I suggest three criteria for responses to abstract problems of evil:

(1) *The Criteria of Philosophical Credibility*: A viable response to abstract problems of evil must be philosophically credible, able to withstand charges of poor explanatory power, fallaciousness, superficiality, etc.

(2) *The Criteria of Biblical Compatibility*: A viable response to abstract problems of evil must be biblically compatible, neither explicitly nor implicitly contradicting successive layers of biblical insight into the nature of reality.

(3) *The Criteria of Existential Consistency*: A viable response to abstract problems of evil must be consistent (though not necessarily identical) with normative methods of existentially engaging the concrete problems of evil.

Are our most cherished responses to the abstract problems of evil philosophically credible, biblically compatible, and existentially consistent?[22]

---

21. See Luke 10:33; Ephesians 4:32; and 1 Peter 3:8.

22. The lack of attention to developing a theodicy that is explicitly consistent with responses to concrete evils is understandable given the phenomenon of *specialization* (i.e., philosophers working on philosophical problems in the academic world). The Christian philosopher, however, still bears a responsibility to "specialize" in the concrete problems of evil. Biblical imperatives to

We now turn to the Free Will Defense, the most pervasive philosophical response to evil within the halls of both historical and contemporary theism.

THE INTRANSITIVITY DIMENSION

According to Gordon Clark,

> From pagan antiquity, through the middle ages, on down into modern times, free will has doubtless been the most popular solution offered to the problem of evil.[23]

In R. K. McGregor Wright's estimation, "the desire to have God freed from responsibility for evil is probably the strongest motivation for assuming free will."[24] In particular, *libertarian* free will is widely viewed as the most promising philosophical response to abstract problems of evil.

We may define libertarian free will as follows: A moral agent has libertarian free will if she has a categorical and irreducible power to act as a first-mover to perform or refrain from performing a given action.[25] When faced with doing some action, A—reading the next sentence—or not-A—refraining from reading on—you have the power to do either. Though you have apparently chosen A (for which I am grateful), you could have chosen not-A. Who or what determined your choice? Neither forces outside you (e.g., physical laws, other people, God) nor forces inside you (e.g., reasons, desires, character) are determinative. You, the choosing agent, and you alone determine

---

"overcome evil with good" apply indiscriminately to all Christians, regardless of their vocation. The Christian philosopher's work on the concrete problems may do a great deal to enrich and humanize his work on the abstract problems.

23. Gordon Clark, *Religion, Reason, and Revelation*, in *The Works of Gordon Clark*, vol. 4 (Unicoi, TN: The Trinity Foundation, 2004), 241.

24. R. K. McGregor Wright, *No Place for Sovereignty: What's Wrong with Free Will Theism?* (Downers Grove, IL: InterVarsity Press, 1996), 189.

25. See Alvin Plantinga, *The Nature of Necessity* (Oxford: Oxford University Press, 1974), 170–71; Thomas Flint, "Two Accounts of Providence," in *Divine and Human Action*, ed. Thomas Morris (Ithaca, NY: Cornell University Press, 1988), 175; and Scott Burson and Jerry Walls, *C. S. Lewis & Francis Schaeffer* (Downers Grove, IL: InterVarsity Press, 1998), 68, 333.

which way to go (and if to go at all). It is the exercise of this self-moving, two-way power that makes good choices rewardable and bad choices punishable.[26]

The last several decades have witnessed a remarkable rise of theists appealing to this libertarian notion of free will as a God-vindicating answer to abstract problems of evil. In 1988, George Schlesinger observed,

> The Free Will Defense has been subject to a greater amount of discussion by analytic philosophers, in the last 25 years or so, than have the rest of the solutions put together.[27]

Yet, the Free Will Defense has a very long history. It can be found in early church fathers like Justin Martyr, Clement of Alexandria, Tertullian, Maximus, and Lactantius. Some trace the genesis of the Free Will Defense before the church fathers into the realms of ancient Greek philosophy. Indeed, there is a deep resemblance between the notion of free will espoused by ancient Greek philosophers and the libertarian free will forwarded in today's theological circles. The following table captures this resemblance:

ANCIENT GREEK PHILOSOPHERS	CONTEMPORARY THEOLOGIANS
"The stick moves the stone and is moved by the hand, which is again moved by the man; in the man, however, we have reached a mover that is not so in virtue of being moved by something else" (Aristotle, *Physics*, 8:256, *The Works of Aristotle*, vol. 9, [Oxford: Clarendon, 1925]).	"Persons are agents and, as such, are first-movers, unmoved movers who simply have the power to act as the ultimate originators of their actions" (J. P. Moreland and Scott Rae, *Body & Soul* [Downers Grove, IL: InterVarsity, 2000], 129–30).

---

26. See Edward Wierenga, *The Nature of God* (Ithaca, NY: Cornell, 1989), 83; and Norman Geisler, *Chosen But Free* (Minneapolis: Bethany House, 1999), 29.

27. George Schlesinger, *New Perspectives on Old-Time Religion* (Oxford: Oxford University Press, 1988), 42.

ANCIENT GREEK PHILOSOPHERS	CONTEMPORARY THEOLOGIANS
"[W]hen acting is up to us, so is not acting, and when No is up to us, so is Yes" (Aristotle, *Nicomachean Ethics*, 5:1113b, 9).	"Minimally, free will is the ability to do otherwise" (Norman Geisler, *Chosen But Free*, 29).
"Hence if acting, when it is fine, is up to us, then not acting, when it is shameful, is also up to us" (Aristotle, *Nicomachean Ethics*, 5:1113b10–13).	"The power to decide between alternatives … must ultimately lie within ourselves"(Greg Boyd, *Satan and the Problem of Evil*, 29–30).
"… praise and blame arise upon such as are voluntary" (Aristotle, *Nicomachean Ethics*, 3:1–2a).	"… praise and blame make no real sense unless those praised and blamed were free to do otherwise" (Geisler, *Chosen But Free*, 31).
"[The prudent person] thinks that with us lies the chief power in determining events … that which is in our control is subject to no master" (Epicurus, *Epicurus to Menoeceus*, 133–35, and *Principal Doctrines*, 4.	"A person is free … only if no causal laws and antecedent conditions determine either that he performs A … or that he refrains from doing so" (Alvin Plantinga, *The Nature of Necessity*, 170–71).
"[Zeus] gave you this faculty of impulse to act and not to act, of will to get and will to avoid" (Epictetus, *Discourses*, 1.1).	"One of the things God gave His good creatures was a good power called free will" (Geisler, *Chosen But Free*, 22).
"The Gods only give us the mere faculty of reason, if we have any; the use or abuse of it depends entirely on ourselves" (Cicero, *Of the Nature of the Gods*, tr. Pierre-Joseph Thoulier Olivet [T. Davies, 1775] 3:237).	"God made the fact of freedom; we are responsible for the acts of freedom. The fact of freedom is good, even though some acts of freedom are evil. God is the cause of the former, and we are the cause of the latter" (Geisler, 23).

Ancient Greek Philosophers	Contemporary Theologians
"Whether we ought to believe, or disbelieve what is said; or whether, if we do believe, we ought to be moved by it, or not; what is it that decides us? Is it not the faculty of Will?" (Epictetus, *The Discourses*, 2.23)	"Ultimately it is up to the person to make a true choice between two or more live options. ... So a free act ... cannot be reduced to anything beyond the choice of the agent." (Scott Burson and Jerry Walls, *C. S. Lewis & Francis Schaeffer*, 68, 333)

The work of atheologians, J. L. Mackie and Anthony Flew, in the 1950s generated much of the current upsurge of libertarian free will as a solution to the abstract problems of evil.[28] Alvin Plantinga emerged as the most vigorous proponent of the Free Will Defense, contending against Flew and Mackie that God could not create free agents who always choose good, since guaranteeing such universal obedience could only be had at the price of abolishing significant freedom, namely, *libertarian* freedom.

The tide of the Mackie-Flew-Plantinga exchange[29] has not ebbed in the last several decades. It has risen within the scholarly community[30] and flowed beyond ivory towers to influence minds on a far wider scale. In what way does libertarian free will function as an answer to abstract evil in so many minds? Roughly stated, the Free Will Defense says that God gave humanity a good gift, a gift that remains

---

28. In 1955 Flew published "Divine Omnipotence and Human Freedom," in *New Essays in Philosophical Theology*, eds. Anthony Flew and Alasdair MacIntyre (New York: Macmillan, 1955), 144–69. That same year J. L. Mackie published his influential "Evil and Omnipotence," *Mind* 64 (1955): 200–12.

29. For Plantinga's responses to Mackie and Flew see part 2 of *God and Other Minds: A Study of the Rational Justification of Belief in God* (Ithaca, NY: Cornell University Press, 1967, reprinted 1990); *God, Freedom and Evil* (New York: Harper and Row, 1974); and chapter 9 of *The Nature of Necessity*.

30. For a range of scholarly responses to Plantinga's version of the Free Will Defense, see Robert Ackerman, "An Alternative Free Will Defense," *Religious Studies* 19 (1982): 365–72; Susan Anderson, "Plantinga and the Free Will Defense," *Pacific Philosophical Quarterly* 62 (1981): 274–81; and Paul Helm, "God and Free Will," *Sophia* 13 (1974): 16–19.

intact after the fall of Genesis 3, namely, libertarian free will to make morally significant decisions. We abuse this gift by actualizing moral evils. Thus, we (the abusers of our free will), not God (the Author of our free will), are blameworthy for the existence of evil.[31]

To approach the Free Will Defense with clarity, it is helpful to distinguish its three fundamental claims, all of which are tied to the notion of libertarian free will. The first two claims appear in early forms of the Free Will Defense set forth by church fathers from the second century onwards. The third claim emerges more in contemporary versions of the Free Will Defense, and will be the primary focus of the present study.

> CLAIM 1—The Intransitivity Dimension: By anchoring moral
> responsibility in two-way, self-moving power, libertarian free
> will places blame for moral evil squarely on creatures without
> indicting the Creator for our immoral actions.

Libertarian free will allows us to trade the frightful claim that "God is the author of evil" for the seemingly more defensible claim that "God is the author of freedom; we are the authors of evil." Geisler says, "God is morally accountable for giving the good thing called free will, but he is not responsible for all the evil we do with our freedom."[32] Libertarian free will allows blame to affix on those creatures who make evil actual, without ascending the ladder of causation up to the Creator, who merely makes evil possible. This will be called the "intransitivity dimension" of the Free Will Defense. It has a discernable ancestry in church

---

31. See Plantinga, *God, Freedom and Evil*, 30.
32. Geisler, *Chosen But Free*, 23.

fathers like Tertullian,[33] Clement of Alexandria,[34] and Augustine,[35] along with their Hellenistic predecessors, including Plato,[36] Cleanthes,[37] and Cicero.[38]

---

33. Tertullian says, "It is not the part of good and solid faith to refer all things to the will of God ... as to make us fail to understand that there is a something in our power" (*Exhortation to Chastity*, 5.1:50 in *Ante-Nicene Fathers*, pt. 4th, eds. Ernest Cushing Richardson, Bernhard Pick [New York: C. Scribner's Sons, 1885]). Tertullian uses the Greek technical terms for free will (e.g., εφ᾿εμιν, αὐτεξούσια=Latin: *liberum arbitrium*) throughout *On the Soul* and *Exhortation to Chastity*. See Alistair McGrath, *Historical Theology: An Introduction to the History of Christian Thought* (Hoboken, NJ: Wiley-Blackwell, 1998); and Max Pohlenz, *Freedom in Greek Life and Thought: The History of an Ideal*, tr. C. Lofmark (Dordrecht: D. Reidel, 1966), 194n28. This Greek notion of freedom factored largely into Tertullian's solution to abstract problems of evil as posed by the dualists of his day (cf. *Against Marcion*), although throughout *Against Marcion* Tertullian attempts to sustain a strict adherence to divine omnipotence.

34. See Clement, *Miscellanies*, 1.17:319 and 5.14:467 in *Ante-Nicene Fathers*, vol. 2., ed. Alexander Roberts (New York: Christian Literature Company, 1885). For Clement's indebtedness to Greek notions of freedom, see William Floyd, *Clement of Alexandria's Treatment of the Problem of Evil* (Oxford: Oxford University Press, 1971), particularly chapter 2.

35. See Augustine, *On Free Choice of the Will* (Indianapolis: Hackett, 1993), 2.17–20; 3.4–5, 16. See also Simon Harrison, "Do We Have a Will?" in *The Augustinian Tradition*, ed. Gareth Matthews (Berkeley: University of California Press, 1999), 195–205; Charles Kahn, "Discovering the Will: From Aristotle to Augustine," in *Eclecticism: Studies in Later Greek Philosophy*, ed. C. Dillon (Berkeley: University of California Press, 1988); and T. Irwin, "Who Discovered the Will?" *Philosophical Perspectives* 6 (1992): 453–73.

36. In what W. C. Greene identifies as the "first distinct statement in Greek literature of the problem of evil" (*Moira: Fate, Good, and Evil in Greek Thought* [Cambridge, MA: Harvard University Press, 1994], 298), Plato says that Zeus is "responsible for a few things that happen to men, but for many he is not. ... The former we must attribute to none else but God; but for the evil we must find some other cause, not God" (*Republic*, 379). While Plato often identifies matter as that "other cause," he continues, "you will choose your genius ... and the life which he chooses shall be his destiny. ... The responsibility is with the chooser—God is justified (αἰτία ἑλομένου. Θεὸς ἀναίτιος)" (*Republic*, 617e). According to Floyd, Clement's intransitivity dimension was "directly derived" from Plato's axiom—αἰτία ἑλομένου. Θεὸς ἀναίτιος (*Clement of Alexandria's Treatment of the Problem of Evil*, 32; cf. *The Instructor*, 1.8:226; and *Miscellanies*, 5.14:475).

37. According to Cleanthes, "[The] acts of bad men constitute one class of events which come about without Zeus' aid" (cited in Josiah B. Gould, *The Philosophy of Chrysippus* [New York: State University of New York Press, 1970], 142). Cleanthes also held, like many contemporary free will defenders, that the intentions of providence can be thwarted by human wickedness (See *Hymn to Zeus*, 17; cf. E. V. Arnold, *Roman Stoicism* [Cambridge: Cambridge University Press, 1911], 207). See also Greene, *Moira: Fate, Good, and Evil in Greek Thought*, 339.

38. Cicero, who influenced Augustine's thinking about God, free will, and evil (Timothy O'Keefe, *Epicurus on Freedom*, [Cambridge University Press, 2005] 159), forwards the intransitivity dimension in *Of the Nature of the Gods*, 3:28, 70; cf. 2:70. See Margaret Y. Henry, "Cicero's Treatment of the Free Will Problem," *Transactions and Proceedings of the American Philological Association*, 58 (1927): 32–42.

THE ANTHROPOLOGICAL DIMENSION

Why would a good God make moral evil possible in the first place? This question evokes the second core claim:

> **CLAIM 2—The Anthropological Dimension:** Libertarian free will, although it may be abused to actualize moral evil, is essential to the humanness of humanity, namely, our capacity for moral goodness.

As Dante says in *The Divine Comedy*, "The greatest gift that God ... made in Creation and the most formidable to His goodness, and that which He prizes most, was the freedom of the will" (*Paradiso*, V.19–24). Claim 2 forms the crux of Plantinga's influential version of the Free Will Defense:

> A world containing creatures who are significantly free (and freely perform more good than evil actions) is more valuable, all else being equal, than a world containing no free creatures at all. To create creatures capable of *moral good*, therefore, He must create creatures capable of moral evil.[39]

C. S. Lewis echoes, "A world of automata—of creatures that worked like machines—would hardly be worth creating."[40]

Libertarian free will is a necessary condition of the capacity for moral goodness, and the capacity for moral goodness is, in turn, a necessary condition of being human. We will call this the "anthropological dimension" of the Free Will Defense, and may trace its lineage

---

39. Plantinga, *God, Freedom, and Evil*, 30. For another contemporary version of the defense featuring the anthropological dimension, see James Petrik, *Evil Beyond Belief* (Armonk, NY: M. E. Sharp, 2000), 32, 52, 78–87; emphasis original.

40. Lewis, *Mere Christianity*, 49.

in early church fathers[41] and their Greek philosophical predecessors.[42] Taken together, the intransitivity dimension and the anthropological dimension form what we may call the "Traditional Free Will Defense," given its far-reaching historical genealogy.[43]

1.1.5 THE RELATIONAL DIMENSION

By adding a third claim, the Traditional Free Will Defense has undergone a significant deepening in recent years. In the words of C. S. Lewis, "free will, though it makes evil possible, is also the only thing that makes possible any love or goodness or joy worth having."[44] Lewis captures the third claim:

> **CLAIM 3—The Relational Dimension:** Libertarian free will, although it opens the door of possibility to moral evil, is a necessary condition for the existence and expression of true love.

---

41. For the indebtedness of the church fathers to Greek philosophy with regard to the intransitivity dimension, see Edwin Hatch, *The Influence of Greek Ideas and Their Usages upon the Christian Church*, 4th ed. (London: Williams and Norgate, 1892), 231–32. For the anthropological dimension in Tertullian see *Against Marcion* 2.5–6:69–74, in *Tertullianus Against Marcion*, tr. Alexander Roberts (Whitefish, MT: Kessinger Publishing, 2004). For commentary see Eric Osborn, *The Beginning of Christian Philosophy* (Cambridge: Cambridge University Press, 1981), 96, 138, 212. For the anthropological dimension in Clement we read, "self-determining choice and refusal have been given by the Lord to men" (*Miscellanies*, 2.4:349 in *Ante-Nicene Fathers*, vol. 2). Epictetus concurs, "I [Zeus] gave you … this faculty of impulse to act and not to act, of will to get and will to avoid" (*The Discourses*, 1.1). See discussion in Floyd, *Clement of Alexandria's Treatment of the Problem of Evil*, 34–35. See also Augustine, *On Free Choice of the Will*, 2.1–2, 18–20.

42. For components of the anthropological dimension in Greek philosophy see Seneca, *On Benefits* (London: George Bell and Sons, 1887), 2.29:45–46; 4.7:90–91; Cicero, *Of the Nature of the Gods*, 3:237; and *On Fate*, 27:279–80, in *The Treatises of M. T. Cicero* (London: George Bell and Sons, 1878); and Epictetus, *Discourses*, 2.23.

43. Church fathers developed the Traditional Free Will Defense to meet the challenge of Gnostic dualisms. These dualisms threatened God's goodness, contributing to the fathers' emphasis on the intransitivity dimension. Dualists also threatened humanity's dignity with an elitist form of determinism, leading to the fathers' emphasis on the anthropological dimension. Mark Larrimore observes, "The most important Western thinking on evil emerged in responses to metaphysical dualists: Plotinus responding to the Gnostics, Augustine to the Manichees" ("Autonomy and the Invention of Theodicy," *New Essays on the History of Autonomy*, ed. N. Brealer [Cambridge: Cambridge University Press 2004], 61–91, 64). We may add, "Tertullian responding to the Marcionites and Valentinians and Clement to the Gnostic thought in Alexandria" to this observation. See P. Ricoeur, "Evil: A Challenge to Philosophy and Theology," *Journal of the American Academy of Religion*, LIII (1985): 633–48, 636.

44. Lewis, *Mere Christianity*, 49.

With this "relational dimension," the Traditional Free Will Defense morphs into the *Relational* Free Will Defense. Real love requires libertarian choice, and real libertarian choice entails the possibility of saying "no" to love. The alternative—a world in which everyone lacks the libertarian power to say "no" to love—would indeed be a world devoid of moral evil. However, it would simultaneously be a relationally vacuous world, no more loving than a warehouse full of computers. In the words of Simone Weil,

> If God did not grant us the ability to sin and cause affliction to him and to one another, we would not have the kind of free and autonomous existence necessary to enter into a relation of love with God and with one another.[45]

For a better approach to the Relational Free Will Defense, it is helpful to clarify its logical flow:

RFD1: For any agent, *A*, to express authentic love for some other agent, *B*, it must be possible for *A* to refrain from loving *B* through an exercise of libertarian power.

RFD2: God does not desire a relationally void world but a world in which agents can express authentic love for Himself and for each other.

RFD3: Therefore, God created agents with libertarian power, making it possible for them to love both Himself and each other or to refrain from doing so.

RFD4: Agents use their libertarian power to refrain from loving God and each other, thereby rendering themselves solely to blame for the actualization of moral evil.

---

45. Simone Weil, *Gateway to God*, 80, cited in Bram Van De Beek's *Why? On Suffering, Guilt, and God* (Grand Rapids: Eerdmans, 1990), 163.

Taken as a whole, the Relational Free Will Defense may be seen less as a new and distinct defense and more as a deepening of the Traditional Free Will Defense, particularly the anthropological dimension. The Relational Free Will Defense tells us something more about the nature of moral goodness that God desires from humanity, namely, that interpersonal love is of paramount importance to the nature of moral goodness.

The Relational Free Will Defense properly emphasizes the centrality of interpersonal love to God's moral vision for His universe (RFD2). What raises questions is the Defense's elevation of libertarian free will as a necessary condition of true love. Is the notion that love requires libertarian freedom philosophically credible? Is it compatible with biblical insights into the nature of love, freedom, and evil? Is it consistent with how we should answer evils in the concrete realm?

These three questions are particularly relevant, given the unchallenged cardinal doctrinal status that RFD1 has achieved within the circles of both academic and popular theology. The claim that love requires libertarian freedom has become a guiding axiom within open theism, process theology, Molinism, and many other contemporary theological paradigms.

From the scholarly literature, Vincent Brümmer argues:

> It is clear that a relationship of love can only be maintained as long as the ... free autonomy of *both* partners is maintained. ... Since love is a reciprocal relation, God is also dependent on the freedom and responsibility of human persons in order to enter into a loving relation with them. Of course, this autonomy is *bestowed* on us by God as our creator. ... Nevertheless, in creating human persons in order to love them God necessarily assumes vulnerability in relation to them.[46]

---

46. Brümmer, *The Model of Love*, 162–63. See also Brümmer, "Ultimate Happiness and the Love of God," in *Religion and the Good Life*, eds. Marcel Sarot and Wessel Stoker (Assen: Royal Van Gorcum, 2004), 248; emphasis original.

Brümmer articulates libertarian free will as a necessary condition of authentic love with great clarity. Likewise, Geddes MacGregor, in developing his theology of divine *kenosis* (God's self-emptying, not merely in the incarnation but also in creation to make room for meaningful love), echoes the assertion of RFD1:

> To provide room for human freedom of choice, or indeed for any kind of freedom within a theistic system, God must not only occasionally restrain himself in the exercise of his power; he must never exercise it at all except in support of love, and love without freedom is impossible. Love *is* the abdication of power.[47]

The claim that "love without freedom is impossible" thrives beyond the academy's towers through a growing number of popular publications and programs. Popular evangelical teacher Chuck Missler states RFD1 in strong terms:

> The dilemma accrues from God's awesome gift of personal sovereignty: our ability to choose entirely on our own. That risk is the price of love—which has to emerge from our own free volition. But that awesome gift carries with it the risk of our choice not to—and the awesome consequences. ... Without the freedom to choose, any concept of "love" is vacuous and bankrupt. ... Love cannot be forced.[48]

Rob Bell echoes, "Love demands freedom. It always has and it always will."[49]

---

47. Geddes MacGregor, *He Who Lets Us Be: A Theology of Love* (New York: The Seabury Press, 1975), 333; emphasis original.

48. Chuck Missler, *The Sovereignty of Man: Supplemental Notes* (Coeur d'Alene, ID: Koinonia House, 1995), 24, 25, 28.

49. Bell, *Love Wins*, 100.

Though there are many examples,[50] I will limit myself to one final case in point from the realm of popular theology. Hank Hanegraaff, a best-selling author and host of internationally syndicated *Bible Answer Man* broadcasts, has declared frequently from his on-air platform, "Love without libertarian free will is meaningless. God did not create us as Chatty Cathy dolls." Hanegraaff lends force to RFD1 with a memorable image—the Chatty Cathy doll, introduced by Mattel in 1960, with a low-fidelity phonograph record inside that would play "I love you" with the pull of a string. Surely God desires more than such artificial affection from His creatures.

These examples give us a sense of what motivates proponents of the Relational Free Will Defense. They seek to meet abstract problems of evil in a way that does not reduce the human-to-God relationship to a mechanistic exchange between the programmed and the programmer. I join them in rejecting any system that reduces our love for God to three mechanical words beckoned from soul-less dolls or any system that diminishes God to an easily amused toddler who takes satisfaction in hearing pre-programmed "humans" express simulated affection.

In sum, the Defense's claim that "love requires libertarian free will" has become highly ubiquitous within the world of contemporary Christian thought from the scholarly to the popular. No matter the context in which we encounter RFD1, it tends to function as an axiomatic starting point. It is more often asserted with common sense appeal than defended through rigorous philosophical, biblical, or existential argumentation. Perhaps the claim that authentic love requires libertarian free will is considered obvious and indubitable, requiring no more evidence than does the claim, "one plus one equals two." Rejecting it would require an abolition of common sense. But why should the notion that love requires libertarian free will be

---

50. See Walls, *C. S. Lewis and Francis Schaeffer*, 239; Hunt, *What Love Is This?*, 138; and Geisler, *Chosen But Free*, 98.

granted such privileged epistemic status in the citadels of contemporary Christian thought?

OVERVIEW

Church history has had its share of detractors who view libertarian free will as hazardous to the Christian faith. In 1757, the philosopher, theologian, and pastor, Jonathan Edwards, wrote in a letter:

> I think the notion of liberty, consisting in a contingent self determination of the will, as necessary to morality of men's dispositions and actions almost inconceivably pernicious. ... Notions of this kind are one of the main hindrances of the success of the preaching of the Word, and other means of grace in the conversion of sinners.[51]

Edwards composed his opus, *Freedom of the Will*, to counteract the libertarian notion of free will, which was gaining momentum in eighteenth-century American Protestantism. Edwards' fellow Puritan, John Owen, viewed libertarian free will as

> a most nefarious, sacrilegious attempt [of humans] to free themselves of the supreme dominion of [God's] all-ruling providence; not to live and move in him, but to have an absolute independent power in all their actions.[52]

Martin Luther wrote in *Bondage of the Will*, the work he considered the most important of all his theological writings, "this false idea of 'free will' is a real threat to salvation, and a delusion fraught with the most perilous dangers."[53]

---

51. Cited in George Marsden, *Jonathan Edwards: A Life* (New Haven, CT: Yale University, 2003), 437–38.

52. John Owen, *A Display of Arminianism* (Edmonton, AB, Canada: Still Water Revival Books, 1989) 12.

53. Martin Luther, *Bondage of the Will*, in John Dillenburger, *Martin Luther: Selections from His Writings* (Garden City, NY: Anchor Books, 1961), 189.

Perhaps these words vilify a helpful idea for Christians engaging the abstract problems of evil. Yet, given the widespread infusion of libertarian free will in the twenty-first century Christian mindset, it is worth looking at the Relational Free Will Defense to ask where problems may lie.

The remainder of part 1, Evil and the Autonomous Heart, offers a friendly philosophical challenge to the common sense appeal of the notion that true love requires libertarian free will. I analyze three distinct ways in which freedom may be understood in relational contexts and their corresponding senses of necessity. Does the common sense appeal of the notion that love requires libertarian free will rest on a failure to carve out these important distinctions? This raises two problems endemic to the notion of libertarian free will. The first problem relates to *who* the choosing agent is: Is a libertarian agent a good candidate for being a true lover? The second problem focuses on *why* agents choose: Is a libertarian choice a credible medium for the expression of true love?

Part 2, Freedom and the Enslaved Heart, assesses the biblical credentials of libertarian free will. In particular, I examine the three possibilities for locating this notion within the Bible: (1) passages in which moral imperatives are directed at choice-making agents, (2) the moral resistance of God's creatures throughout the biblical narrative, and (3) the picture of God's relational vision for His world. These attempts rest on extra-biblical premises that stand logically between biblical insights and the conclusion of libertarian free will. Are these extra-biblical premises defensible?

Part 3, Love and the Reformed Heart, asks how the Relational Free Will Defense fares relative to the scope of divine action in human love. After introducing the primary theological alternatives, I enter biblical analysis with a focus on John's Gospel. Does God's role in bringing about authentic love in human hearts go deeper than the Relational Free Will Defense allows? I close with an existential critique. Does the Defense's claim that love requires libertarian free will hinder us as we seek to embody a loving response to concrete evils?

The overarching goal of this work is to make progress against the problems of evil, progress that illumines God's goodness, humanity's value, and the authenticity of love without undercutting the philosophical credibility of a Christian worldview, straying from biblical insights, or derailing us in our efforts to meet the multifronted challenges of concrete evils. This goal, I hope, will be pursued in dialogue by both those who endorse the Relational Free Will Defense and those who do not.

1.2

The Axiom of Libertarian Love

*I am well aware of how much more needs to be done,
especially on the issue of free will, the solution of which
seems to me to require a set of new conceptual tools, a
break with traditional terminology.*

—*Isaiah Berlin,* Four Essays on Liberty

THREE NECESSITIES

According to W. S. Anglin,

> No one can love truly unless, at some time or another, he is
> free not to love, and in a sense which precludes any arrange-
> ment which would be a sufficient cause of love-like behavior.
> If love is ensured or made necessary ... then it is not true love
> but mere love-behavior. To have real love between persons,
> we must have libertarian free will.[1]

---

1. W. S. Anglin, *Free Will and the Christian Faith* (Oxford: Oxford University Press, 1990), 20.

As we have seen, Anglin is far from alone in his conviction. He is one voice within the vast transdenominational and transcultural choir in which libertarian free will is proclaimed in unison as a necessary condition of authentic love (RFD1). Let us call this melody captured by Anglin and so many others, "The Axiom of Libertarian Love":

> Any agent, A, must possess libertarian free will to love or refrain from loving another agent, B, if A's love for B is to count as authentic.

To test the philosophical credibility of this Axiom we must distinguish between love as an expression of *freedom* and love as an expression of *necessity*. Gottfried Leibniz recognized the need for terminological precision in navigating the tangle of problems surrounding freedom and necessity:

> I find that it is principally the use of terms like "necessary" or "contingent," or "possible" or "impossible," which sometimes gives a handle and causes much ado. That is why ... Luther desired, in his book *On the Will in Bondage*, to find a word more fitting for that which he wished to express than the word "necessity."[2]

This work joins Luther in his quest for a less problematic rendition of necessity. I develop the thesis that *there exists a necessity that is not only compatible with free action and true love but serves as an integral and essential element for the freest of actions and the truest of loves.* I will argue that this counterthesis of the Axiom is not only philosophically viable but also deeply biblical and vital to meeting concrete problems of evil. Any slant of common sense in favor of the Axiom can

---

2. Leibniz, *Theodicy*, tr. E. M. Huggard (LaSalle, IL: Open Court, [1710] 1985), 135.

be traced to equivocations, conflations, and ambiguities that engulf the notion of necessity.[3]

How may we secure some grip on this slippery term? In the broadest sense, something is necessary if it is impossible for that something to be other than it is. It *must* be. This "must-ness" may be cashed out in terms of *logical* necessity, the kind that attaches to propositions and their logical relationships to one other (e.g., If "all men are mortal," and "Socrates is a man," then "Socrates is mortal" is logically necessary). Philosophers in recent years have added to logical necessity a growing list of ways in which something must be.[4] When it comes to questions surrounding the Relational Free Will Defense, we are in the realm of moral agency—how agents choose to act. There are three senses of necessity that are most salient to philosophical discussions surrounding moral agency. As we distinguish these three necessities, the Axiom of Libertarian Love loses much of its force as an indubitable axiom, thereby making room for alternative understandings of love and freedom.

I introduce these three forms of necessity with three cases of "love" expressed between two persons, Jim and Claudia:

CASE 1: Jim, a mad scientist desperate for love, installs A. A. (Artificial Affection) hardware in Claudia's brain that programs her to "love" him. Claudia says, "I love you," and cannot do otherwise.

---

3. Edwards echoes,

> The words necessary, impossible, &c. are abundantly used in controversies about Free-Will and Moral Agency; and therefore the sense in which they are used should be clearly understood. ... Though we use the words, as terms of art, in another sense, yet, unless we are exceedingly circumspect, we shall insensibly slide into the vulgar use of them, and so apply the words in a very inconsistent manner, which will deceive and confound us in our reasonings and discourses (*Freedom of the Will*, in *The Works of Jonathan Edwards*, vol. 1 [Peabody, MA: Hendrickson, 2000], 8).

4. See Richard Swinburne, *The Christian God* (Oxford: Oxford University Press, 1994), 96–116; "Necessary A Posteriori Truth," *American Philosophical Quarterly* 28 (1991): 113–23; and Saul Kripke, *Naming and Necessity* (Cambridge, MA: Harvard University Press, 1980).

CASE 2: Jim, a neurotic desperate for love, holds a gun to Claudia's back and commands her to love him. Claudia says, "I love you," and cannot do otherwise.

CASE 3: Claudia has a powerful internal desire to maximize Jim's welfare, a propensity so strong that she cannot bring herself to reject him. Claudia says, "I love you," and cannot do otherwise.

In all three cases Claudia says "I love you" to Jim and cannot do otherwise. Claudia expresses "love" by way of *necessity* in each case. She *must* "love." In the first two cases it is clear that the expressed "love" falls short of true love. Why? Her heart has been bypassed in both cases, first by Artificial Affection hardware and second by the threat of a gun. Behind the first "I love you" we do not find a heart willingly committed to Jim but a functioning piece of cold, impersonal technology. The second "I love you" is not motivated by an altruistic desire to maximize Jim's welfare but a sensible desire to avoid a bullet.

The third case stands apart. Claudia does not merely *say* "I love you." She *means* it. Her heart has not been bypassed but is so deeply intertwined with her action that it serves as the very reason that she cannot do otherwise. Her expression of love follows necessarily from her internal propensities. From these cases we encounter three distinct senses of necessity.

The case of Artificial Affection hardware captures physical necessity in which a purely physical phenomenon is causally sufficient to propel the agent's action. This is essentially the necessity championed as the sole causal factor in human action by Democritus in Greek antiquity, Diderot during the Enlightenment, B. F. Skinner in the twentieth century, and many contemporary philosophers and neuroscientists who reduce the mind to the brain in a quest for an ontologically pure naturalism. In this view, an agent's actions (if indeed one can meaningfully speak of an "agent" in such a paradigm) result deterministically from physical processes. In Jacques Monod's words,

"Anything can be reduced to simple, obvious mechanical interactions. The cell is a machine. The animal is a machine. Man is a machine."[5]

Don DeLillo questions this mechanistic view in his novel, *White Noise*:

> They can trace everything you say, do, and feel to the number of molecules in a certain region. ... What happens to good and evil in this system? Passion, envy and hate? Do they become a tangle of neurons? ... What about murderous rage? A murderer used to have a certain fearsome size to him. His crime was large. What happens when we reduce it to cells and molecules?[6]

We may extend DeLillo's point on human evil to the triumphs of human love. What happens to love "when we reduce it to cells and molecules?" As captured in Case 1 above, such impersonal physical interactions move Claudia to say "I love you" to Jim and prevent her from doing otherwise. If a love relationship is reduced to such necessity, then we are no longer dealing with a lover and a beloved but with cogs in the deterministic machinery of the natural cosmos. I will call such physical necessity, when determining action, "Necessity of the Machine."

The second case in which Jim holds a gun to force "love" from Claudia illustrates coercive necessity. In this form of necessity an agent does some action because some other agent exercises power that moves the first agent to do that action *contrary to what she wills*. This is the form of necessity exploited by slave owners, abusive spouses, and totalitarian governments. This necessity parallels Philip Hallie's analysis of cruelty as "an imbalance of power wherein the stronger

---

5. Jacques Monod, *Chance and Necessity* (New York: Vintage Books, 1972), 180. It follows from the quote above that "Monod is a machine," in which case his own view is not the product of a valid process of reason and deliberation but of "simple, obvious mechanical interactions."

6. Don DeLillo, *White Noise* (New York: Penguin Books, 1986), 190.

party becomes the victimizer and the weaker becomes the victim."[7] Jim's power as an armed and threatening assailant motivates Claudia to say "I love you" and prevents her from doing otherwise. Such a coerced-to-coercer relationship is qualitatively different from a lover-to-beloved relationship. Such coercive necessity when determining action will be called "Necessity of the Gunman."[8]

The third case highlights an altogether different kind of necessity. Claudia is free from both Necessity of the Machine and Necessity of the Gunman. Neither physical powers nor coercive agents determine that she love Jim. Rather, being a Jim-lover is part of who Claudia is, one aspect of her internal teleological (goal-oriented) makeup. This represents a case of intrapersonal necessity in which the agent's internal propensities evoke the action and render it impossible for her to refrain. Such intrapersonal necessity when determining human action will be called "Necessity of the Heart."

THREE FREEDOMS

Before analytically refining the three necessities sketched above, we will distinguish their corresponding freedoms. In Edwards' terminology, freedom is "relative," requiring us to specify what exactly the agent is free *from* (i.e., freedom relative to some object, person, or power). In distinguishing various freedoms we must answer the

---

7. Philip Hallie, "From Cruelty to Goodness," in *Vice & Virtue in Everyday Life: Introductory Readings in Ethics*, 6th ed., eds. Christina Sommers and Fred Sommers (Belmont, CA: Wadsworth, 2004), 4–16, 8.

8. Throughout the Bible, threats of divine punishment are frequently attached to divine imperatives (e.g., Deut 28:15–68). It may be argued that such threats exhibit no qualitative difference from Necessity of the Gunman. In response, there are fundamental distinctions between these cases. The most crucial distinction lies between a morally warranted threat and a threat lacking moral warrant. When Jim threatens Claudia with a bullet, he possesses no moral warrant to demand her response of love. Lack of moral warrant is a distinguishing feature of Necessity of the Gunman. A slave owner does not possess moral warrant to demand wage-free labor, and his slaves are under no moral obligation to provide it. By contrast, when God issues a moral demand enforced with a threat, He possesses moral warrant as God to do so, and humans are under a proper moral obligation to obey. Thus, such threats do not meet the criteria of Necessity of the Gunman. Moreover, I argue in 3.2 that God does not evoke love by coercively bypassing the human heart but by an act of grace that reorients the human heart.

relativity question—*free from what?* With this question, three distinct freedoms emerge:

> Claudia has "Freedom from the Machine" to do some action x or refrain from x if *relative to all powers of the physical world*, she can still do x or refrain from doing x.[9]

> Claudia has "Freedom from the Gunman" to do some action x or refrain from x if *relative to all powers of coercive persons*, she can still do x or refrain from doing x.

> Claudia has "Freedom from the Heart" to do some action x or refrain from x if *relative to all of her internal character propensities*, she can still do x or refrain from doing x.

It is logically possible for Claudia to possess Freedom from the Machine and Gunman while lacking Freedom from the Heart. In such cases, there is still a meaningful sense in which she retains the ability to do otherwise. Namely, *relative to all physical and coercive powers*, Claudia can still go one way or another.[10] With the cumulative powers of physical causation and coercive agents exerted on Claudia, she may still love or refrain from loving Jim. Nevertheless, she may possess this two-way freedom relative to the Machine and Gunman, while at the same time the prevailing dispositions of her internal makeup—her heart—are such that she cannot refrain from loving Jim. In this case, Claudia's ability to do otherwise is not absolute. She cannot actualize both the state of affairs "I love Jim" or "I

---

9. In the words of Arthur Schopenhauer,

> In this physical meaning of the concept of freedom, animals and human beings are called free when neither chains, dungeon, nor paralysis, and thus generally no physical, material obstacle impedes their actions, but these [actions] occur in accordance with their will." (*Prize Essay on the Freedom of the Will*, ed. Günter Zöller, tr. Eric Payne [Cambridge: Cambridge University Press, 1999], 4)

10. In a philosophical analysis that parallels my own on this point, see John Martin Fischer's notion of "regulative control" in *The Metaphysics of Free Will: An Essay on Control*, Aristotelian Society Series, vol. 15 (Oxford: Blackwell Publishers, 1994), 189–215.

refrain from loving Jim" because her internal states preclude her from actualizing the latter.

Such an account will not suffice for those who espouse the Axiom of Libertarian Love. When libertarians champion two-way power they do not mean mere Freedom from the Machine and Gunman, but also Freedom from the Heart. This point is critical to understanding what the Axiom is really saying—libertarian free will *entails* Freedom from the Heart.

Why is Freedom from the Heart a built-in feature of the libertarian notion of free will? Robert Kane answers:

> If the agent might either make a choice or do otherwise, given all the same past circumstances, and the past circumstances include the entire psychological history of the agent, it would seem that no explanation in terms of the agent's psychological history, including prior character, motives and deliberation, could account for the actual occurrence of one outcome rather than another.[11]

For Claudia to have libertarian free will to love Jim or to refrain from loving him, there can be no power beyond her own irreducible active power determining her choice, including (as Kane clarifies) her "prior character, motives and deliberation."

If such internal factors render it necessary for her to love Jim, then her two-way freedom is hypothetical. The libertarian, however, seeks an *actual* ability to realize either the state of affairs "Claudia loves Jim" or that of "Claudia does not love Jim." J. P. Moreland clarifies;

> If Smith freely does (or wills to do) action *a*, then he could have refrained from doing (or willing to do) *a* or he could have done (or willed to have done) *b* without any conditions whatever being different. No description of Smith's desires, beliefs, character or other things in his make-up and no description

---

11. Robert Kane, *Free Will and Values* (Albany: State University of New York Press, 1985), 53.

of the universe prior to and at the moment of his choice to do
b is sufficient to entail that he did *a*.[12]

Moreland sets forth Freedom from the Heart (Smith's capacity to
choose contrary to his "desires, beliefs, character, or other things in his
make-up") as a necessary condition of libertarian free will. Freedom
from the Machine and from the Gunman without Freedom from the
Heart fails to capture what Richard Double calls "the [libertarian's]
intuition that moral responsibility requires *actual* categorical ability
to choose otherwise" (emphasis added).[13]

Libertarian free will is better understood as the sum of the three
freedoms sketched above. The Axiom of Libertarian Love may be
further refined from

> Any agent, *A*, must possess [libertarian free will] to love or
> refrain from loving another agent, *B*, if *A*'s love for *B* is to count
> as authentic

to the following:

> Any agent, *A*, must possess [Freedom from the Machine, the
> Gunman, and the Heart] to love or refrain from loving another
> agent, *B*, if *A*'s love for *B* is to count as authentic.

There is a common misconception to avoid. Libertarianism does
not require Freedom from the Heart in the radical sense that the agent's
propensities are irrelevant to her actions. Contemporary libertarians
are careful to grant that the agent's character, reasons, and other internal states do play a significant role in an agent's free choice, though
they may define the nature and scope of this role differently. Many
contemporary libertarian theorists, including Roderick Chisholm
and Timothy O'Conner, follow the Leibnizian dictum that "reasons

---

12. J. P. Moreland and Scott Rae, *Body & Soul: Human Nature & Crisis in Ethics* (Downers
Grove, IL: InterVarsity, 2000), 126.

13. Richard Double, "Libertarianism and Rationality," in *Agents, Causes, & Events: Essays on
Indeterminism and Free Will*, ed. Timothy O'Conner (Oxford: Oxford University Press, 1995), 65.

may incline without necessitating," forwarding various probabilistic models of libertarian freedom.[14] What unites libertarians is the claim that when all powers that might move an agent to choose a course of action are taken into account—including the agent's own character, dispositions, reasons, and desires—the agent can still refrain from that course of action. If the libertarian were to grant that these internal states not only influence but also *determine* which direction the agent will choose, then the libertarian is no longer a libertarian.

NECESSITY OF THE HEART

We must further contrast the libertarian's Freedom from the Heart with its opposite, Necessity of the Heart, if we are to avoid conflating this form of necessity with love-abolishing forms of necessity. A nuanced analysis of Necessity of the Heart begins with three conditions:

Claudia chooses to love Jim from Necessity of the Heart if she has (1) an internal, convergent, and prevailing reason to love Jim, (2) freedom to either love or refrain from loving Jim relative to the cumulative causal powers of both the physical world and coercive agents, and (3) Claudia does not stand in a transcendent relation to her inner *telos*.

I will call (1) the "Reason Condition," (2) the "Freedom Condition," and (3) the "Teleological Condition."

1. *The Reason Condition.* A choosing agent simply cannot be said to make a *choice* from Necessity of the Heart if the agent has no reason for making that choice. Reason-less, and therefore arbitrary, action

---

14. We return to an analysis of these probabilistic models in 3.3.4. One of the most developed proposals comes from Timothy O'Conner, *Persons and Causes: The Metaphysics of Free Will* (Oxford: Oxford University Press, 2000), chapter 5, particularly pp. 95–98. O'Conner says, "My reasons structure my activity … in the more fine grained manner of giving me, qua active cause, relative tendencies to act" (97). Yet, these "relative tendencies to act" are still not determinative in O'Conner's view. "These are tendencies that it remains entirely up to me to act on or not" (97). Even within O'Conner's probabilistic model of libertarianism, Freedom from the Heart remains a crucial ingredient.

does not count as a choice in this paradigm.[15] By "reason" I simply mean some perceivable end as to why the agent should choose the action in question.[16] Three things can be said of this reason that is our first condition for Necessity of the Heart type choices.

First, the "reason" must be *internal*, residing within the conscious or subconscious borders of the agent's own mental life. It is the *agent's* reason, not an abstract proposition floating in a Platonic realm of forms. Second, the reason must be *convergent* with the propensity-rich character structure of the agent herself. The agent is not an indifferent spectator who views all reasons with equal action-worthiness. Rather, the agent is inclined in such a way that certain reasons appear worthy of her action and others do not. In Edwards' words:

> In every act, or going forth of the Will, there is some preponderation of the mind, one way rather than another; and the soul had rather have or do one thing, than another, or not have or do that thing; and that where there is absolutely no preferring or choosing, but a perfect, continuing equilibrium, there is no volition.[17]

Reasons are like agents in that they also include a teleological element; both aim at certain goals, ends, or purposes. There are cases in which the teleology of an agent converges with the teleology of a reason, i.e., both the agent and the reason aim at the same purpose. An agent may be sympathetic to the plight of single mothers and desire to ease their suffering. A reason to purchase groceries for a

---

15. Reasons are also viewed as an essential element in libertarian accounts of freedom. Every concept of free agency in the contemporary philosophical literature stipulates some reason condition that must be fulfilled in cases of free action.

16. The reason within the account I am sketching need not be singular. "Reason" may stand for a complex, interweaving set of diverse reasons that are teleologically aimed at the same action.

17. Edwards, *Freedom of the Will*, 5.

single mother is that such an act would ease her suffering. Thus, the agent's *telos* and the reason's *telos* converge.[18]

This leads to a third feature of a "reason" in Necessity of the Heart type choices. In addition to being internal and convergent with the agent, the reason must also be *prevailing*. From the perspective of the agent, it is the most action-worthy reason. The agent views the reason (with relative degrees of accuracy or inaccuracy) as resonating more closely with her own teleological propensities than all other reasons. This entails that agents are not only teleological but that an agent's teleology is *hierarchical*. The agent does not aim at all goals equally, but some goals are more prevalent within her character structure.

2. *The Freedom Condition.* In Necessity of the Heart type choices, I add the Freedom Condition: *The agent must be free to actualize or refrain from that choice relative to the cumulative causal powers of both the physical world and coercive agents.* Agents choosing from Necessity of the Heart must make that choice with Freedom from the Machine and Gunman.

This Freedom Condition does not require us to reduce the role of all physical influence to zero, especially in the case of physical influence exerted by the neurological components belonging to the agent (e.g., the native brain constituents *owned by* the agent in contrast to foreign A. A. hardware *imposed on* the agent). Neither must we eliminate the role of social influences surrounding Necessity of the Heart type choices. The physiosocial network may confront the agent with

---

18. It is important to recognize that within this model, it is *not* the reason that causes the choice. I believe that Swinburne, Brümmer, and Geisler are correct in contending that reasons do not function as efficient causes. An agent has choice-making power, whereas a reason does not. Given the success of the internal, convergent, prevailing reason, it has appeared to many philosophers that the reason itself is the salient causal factor in the choice being made. Reasons, however, are causally impotent (i.e., a reason cannot rob a liquor store, but an agent can rob since he acts on reasons with a prevailing teleological convergence to his character). The reason's success is not due to its causal power but to the deep connection between the agent, as a propensity-rich actor who can usher reasons into the realm of action, and the reason, which takes on a prevailing charge from the agent's character.

the raw ontological contours within which her heart's *telos* can be expressed (or perhaps distort those contours/constrictions), and may even push the agent toward a given course of action.

Nevertheless, the Freedom Condition ensures that it is really the agent's heart—her teleological character—that is being expressed in the choice and not merely physical or coercive causal forces. Since neither the Machine nor the Gunman necessitate the agent's choice, the element of necessity in these choices is must be located elsewhere. The necessity is found within the agent herself, or more precisely, in the prevailing teleological convergence between a given reason and the agent's own character.[19]

3. *The Teleological Condition.* This leads to the third condition, which elaborates on the central role occupied by the agent's character in Necessity of the Heart type choices—the Teleological Condition. This condition relates to Richard Taylor's description of a libertarian agent. If an agent transcends all teleological pushes and pulls, then in Taylor's estimation, "The conception that now emerges is not that of a free [agent], but of an erratic and jerking phantom, without any rhyme or reason at all."[20] If an agent has two-way power over every *telos* to choose for or against them, then the agent herself must transcend every *telos*. Thus, there is no "rhyme or reason" to her choices.

The power to act as an "erratic and jerking phantom" is the kind of meaningful action-threatening power that an agent choosing

---

19. Nothing in this view requires that the agent always (or even often) acts from Necessity of the Heart. There are cases in which physical or coercive necessities rather than the agent's character play the determinative role in her "action." See the Epilogue of this work for additional explanation.

20. Richard Taylor, *Metaphysics* (Englewood Cliffs, NJ: Prentice Hall, 1974), 51. For more on why the libertarian view of the agent is "positively mysterious" in Taylor's estimation, see *Metaphysics*, 51–57. In a similar vein are the words of James Thornwell: "As well might a weather-cock be held responsible for its lawless motions as a being whose arbitrary, uncontrollable will is his only law" (cited in John Frame, *No Other God: A Response to Open Theism* [Phillipsburg, NJ: P&R Publishing, 2001], 126n19). R. E. Hobart echoes, "In proportion as [a person's act] is undetermined, it is just as if his legs should suddenly spring up and carry him off where he did not prefer to go" (also cited in *No Other God*, 127).

from Necessity of the Heart does not succumb to. This Teleological Condition, like the Reason and Freedom Conditions, ensures that it is really the agent's heart expressed in the choice, and not some *telos*-overriding power beyond the agent's character.

From the foregoing analysis, we are able to see what led Luther on a quest for a more satisfactory term than "necessity" to describe these kinds of choices. Freedom and necessity are so often pictured in an oil-and-water relation, as modalities that cannot be mixed. In the account above, however, Necessity of the Heart *requires* the agent to possess Freedom from the Machine and Gunman. The heart is free to choose one way or another *relative to physical and coercive powers.* The heart is free to choose in accord with *internal, convergent, and prevailing reasons.* The heart is free to express its own teleology by translating reasons into the realm of action *without a power to transcend one's teleology derailing the process.*

Therefore, Necessity of the Heart may be more accurately described as "Freedom *of* the Heart" (not to be confused with the libertarian's Freedom *from* the Heart).

TELEOLOGY AND TRANSCENDENCE

With Necessity of the Heart better understood as Freedom *of* the Heart, we are in a better place to appreciate the distinction between this notion of freedom and the libertarian notion. This distinction centers on two pictures of who the choosing agent is: a *teleological* or a *transcendent* substance.

To appreciate this distinction, let us introduce a fourth case of Claudia expressing love for Jim, one in which Claudia possesses libertarian free will and, therefore, Freedom *from* the Heart. Not only is there no Necessity of the Machine and Gunman forcing Claudia to love Jim; she can also go one way or the other relative to her character states. In the words of libertarian Clark Pinnock,

It is not enough to say that a free choice is one which, while not externally compelled, is nonetheless determined by the psychological state of the agent's brain or the nature of the agent's desiring. To say that Harry stole the candy bars because he wanted them is obvious—the question is, could he have refrained from stealing them in spite of his desire? The idea of moral responsibility requires us to believe that actions are not determined either internally or externally.[21]

It is in this requirement of Freedom *from* the Heart, the agent's autonomy from her "psychological state" and "desiring," that problems arise for the Axiom of Libertarian Love.

If Claudia transcends her inner propensities in order to possess non-hypothetical two-way power, then who, we may ask, is this heart-transcending, choice-making Claudia? Does she have her own set of internal propensities that move her to act on certain propensities rather than others? If we ascribe a teleological heart orientation for or against loving Jim to this transcendent Claudia, then those propensities either determine her or merely influence her such that she can resist them. If they determine her, then we have abandoned libertarianism. On the other hand, if this transcendent Claudia can act in concert or discord with this teleology, then there is a still more transcendent Claudia. We may ask of that Claudia: Does she have a determining heart or merely an influencing heart whose teleology may be resisted? A positive answer requires an abandonment of libertarianism and a negative answer requires us to posit an even more transcendent Claudia on pain of infinite regress.[22]

Another way of expressing the implications of the libertarian demand for Freedom *from* the Heart is to speak of what libertarians

---

21. Clark Pinnock, "God Limits His Knowledge," in *Predestination and Free Will: Four Views of Divine Sovereignty and Human Responsibility*, ed. David Basinger and Randall Basinger (Downers Grove, IL: InterVarsity, 1986), 149.

22. In Susan Wolf's words,

> In order for an agent to be autonomous, it seems, not only must the agent's behavior be governable by her self, her self must in turn be governable by her self—her deeper self, if you like—and this must in turn be governable by her (still deeper?) self, *ad infinitum*. (*Freedom within Reason* [New York: Oxford University Press, 1990], 14).

of past centuries often called "indifference" (*liberum arbitrium indif-ferentiae*). Schopenhauer in his *Prize Essay on the Freedom of the Will*, Malebranche in his *Search after Truth*, and Descartes in his *Meditations*[23] used the term "indifference" to describe the free agent (though libertarians avoid that term in the contemporary literature). To be in a state of indifference *is* to be in a transcendent state over all desires and aversions. To hint at a problem that will unfold in 1.3: If the choice to love originates in the active power of an *indifferent* agent, is true love really being expressed? Is there not something profoundly oxymoronical about an indifferent lover?

BOYD'S CHIP, HANEGRAAFF'S CATHY, BRÜMMER'S DOLL

Perhaps we can avoid the problematic picture of a heart-transcending, indifferent agent by making a single modification to the Axiom of Libertarian Love. If we subtract the libertarian demand of Freedom *from* the Heart, we reach the following:

> Any agent, A, must possess Freedom from the Machine and
> from the Gunman when loving another agent B if A's love for
> B is to count as authentic.

Let us call this the "Axiom of *Unforced* Love." On this new Axiom, a father's love for his daughter may count as authentic even if his heart renders it impossible for him to refrain from loving her (provided he retains Freedom from the Machine and Gunman). On the Axiom of Libertarian Love, by contrast, such love must be deemed inauthentic because the father does not possess Freedom *from* the Heart. Would a father's love cease to be authentic if he lacked Freedom *from* the Heart? If his internal *telos* were so strong that he simply could not bring himself to say "no" to loving his daughter, then is his

---

23. There are some passages in the *Meditations* where Descartes seems to reject freedom as consisting in indifference, while in later passages he "practically equated freedom with indifference" (Tad Shmaltz, "The Science of Mind," in *The Cambridge Companion to Early Modern Philosophy*, ed. Donald Rutherford [Cambridge: Cambridge University Press, 2006], 161).

love rendered null and void? We cannot easily dismiss such love as inauthentic.

Here we are able to see where the Axiom of Libertarian Love gains its common sense appeal. The Axiom of Unforced Love rings true to common sense. If a person is reduced to a cog in a physical machine or a victim of manipulation, then love loses its authenticity. Freedom from the Machine and the Gunman are indeed necessary conditions of true love. The Axiom of Libertarian Love, however, ventures farther than the Axiom of Unforced Love. It secures libertarian free will by adding the heart to the list of powers from which the will must be free, and thereby becomes less obviously true. It is not beyond doubt that a father's love is inauthentic if his inner *telos* makes it impossible for him to refrain from loving his daughter. There is a bait-and-switch pattern detectable in the libertarian literature by which the Axiom of Unforced Love is conflated with the Axiom of Libertarian Love in such a way that the latter parasitically takes on the common sense force of the former.[24]

Consider three examples in which the Axiom of Unforced Love is conflated with the Axiom of Libertarian Love. Gregory Boyd offers the following argument:

> Suppose I were able to invent a computer chip that could interact with a human brain in a deterministic fashion, causing the person who carries the chip to do exactly what the chip dictates without the person knowing this. Suppose I further programmed this chip to produce "the perfect wife" and inserted it in my wife's brain while she was sleeping. ... Owing to the sophistication of this chip, she would believe that she was voluntarily choosing to love me in this fashion, though in truth she could not do otherwise. Would my wife genuinely love

---

24. It is important to recognize the fundamental unity between those on both sides of the free will question. Libertarians and non-libertarians may find unity in the belief that love is too deeply personal to be reduced to a mechanical process or coercive manipulation. The Axiom of Unforced Love serves as this unity point.

me? I think not. ... My wife's behavior would not be chosen by *her*, so *she* would not really be loving me at all. She would become the equivalent of a puppet. If I want love from *her*, she must personally possess the capacity to choose *not* to love me.[25]

What forms of necessity serve as the counterpoints of authentic love in Boyd's scenario? Boyd combines Necessity of the Machine—a sophisticated computer chip—and Necessity of the Gunman—his coercively installing the chip while she sleeps in a misguided effort to achieve the "perfect wife." Since Boyd has overthrown her Freedom from the Machine and from the Gunman, she does not love authentically, precisely as the Axiom of Unforced Love maintains and exactly as common sense confirms.

Boyd concludes that she must be free "to choose *not* to love me" for any love he receives to be authentic. This conclusion would reasonably follow if this freedom "to choose *not* to love me" were defined in terms of Freedom from the Machine and Gunman. Boyd, however, is arguing for libertarian free will, which also requires Freedom from the Heart. What if Mrs. Boyd lacks the power to "choose not to love" Dr. Boyd because her character qualities and internal dispositions render it impossible for her to refrain from loving him?[26] Is it possible for her to love without Freedom *from* the Heart and still love authentically? Arguing against such a possibility would drastically reduce the persuasive force of Boyd's argument. Her Freedom *from* the Heart must be somehow demonstrated in order to turn Boyd's compelling case for the Axiom of *Unforced* Love into what it actually purports to be—a case for the Axiom of *Libertarian* Love.

---

25. Gregory Boyd, *Satan and the Problem of Evil* (Downers Grove, IL: InterVarsity, 2001), 55; emphasis original.

26. Boyd could perhaps counter this point with his view articulated in *Satan and the Problem of Evil* that through libertarian choices we can actually "resolve our characters." It may be argued that his wife has such a resolved character and, therefore, loves him authentically though without libertarian free will. This calls for a drastic revision of the Axiom as Boyd affirms it. I respond to Boyd's notion of self-resolved characters in 2.2.

The same conflation occurs in Hank Hanegraaff's Chatty Cathy Doll argument. This image confronts us with Necessity of the Machine in which the physical forces at work between a pulled string and a low fidelity phonograph inside Chatty Cathy ensure that "love" will be expressed (unless, of course, the toy is broken). We recognize this "love" as artificial. Hanegraaff concludes that non-artificial love requires libertarian free will.

Cannot someone who rejects the Axiom of Libertarian Love use Hanegraaff's Chatty Cathy image to highlight salient features of authentic love, namely, that love is a deeply *personal* reality? Authentic lovers have certain irreducible properties to them, aspects of volition and consciousness that transcend physical necessity. The Chatty Cathy image captures these intuitions about the nature of love as something essentially personal, the very intuitions behind the Axiom of Unforced Love. By failing to distinguish Freedom *of* the Heart from Necessity of the Machine, Hanegraaff is able to conclude from Chatty Cathy that libertarian free will is a condition of authentic love. The Axiom of Libertarian Love has once again parasitically attached to the intuitive appeal of the Axiom of Unforced Love.

As a third case in point, Vincent Brümmer says, "[love relationships] can only be established and maintained in mutual freedom."[27] He illustrates with the song "Paper Doll":

I'm goin' to buy a paper doll that I can call my own,
A doll that other fellows cannot steal.
And then those flirty flirty guys
With their flirty flirty eyes
Will have to flirt with dollies that are real.
When I come home at night she will be waiting.
She'll be the truest doll in all the world.
I'd rather have a paper doll to call my own
Than have a fickle-minded real live girl.

---

27. Vincent Brümmer, *Brümmer on Meaning and the Christian Faith: Collected Writings of Vincent Brümmer* (Farnham: Ashgate Publishing, 2006), 297.

Brümmer comments,

> Far from being a love song, this is a lament on the absence of
> love. In the words of Sartre, if the beloved is transformed into
> an automaton, the lover finds himself alone—alone with his
> paper doll. It is clear that a relationship of love can only be
> maintained as long as the personal integrity and free auton-
> omy of *both* partners is maintained. As soon as I try to con-
> trol you as an object or allow you to treat me as an object, our
> relationship is perverted into something other than love. Love
> must by its very nature be a relationship of free mutual give
> and take, otherwise it cannot be love at all.[28]

Brümmer cites "Paper Doll" to contrast authentic love relationships with those rendered counterfeit through coercion. In doing so,
Brümmer captures a deep intuition that there is a qualitative difference between love and coercion. Controlling someone as an object to
guarantee reciprocated "love" is hardly worthy of the word.

The incompatibility of love and coercion is precisely what the
Axiom of Unforced Love affirms, and Brümmer sheds light on why
this is so. The extent to which I coerce you to love me is the extent
to which I have trampled your integrity as a person and attempted
to reduce you to a doll. Just as Boyd and Hanegraaff, Brümmer has
helped us to see love for the profoundly *personal* reality that it is.
Like Boyd and Hanegraaff, Brümmer is also arguing for more than
Freedom from the Machine and Gunman. When Brümmer speaks
of "free autonomy" he means libertarian free will, which includes
Freedom *from* the Heart.

Brümmer rightly calls "Paper Doll" a "lament on the absence of
love." What if the lyrics are altered so that the song is no longer
about coercion? Would it remain a "lament on the absence of love"?
Consider the following attempt to lyrically capture the love enjoyed

---

28. Brümmer, *Brümmer on Meaning and the Christian Faith*, 297; emphasis original.

within the Trinity between the Father and the Son "before the creation of the world" (John 17:24b):

> I've always had a loving Father whom I call my own,
> A Father who cannot fail to love Me.
> And when all the love-hungry guys
> With all their love-hungry eyes
> Seek love in characters savvy to lies,
> His Goodness flows inevitably toward Me as love unabating.
> He's been the truest Lover since before the world.
> I'd rather Him be a loving Father always my own
> Than a libertarian agent free to disown.

If these lyrics capture a truth about the intratrinitarian love relationship[29]—namely, that the Father's heart makes it impossible for Him to
refrain from loving the Son—would this be a "lament on the absence
of love" like "Paper Doll"? On the contrary, it could be viewed as a
celebration of the presence of love, an authentic, eternal, and irre-
vocable love.

While Freedom from the Machine and the Gunman are indeed
conditions of true love, as Boyd's "perfect wife" chip, Hanegraaff's
"Chatty Cathy Doll," and Brümmer's "Paper Doll" remind us, it is not
so clear that Freedom *from* the Heart is essential to true love. Freedom
from the Heart is precisely what is required by the libertarian notion
of free will and precisely what these three cases for the Axiom of
Libertarian Love do not address. Given the foregoing analysis, we
can better grasp the "grand illusion" described by Edwards,

> There is a grand illusion in the pretended demonstration of
> *Arminians* [read: libertarians] from common sense. The main
> strength of all these demonstrations lies in that prejudice, that

---

29. A treatment of competing Trinitarian models (i.e., Social Trinitarianism, Latin
Trinitarianism, Salvation-history Trinitarianism) lies beyond the scope of this work. The point
above, however, does not exclusively rest on any one of these Trinitarian models but on the
insight from John 17:24b that love has existed before creation between Father and Son. We
will return to this insight for exegetical analysis in 3.2.

arises through the insensible change in the use and meaning of such terms as *liberty, able, unable, necessary, impossible, unavoidable, invincible, action, etc.,* from their original and vulgar sense, to a metaphysical sense, entirely diverse. ... This prejudice and delusion, is the foundation of all those positions they lay down as maxims.[30]

---

30. Edwards, *Freedom of the Will,* 66–67; emphasis original.

1.3

True Love

Is Freedom from the Heart Indubitable or Dubious?

The most tragic problem in philosophy is to reconcile intellectual necessities with the necessities of the heart and the will.

—*Miguel de Unamuno*, The Tragic Sense of Life

THE NON-INDIFFERENCE
CONDITION OF TRUE LOVE

The Axiom of Libertarian Love not only fails to share the indubitable force of the Axiom of Unforced Love but may also turn out to be deeply counterintuitive upon closer inspection. This chapter highlights two philosophical problems with the libertarian requirement of Freedom *from* the Heart for true love. The first problem focuses on *who* the agent is—an indifference endemic to libertarian agents that renders them questionable candidates for being true lovers. A second problem centers on *why* such an agent chooses—an arbitrariness underlying libertarian choices that makes them a poor medium for the expression of true love.

To the first problem, consider a rather minimal and uncontroversial condition of true love:

> For any agent A to be a true lover of some agent B, A must not be indifferent with regard to B's welfare.

One can no more be indifferent to a person's welfare and simultaneously be a lover of that person than one can be ambivalent about the Lakers' record and simultaneously be a Laker fan. Since being a Laker fan logically entails a desire for the Lakers to win, so, as a matter of analytic *a priori* truth, being a lover entails a desire for the welfare of the beloved.[1]

Reinforcing this point is Philip Hallie's ethical analysis of various responses to Nazi cruelty. Hallie contrasts the liberation of the death camps with the risky hospitality practiced by the Jew-sheltering French Protestants in the city of Le Chambon:

> The opposite of cruelty is not simply freedom from the cruel relationship. ... It lies not only in something negative, an absence of cruelty or of imbalance; it lies in unsentimental, efficacious love. ... The opposite of the cruelties of the camps was not the liberation of the camps. ... All of this was the *end* of the cruelty relationship, not the opposite of that relationship. ... The opposite of cruelty was the kind of goodness that happened in Chambon.[2]

---

1. This desire, however, does not necessarily require an intense emotional component (though it certainly may). I am using the term broadly enough to include cases in which one's desire for the beloved's welfare may be more a reflection of faithful duty than of immediate delight.

2. Philip Hallie, "From Cruelty to Goodness," in *Vice & Virtue in Everyday Life: Introductory Readings in Ethics*, 6th ed., eds. Christina Sommers and Fred Sommers (Belmont, CA: Wadsworth, 2004), 11; emphasis original.

We will further appreciate "the kind of goodness that happened in Chambon" as our analysis of love develops in 1.3. For our present purposes, Hallie's insight is this: Love is not a midpoint between cruelty at one pole and some *tertium quid* at the other. Rather, love stands at the opposite pole of cruelty, with indifference—an absence of cruelty and love—as the midpoint. This is another way of seeing that "love" and "indifference" are qualitatively distinct. Love entails the lover's desire for the beloved's welfare. Let us call this condition for being a true lover the "Non-Indifference Condition."

This qualitative distinction between love and indifference evokes the question: *Can an agent with libertarian free will meet the Non-Indifference Condition?*

LEIBNIZ'S INDIFFERENT QUEEN

In approaching this question, let us recall our case of Claudia loving Jim with libertarian free will—Freedom from the Machine, the Gunman, *and* the Heart. Claudia's inner propensities, character traits, and deliberations may strongly influence her to love Jim. All of those teleological factors must be resistible for Claudia to possess libertarian free will. She must stand in a transcendent relationship above all teleological factors. This transcendence is tantamount to being indifferent or being devoid of desire. Desires are teleological; they are goal-oriented mental states. Is it a matter of common sense that true love must originate in the active power of an indifferent agent? Would we bestow the title of "lover" on an agent devoid of any desire for another's welfare?

Gottfried Leibniz offers an image that clarifies this problematic notion of an indifferent agent:[3]

---

3. Leibniz attempts to "rid [us] of the chimera of complete indifference, which can only be found in the books of philosophers. ... For they cannot even conceive the notion in their head, or prove its reality by an example in things" (*Theodicy* [LaSalle, IL: Open Court, 1985], 345). Leibniz adopts more of a probabilistic view of freedom in which reasons may "incline without necessitating." I analyze this view in 2.2 and 3.3 of this work.

One will have it that the will alone is active and supreme, and one is wont to imagine it to be like a queen seated on her throne, whose minister of state is the understanding, while the passion are her courtiers or favourite ladies, who by their influence often prevail over the counsel of her ministers. One will have it that the understanding speaks only at the queen's order; that she can vacillate between the arguments of the ministers and the suggestions of her favourites, even rejecting both, making them keep silence or speak, and giving them audience as it seems good to her.[4]

Leibniz's image raises an important question: If the libertarian agent is pictured as a queen presiding over all teleological elements such as understanding and passion (Leibniz's "ministers" and "favourite ladies"), then what teleology can be attributed to the queen herself?

Suppose that the Leibnizian queen is Queen Claudia. Queen Claudia's ministers and favourite ladies represent the cumulative teleological factors for and against loving Jim. Imagine a virtual consensus among these ministers and favourite ladies for loving Jim, though a few desires are against it. Queen Claudia can exercise royal authority toward either side with the majority and love Jim, or with the minority and refrain from love.

Suppose that she sides with the majority, choosing to endorse the Jim-loving teleologies in her courtyard. Did Queen Claudia choose to act on Jim-loving teleologies because she *desires* those teleologies over their opponents? If we maintain a pure libertarian view of free will, then the answer is "no." Any such desire is itself a teleological factor. It resides not within the queen on her throne but within the courtyard with all other desires, where it may be endorsed or rejected.

---

4. Leibniz, *Theodicy*, 421.

We can approach this point from a different angle with help from Harry Frankfurt's concept of first and higher-order desires.[5] A first-order desire—a desire to love Jim—resides in Queen Claudia's courtyard. If she chooses for the first-order desire to love Jim, then she either desires to choose the first-order desire to love Jim or she does not. If not, then she is indifferent toward the first-order desire to love Jim, and it is difficult to see why she would choose in favor of that desire at all. If, on the other hand, she does desire to choose the first-order desire to love Jim, then libertarian free will demands that this second-order desire is resistible (i.e., non-determinative). For this second-order desire to be resistible, Queen Claudia must preside over it in such a way that she may endorse or reject it. Thus, the second-order desire moves outside of Queen Claudia and into the courtyard with all other desires.

If she chooses in favor of that second-order desire, then she either desires that second-order desire to be chosen or she does not. If not, then we have slipped back into indifference. If so, then that third-order desire is either determinative (in which case libertarian free will is abandoned) or resistible (in which case it joins ranks with all other desires in the courtyard). If chosen, then this third-order desire must be desired by the queen (with a fourth-order desire) or not; and so the infinite regress continues.

This tiresome story reveals a trilemma regarding the agent in to-love-or-not-to-love choices. Either:

(1) Queen Claudia desirelessly chooses to endorse the first-order desire to love Jim. In this case, we are left with an *indifferent* agent whose choices are arbitrary. Or:

(2) Queen Claudia faces the task of actualizing an infinite amount of higher-order desires. In this case, we have an *exhausted* agent whose choices could never make it into the

---

5. See Harry Frankfurt, "Freedom of the Will and the Concept of a Person," in *Free Will*, 2nd ed., ed. Gary Watson (Oxford: Oxford University Press, 2003), 81–95.

real world (given the impossibility of instantiating an actual infinite series of antecedent desires). Or:

(3) Queen Claudia has prevailing desires to love Jim within her character, desires that she does not transcend. In this case, we have an *inherently teleological* agent whose choices are reflections of her internal *telos*.

The third option represents Freedom *of* the Heart (also known as "compatibilism"), which I developed in 1.2.4. Hendrik Vroom captures this option with an alternative to the Leibnizian queen:

We can imagine our self or "soul" as a kind of conference room in which all those urges, needs, obligations, possibilities and ideals have a voice and try to attract our attention. ... The "I" resembles that conference room more than it does an old throne room with our "I" on the throne, ruling wisely and justly amongst these impulses. ... We are that bundle of urges, pulses, needs, obligations, ideals, memories and schemes of acts. ... The real "me" is the whole of this process and not a free floating "I" in (sub)consciousness above the hustle and bustle.[6]

Such a view is off limits to the libertarian because it lacks the transcendent "I" who floats "above the hustle and bustle."

Rejection of this third option leaves the libertarian with two other possibilities. An exhausted agent is not the kind of entity whom libertarians would wish to make their champion of freedom. This leaves the libertarian with an indifferent agent, one who must transcend all desires in order to accept or reject them.[7] If we are to avoid the Scylla

---

6. Hendrik Vroom, "Sin and Decent Society: A Few Untimely Thoughts," *International Journal of Public Theology* 1 (2007): 471–88, 475–76.

7. There are two senses of the "agent" that must be kept distinct. First, the libertarian may speak of the "agent" as the center of active power (i.e., the Leibnizian queen) who presides over all desires. "Agent" may also refer to both the center of active power and the desires over which she presides, i.e., the queen and her courtyard. In this second sense of the "agent," libertarianism does not require the agent to be indifferent. It is the first sense, essential to two-way power, to which my critique applies.

of an infinite regress on one side and the Charybdis of compatibilism on the other, then this indifferent agent may choose for desires *but must remain desireless when so choosing*.[8]

EDWARDS ON INDIFFERENCE AND LOVE

From this analysis the question arises: *Could an indifferent queen be a true lover of Jim?* Given the Non-Indifference Condition, with its modest requirement that a true lover not be indifferent with regard to the beloved's welfare, the answer is "no." The agent could choose in favor of the desire-for-the-welfare-of-the-beloved as it resides in the courtyard but must lack any such desire within herself if our picture is to remain consistently libertarian. Since Queen Claudia is devoid of any internal desire for Jim's welfare, she fails to meet the Non-Indifference Condition and cannot, therefore, be accurately described as a "true lover" of Jim (or anyone else).

Jonathan Edwards reinforces this assessment. "Virtue" language in the quote below may be read as "love" language to clarify the main thrust of Edwards' analysis relative to my own:

> If Indifference belong to Liberty of the Will ... and it be essential to virtuous action, that it be performed in a state of Liberty ... it will follow, that it is essential to a virtuous [read: loving] action, that it be performed in a *state* of indifference. ... And so it will follow, that ... the more indifferent and cold the heart is with relation to the act performed, so much the better; because the act is performed with so much the greater liberty. But is this agreeable ... to the notions which mankind in all ages have of Virtue [Love], that it lies in what is contrary to

---

8. The libertarian may reply that the agent still exercises active power to choose for a desire. Libertarianism can offer an agent who chooses to act on a (first-order) desire for another's welfare. However, there is a distinction between *desirously choosing* (as required by the Non-Indifference Condition) and *desirelessly choosing for a desire* (as required by libertarian free will). In the former case, the desire is an intrinsic property of the agent as a nexus of active power (i.e., the inherently teleological agent). In the latter case, the desire does not enter into that nexus of active power known as the agent (i.e., the indifferent agent).

indifference, even in the *tendency* and *inclination* of the heart
to virtuous [loving] action; and that the stronger the inclination, and so the further from Indifference, the more virtuous
[loving] the *heart,* and so much more praiseworthy the *act*
which proceeds from it?[9]

Edwards' insight is that "virtue," which "most essentially consists in
love,"[10] exists in an inverse proportion to indifference: The greater the
degree of indifference within the agent, the lesser the degree of love
within that agent. Love entails an inherently teleological agent, an
agent with "the *tendency* and *inclination* of the heart to virtuous action."
Edwards continues,

> Moreover, that it is necessary to a virtuous [loving] action
> that it be performed in a state of Indifference … is contrary
> to common sense; as it is a dictate of common sense, that
> Indifference itself, in many cases, is vicious, and so to a high
> degree. As if when I see my neighbour or near friend … in
> extreme distress, and ready to perish, I find an Indifference in
> my heart with respect to anything proposed to be done, which
> I can easily do, for his relief. So if it should be proposed to me
> to blaspheme God, or kill my father, or do numberless other
> things, which might be mentioned, the being indifferent, for a
> moment, would be highly vicious and vile.[11]

To illuminate Edwards' point, we return to Le Chambon in 1941, two
years after the fall of France to Nazi forces. A Jewish refugee knocks
on the door of a farmhouse seeking shelter for her family from the
German SS. A Chambonais woman opens the door. Upon hearing
the refugee's pleas, the heart of the Chambonais woman is such that

---

9. Edwards, *Freedom of the Will,* in *The Works of Jonathan Edwards,* vol. 1 (Peabody, MA:
Hendrickson, 2000), 53–54; emphasis original.

10. Edwards, *A Dissertation Concerning the Nature of True Virtue,* in *The Works of Jonathan
Edwards,* vol. 1, 122–42, 122.

11. Edwards, *Freedom of the Will,* 53–54.

she can do nothing else than extend help.[12] Does the lack of non-hypothetical two-way power due to the Chambonais' inner *telos* render her life-saving actions sub-loving or sub-virtuous? Or does the fact that refusing to help the endangered family is not even a live possibility for her, given her inner *telos*, count even more toward her being virtuous and loving?

Let us envision an indifferent agent responding to the refugee's knock. Upon hearing her requests, this agent faces the woman on his porch suspended in perfect equipoise, equally capable of bringing about love or cruelty toward his imperiled neighbor. With no internal *telos* to converge with the reason to help the refugee before him, how could this agent operating with such Freedom *from* the Heart merit the title of "true lover"? If he is equally able to welcome her hospitably or to stand idly by, would not common sense view such an agent as "vicious and vile,"[13] rather than loving and virtuous? Even if our indifferent agent were to exercise his libertarian power to shelter the refugee, he could have just as easily (from his state of *telos* transcendence) turned her over to the SS. The Chambonais woman whose help overflows from her heart automatically and without transcendent deliberation comes closer to the mark of true lover than the libertarian agent for whom Nazi collaboration was a live possibility.

We might add the perspective of the Jewish refugees to the foregoing analysis. The roughly six thousand Jewish lives saved at Le Chambon were not indifferent to the fact that nearly thirty-five hundred residents gave them life-saving nourishment, shelter, and respect. In such cases, love's core component is not desire for the welfare of

---

12. In the historical account of this episode as told by Philip Hallie, the woman, a Protestant fundamentalist from the Darbystes tradition, warmly welcomed the Jewish refugee into her home and called up the stairs, "Husband, children, come down, come down! We have in our house at this very moment a representative of the Chosen People!" (Hallie, "From Cruelty to Goodness," 13).

13. If *we* were the refugees, which agent would we rather have encountering our peril—an agent with a prevailing inherent *telos* to help his neighbors or an indifferent agent with equal power to help or not help his neighbors? Would we prefer an agent choosing with Freedom *of* or Freedom *from* the Heart pondering our plight? Which agent would we rather be married to, friends with, etc.?

others; rather, it is grateful recognition that someone has done much for our welfare while we have done little or nothing for his (and perhaps even caused him pain). Love for God motivated by a realization of His grace falls into this category. In this model of love there remains an inescapable element of non-indifference. One of the "hidden children of the Holocaust," a Jewish woman saved at the age of eleven from Nazi forces in southern France, exclaimed, "I'm alive! I'm grateful for each and every day, grateful that I was married for fifty-eight years, grateful that I have three children and nine grandchildren! I'm grateful!"[14] These are not the words of an indifferent agent but of a woman whose heart overflows with gratitude. Likewise, we are not indifferent to the fact that God has done so much for our welfare but deeply grateful for it. On this grace/gratitude analysis of love, the indifference endemic to libertarian agents remains a troublesome problem.

In sum, we have seen an important reason to question the philosophical credibility the Axiom of Libertarian Love. If being a true lover requires libertarian free will, and libertarian free will requires an indifferent agent, then it follows that being a true lover requires an indifferent agent. What appeared from a pre-analytical perspective to be a necessary condition for being a true lover is, on closer analysis, *incompatible* with being a true lover. True love is not the feat of indifferent agents. These conclusions, however, do not demand a wholesale abandonment of the Axiom of Libertarian Love. It is not *all* misguided. We can retain its kernels of truth—that love is far too personal a reality to be reduced to either physical or coercive necessities—by holding instead to the Axiom of Unforced Love.

---

14. Madeleine Nussen in a personal interview conducted on April 8, 2011. At the age of eleven, Madeleine Rozenfeld became Madeleine "Rousseau" to evade Nazi detection. In November of 1942, her loving father, Henri, escaped Paris with his family by bribing a train operator to ride a midnight freight to southern France where they found life-saving shelter.

WIGGINS AND HASKER ON
CONTRASTIVE EXPLANATIONS

To encourage further thinking in this direction, I add a second problem with the Axiom of Libertarian Love. Kane introduces this second problem:

> If an agent's reasons incline her toward choosing A rather than B, it must still be possible on an incompatibilist [i.e., libertarian] view ... for her to choose A or to choose B all circumstances remaining the same. Now if the agent chooses A, we can explain the choice by saying that the agent's reasons inclined to the choice of A rather than B. But what if B is chosen? How will this be explained, given exactly the same reasons that inclined to A?[15]

Libertarians offer two answers to Kane's question of why agents choose one way rather than another. First is the appeal to quantum indeterminacy, as typified by David Wiggins.[16] For Wiggins, Claudia choice either to love Jim or to refrain from loving him, is explicable in terms of the indeterministic behavior of subatomic particles in her brain matter. Saul Smilansky counters:

> Presumably, the indeterminacy of a subatomic particle in the brain "triggers" the person's macro-level action. Action here "can be otherwise in exactly the same situation" only because a randomly indeterminate subatomic particle happened to be effective on the macro-level. We find nothing here that makes

---

15. Robert Kane, "Two Kinds of Incompatibilism," in *Agents, Causes, and Events: Essays on Indeterminism and Free Will*, ed. Timothy O'Conner (Oxford: Oxford University Press, 1995), 115–50, 124.

16. See David Wiggins, "Freedom, Knowledge, Belief and Causality," in *Knowledge and Necessity*, ed. G. Vesey, Royal Institute of Philosophy Lectures 3 (London: Macmillan, 1970), 52. This approach is reminiscent of Epicurus' ancient doctrine of the atomic "swerve," in which room for free moral agency is postulated and fear of fatalism abated on the basis of physical indeterminacies.

a person (or anything else) truly free or a suitable candidate for the attribution of moral responsibility.[17]

How can the expression "I love you" retain relational significance if it ontologically reduces to: "A subatomic particle in my brain matter happened to move one way rather than another, thereby triggering my macro-level love-response to you." A husband invoking such a quantum explanation of his love to his wife would soon find himself sleeping on the couch. By tracing love's origin to quantum phenomenon, he has trivialized the relationship.

Whether Monod's impersonal physics determine our actions or our actions are explicable in terms of Wiggins' indeterministic quantum physics, equally as impersonal, we still lose the personhood essential to true love. In Kane's words,

> If choices or decisions result from ["quantum uncertainties in the brain"], those choices or decisions would be chance occurrences, neither predictable nor within the agent's control—more like epileptic seizures than free, responsible choices or actions.[18]

William Hasker, Robert Nozick, J. P. Moreland, and Gregory Boyd offer a second answer to the question of why an agent with libertarian free will chooses one course of action over another. They do not make the appeal to quantum physics that Wiggins does but reject the need for such explanations altogether. Says Hasker,

> It is not enough, we will be told, that an action can be given a rational explanation after the fact. What we need is a *contrastive explanation* that explains, in terms of antecedent conditions *why one alternative was chosen rather than another*. And if the reply is "Well, that's the way I decided," ... the challenge will simply be repeated. The proper response for a libertarian, of

17. Saul Smilansky, *Free Will and Illusion* (Oxford: Oxford University Press, 2000), 70.
18. Kane, "Two Kinds of Incompatibilism," 125.

course, is to simply *reject* the demand for a contrastive explanation in such cases.[19]

When explaining why an agent chooses one alternative rather than another, the "proper response," according to Hasker, is simply to reject the need to explain the choice contrastively.[20] It is clear why Hasker and other libertarians deem contrastive explanations superfluous. Such explanations, if they appealed to antecedent factors within the agent that were sufficient to tilt the scales of action toward one alternative over another, would be tantamount to an abandonment of libertarian free will.[21]

Rejecting the need to explain our actions contrastively moves us still farther from the realm of common sense where such explanations factor largely into our understanding of our selves and one another. In everyday discourse, we frequently offer contrastive explanations for our actions in terms of antecedent character states. Examples abound: John spent his Sunday at Torrey Pines rather than at church *because he is more of a golf-lover than a religious man.* Aron did not demand repayment and never asked for the loaned money back *because he is a generous friend.* Brian buys lottery tickets the seventh of every month but never on the thirteenth *because he is so superstitious.*

---

19. William Hasker, *The Emerging Self* (Ithaca, NY: Cornell University Press, 1999), 103–4; emphasis original. For a further defense of this position see J. P. Moreland, "Miracles, Agency, and Theistic Science: A Reply to Steven B. Cowan," *Philosophia Christi* 4 (2002): 139–60, 151–55.

20. A non-contrastive explanation may be offered by the libertarian in terms of reasons that "impressed" the agent to choose a course of action. However, a contrastive explanation of why the agent chose to act on that reason set rather than another is withheld. For example, there may be a reason-desire set, RD_1, for Claudia to choose to love Jim, and a reason-desire set, RD_2, why Claudia should refrain from loving Jim. If Claudia chooses to love Jim and we ask why she so chose, the libertarian may respond with a non-contrastive explanation by simply citing RD_1. However, if we refine the question and ask why she chose to act on RD_1 rather than RD_2, no answer is offered beyond Hasker's "Well, that's the way [she] decided."

21. There is a qualitative difference between rejecting the demand to solve a problem and actually solving it. For example, an atheist who believes the natural world to be the self-sufficient, all-encompassing reality, does not solve the problem of explaining how the natural universe began without a Beginner by simply rejecting the demand for an explanation, since such an explanation would require an abandonment of his theory.

We operate in our relational worlds as if actions originate in who we are as genuinely teleological actors rather than thinking in terms of "Well, that's the way I decided." The burden of proof falls on the libertarian to demonstrate why our common sense use of contrastive explanations in terms of antecedent character states is misguided. Why should we content ourselves with merely non-contrastive explanations when describing free actions?[22]

CONTRASTIVE EXPLANATIONS
AND LOVE IN LE CHAMBON

To deepen this point, we return once more to Le Chambon for a concrete case of expressed love in which nearly thirty-five hundred French Protestants saved nearly six thousand Jews from Nazi extermination. Why did the Chambonais choose to help rather than refrain from helping? In a compatibilistic picture in which agents choose by Freedom *of* the Heart, we have a straightforward answer: The Chambonais expressed loving action for the Jews rather than refrained from doing so because of the teleological makeup of their hearts. The moral fabric of their internal *telos* converged more closely with the *telos* to help the Jews than it did with the *telos* to capitulate to Nazi pressure. A contrastive explanation is readily available by pointing to salient features of the agents' characters.

This explanation fits precisely the accounts offered by the residents of Le Chambon. Hallie narrates:

> When I asked [the Chambonais] why they helped these dangerous guests, they invariably answered, "What do you mean,

---

22. We think not only of actions but also of agents in teleological rather than transcendent terms. When we call someone good, generous, and honest, or bad, greedy, and deceitful we ascribe teleology to agents themselves. A generous agent is teleologically aimed toward liberally giving to others; an honest agent is teleologically aimed toward telling it like it is, and so on. In the libertarian picture, none of these teleological qualities can be ascribed to agents themselves. If generosity is something the agent can equally choose to act on or not, then generosity is not part of the agent herself. She can choose for or against that teleology, and therefore transcends it. Are our teleological descriptions of agents misguided? What alternative descriptions of a *telos*-transcendent agent can we offer from within a libertarian paradigm?

'Why'? Where else could they go? How could we turn them
away? There was nothing else to do". ... They saw no alternative to their actions and to the way they acted, and therefore
they saw what they did as necessary. ... Helping for them was
as natural as breathing or eating—one does not think of alternatives to these functions; they did not think of alternatives
to sheltering people.[23]

Given the loving characters found among the farming community of
Le Chambon, shunning Jewish refugees was incomprehensible. They
did not transcend their endangered human-loving propensities in a
position of indifference from which they could either help or not help.

On the libertarian account, by contrast, the residents of Le
Chambon, as centers of active power, transcended whatever loving
teleologies may have been part of their broader fields of consciousness. These transcendent Chambonais had no *intrinsic* desires to
love refugees but presided over any such desires to act on them or
not. Why did these transcendent Chambonais choose to act on ref-
ugee-loving desires rather than refrain from doing so? With no compatibilistic explanation in terms of their antecedent *telos* available to
the libertarian, we are left with Hasker's answer, "Well, that's the way
[they] decided." The causal connection between *what the Chambonais
hearts were like* and *the way the Chambonais chose* has been severed.
However, we commonly assume such causal connections between
people's hearts and their actions everyday as we attempt to navigate
our relational worlds.

Is the libertarian rejection of contrastive explanations the best
we can do when seeking to understand the phenomenon of love? If
we think in very personal terms of those whom we dearly love, are
we content to say, "Well, that's just the way we decided," when we
could have just as easily refrained from loving them? The Freedom
from the Heart required by the Axiom of Libertarian Love ushers us

---

23. Hallie, "From Cruelty to Goodness," 13.

farther from the realm of common sense, not only in explaining *who* choosing agents are as lovers but also in explaining *why* we choose to love. We can jettison these problems and simultaneously hold on to the gems of insight within the Axiom of Libertarian Love by opting instead for the Axiom of Unforced Love.

Part 1:
Evil and the Autonomous Heart

Summary and Conclusions

Part 1 opened by dispelling the misnomer that there is a problem of evil. We face a tangled web of problems, both abstract and concrete. Successful answers to abstract problems of evil should be not only credible philosophically but also compatible with biblical insights and consistent with how we meet the concrete problems of evil.

We then turned to the Relational Free Will Defense and its crucial claim that love requires libertarian free will. I challenged this Axiom of Libertarian Love by distinguishing three senses of necessity and their corresponding freedoms. I concur with libertarians that the lover-to-beloved relationship cannot be reduced to a programmed-to-programmer or coerced-to-coercer relationship. The Axiom of Unforced Love captures this significant point of unity.

By requiring Freedom *from* the Heart, the Axiom of Libertarian Love is not as obviously true as the Axiom of Unforced Love. I offered examples from Gregory Boyd, Hank Hanegraaff, and Vincent Brümmer that demonstrate how the two are often conflated in such a way that the Axiom of Libertarian Love parasitically takes on the indubitable force of the Axiom of Unforced Love. It is only by confusing Necessity of the Machine and of the Gunman with that of the Heart that we reach the conclusion that love requires *libertarian* free will.

Two additional problems threaten the credibility of the Axiom of Libertarian Love. First was the problem of positively defining who the choosing agent is if she stands in a transcendent relationship over all teleologies. Such indifferent agents serve as poor candidates for being true lovers. Second was the related problem of explaining why such transcendent agents choose to love rather than refrain from loving without resorting to quantum indeterminacy ("Well, that's the way the subatomic particles happened to move.") or Hasker's non-contrastive explanation ("Well, that's the way I decided.").

Libertarian free will, which seemed like a requirement of authentic love from a pre-analytical perspective, turns out to be a significant threat to authentic love. Such freedom does not enter deeply enough into how we love as genuinely teleological agents. I conclude that the Axiom of Libertarian Love is not an axiom at all (although it may *function* that way in various theological systems). The notion that authentic love requires libertarian free will is not an indubitable starting point beyond reasonable challenges. I will no longer refer to this notion as the *Axiom* of Libertarian Love, but as the *"Assertion* of Libertarian Love" (or simply as the "Assertion").

We will move on to the question: Does the Assertion face problems in the realms of biblical insight and the existential confrontation of concrete evil?

PART 2

Freedom and the Enslaved Heart

Depth Capacity and the Case for Libertarian Free Will

2.1

The Moral Imperative Argument

Does "Ought" Imply "Can"?

Why should that be commanded which cannot at all be done? The answer is, that man is most wisely commanded to walk with right steps, on purpose that, when he has discovered his own inability to do even this, he may seek the remedy which is provided for the inward man to cure the lameness of sin, even the grace of God, through our Lord Jesus Christ.

—*Augustine,* On Man's Perfection in Righteousness

DEPTH CAPACITY

To assess if the Defense's claim that "authentic love requires libertarian free will" is successful in terms of biblical insight, we must first ask: What is the measure of success here? Otherwise, we slide into superficial proof texting and premature conclusions. In this analysis, success is measured in terms of "depth capacity." By depth capacity, I mean the ability of a given notion to be integrated through successive levels of biblical insight without the force of biblical insight exerting fatal logical pressure on that notion.

An analogy from diving offers clarification of depth capacity. Beginning divers risk serious problems if they descend below forty feet underwater. Veteran divers may descend to a depth of around one hundred and thirty feet. Roughly a dozen professional divers, with proper equipment, have surpassed eight hundred feet—a depth that would prove fatal for beginning divers given their limited depth capacity.

Similarly, certain theological notions fare well when initially submerged in the text, but suffer fatal logical pressure at greater depths of biblical insight. The notion that Jesus was *merely* human survives without complication in John's Gospel when we read of Jesus enduring fatigue beside a well in the heat of Samaria (John 4:6), and exhaling a terminal breath on the cross (John 19:30). Pressure builds when Jesus promises the quenching water of eternal life to a Samaritan woman at the well and offers superhuman insight into her clandestine relational life (John 4:11–19). The notion of a merely human Jesus suffers further pressure when He rises from the dead by His own authority (John 10:17–18; 20:1–9). As John's narrative moves deeper, we read of Jesus as the "Word" who stands in an identity relation to God (John 1:1), the Father's "equal" (John 5:18–20), the "I Am" who existed before Abraham (John 8:58), and Thomas' "Lord and God" (John 20:28). At this depth, the notion of a merely human Jesus fatally succumbs to the force of biblical insight and, therefore, lacks depth capacity.[1]

Assessing depth capacity does not require us to conclude with hubris that we have exhausted the text's meaning "with Cartesian

---

1. Certain theological conclusions such as "God exists," "there is one God," "God is morally pure," "humankind needs a Redeemer," and "God is at work in time-space history," exhibit a strong depth capacity. Such conclusions do not require additional premises beyond the biblical text or logically implode when immersed within greater depth of biblical insight. Conversely, theological notions like, "man is intrinsically good," "God is devoid of all emotion," and "God promises you health and wealth," may breathe in isolated contexts, but collapse the deeper they are pushed into the text (i.e., they lack depth capacity).

cleanliness or Baconian precision."[2] Rather, depth capacity can be assessed relative to biblical insight *as far as our most exegetically faithful interpretations go*. We interpret the text as accurately as we can (without confusing our interpretations with the final word on the text) and then ascertain how a given theological notion logically withstands what depths have been reached.

The following chapters gauge the depth capacity of the three most common attempts to find biblical warrant for libertarian free will. Norman Geisler offers an argument from passages in which humans are commanded to exercise choice-making power in an obedient love relationship with God. Such biblical commandments are meaningless, Geisler contends, if we lack the libertarian power to obey them. "If God demands it, then we can do it."[3] We will call this the "Moral Imperative Argument," which is the focus of 2.1.

Clark Pinnock articulates a second libertarian argument, focusing on passages in which humans stubbornly resist God's commands to love Him. We rebel against God and He is genuinely grieved when we do so. For Pinnock, "our rebellion is proof that our actions are not determined but significantly free."[4] In Pinnock's view, "significantly free" is synonymous with libertarian free will. We will call this the "Grievous Resistance Argument," which is the focus of 2.2.

A third argument comes from I. Howard Marshall, who attempts to reach the libertarian conclusion from passages on God's relational vision for His creatures. God desires meaningful relationships, but "when we try to think of a person foreordaining the course of

---

2. See Roger Lundin, *The Responsibility of Hermeneutics*, with A. C. Thiselton and C. Walhout, (Grand Rapids/Exeter: Eerdmans/Paternoster, 1985), 23. The interpretive task begins with the recognition that the object of scriptural study—God and His ways—is too vast to be circumscribed by our analytical attempts at objectification. This recognition does not call for a theological agnosticism. It is not a black vacuum that we behold through the mirror. Rather, we may see true reflections of God that He has condescended to reveal. We know neither nothing nor fully but "in part."

3. Geisler, *Chosen But Free* (Minneapolis: Bethany House, 1999), 30.

4. Pinnock, "God Limits His Knowledge," in *Predestination and Free Will: Four Views of Divine Sovereignty and Human Responsibility*, eds. David Basinger and Randall Basinger (Downers Grove, IL: InterVarsity, 1986), 149.

a relationship ... the concept is logically contradictory."[5] Therefore, Marshall concludes, we must have libertarian free will to embrace or shun God's relational vision for our lives. We will call this the "Relational Vision Argument," which is the focus of 2.3.

In gauging the depth capacity of the Moral Imperative, Grievous Resistance, and Relational Vision Arguments, we will ask a series of questions of each. To shed light on the logical structure of each argument, we will ask: Does reaching the libertarian conclusion from a biblical premise require an additional premise in order to be logically valid? If such an additional premise is required to reach the libertarian conclusion, does this premise succumb to logical pressure from biblical insight? We will engage the best efforts of libertarian theologians to relieve any such pressure. Our assessment of depth capacity will close by clarifying the existential implications of the libertarian arguments.

THE PELAGIAN-ERASMIAN-KANTIAN-FINNEYAN DICTUM

A first argument for libertarian free will stems from such passages as "Choose life" (Deut 30:19), "Choose this day whom you will serve" (Josh 24:15),[6] and "Three things I offer you. Choose one of them" (2 Sam 24:12). Norman Geisler and others[7] argue that such imperatives are meaningless if humanity lacks the libertarian power to heed them.

We will begin our assessment of depth capacity by asking: What is the logical structure of this Moral Imperative Argument? It is logically possible that the commands, invitations, and calls of the Bible do not gauge our ability to heed them but expose an utter inability to respond positively to God. In this logically possible scenario, the

---

5. Marshall, "Predestination in the New Testament," in *Grace Unlimited*, ed. Clark Pinnock (Minneapolis: Bethany House, 1975), 132.

6. Any viable interpretation of Joshua's call to "choose" must include the tension entailed by Joshua's claim, "You are not able to serve the LORD" (24:19). The immediate context of the "choose" imperative of Joshua 24:15 is not choosing to love God but a choice between the false "gods your fathers served beyond the River" and the false "gods of the Amorites."

7. See Richard Ruble, "Determinism vs. Free Will," *Journal of the American Scientific Affiliation* 28 (1976): 70–76, 73.

Bible's moral imperatives do not lead to the libertarian conclusion. Therefore, an additional premise is required to render the induction from moral imperatives to libertarian free will logically valid.

The additional premise—"ought implies can"—fills this void. Geisler clarifies,

> Logic seems to insist that such moral obligations imply that we have self-determining moral free choice. For *ought* implies *can*. ... Otherwise, we have to assume that the Moral Lawgiver is prescribing the irrational, commanding that we do what is literally impossible for us to do. ... Moral obligation implies moral freedom.[8]

From Geisler's logic, the Moral Imperative Argument takes the following form:

MIA1 (The Biblical Premise): According to biblical insights, humans are proper subjects of divine imperatives.

MIA2 (The Additional Premise): Ought implies can, i.e., being subject to divine imperatives requires humans to have the power to respond positively to those imperatives.

MIA3 (The Libertarian Conclusion): Therefore, humans have the libertarian free will to respond positively to divine imperatives.

"Ought implies can" (MIA2), the crucial premise between biblical imperatives and the libertarian conclusion, is often credited to Immanuel Kant. Kant argues that human agents are plagued by a self-incurred (versus inherited) "inversion" of our "maxims." Rather than the intrinsic rightness of a given action (i.e., the "categorical imperative") as our fundamental moral motivation in choice making, we allow self-centered goals to steer our choices. We do what is "right" for the wrong reason, allowing self-aimed agendas to masquerade as

---

8. Geisler, *Chosen But Free*, 30; emphasis original.

moral action to both others and ourselves.[9] Kant calls this phenomenon "radical evil." Just as this state of radical evil is self-incurred for
Kant, so it may be self-cured through a "moral conversion" brought
about by our appropriate exercise of free will. That we *ought* to
undergo a moral conversion from radical evil implies that we *can* do
so. In Kant's words,

> Duty demands nothing of us which we cannot do. ... When the
> moral law commands that we ought now to be better men, it
> follows inevitably that we must be able to be better men ... we
> ought to conform to it; consequently we must be able to do so.[10]

The "inversion" of "maxims" can be realigned, self-centeredness
resisted, and radical evil defeated, because "ought implies can."[11]

The Kantian connection between moral duty and moral ability
gained momentum in American theology through the nineteenth-
century "revivalist" Charles Finney. Finney expounds Kant's argument
for human ability not in the context of the rationally achieved categorical imperative but in the context of biblically-revealed imperatives:

> The human will is free, therefore men have power or ability to
> do all their duty. The moral government of God everywhere
> assumes and implies the liberty of the human will, and the
> natural ability of men to obey God. Every command, every
> threatening, every expostulation and denunciation on the Bible

---

9. P. Rossi expounds, "We thus inculcate in ourselves a propensity to make exceptions to
the demand of the categorical imperative in circumstances when such an exception seems to be
in our own favor" ("Kant's Philosophy of Religion," in *The Stanford Encyclopedia of Philosophy*,
ed. Edward Zalta [Stanford, CA: Stanford University, 2004], 3.6).

10. Immanuel Kant, *Religion within the Limits of Reason Alone*, tr. Theodore Greene and Hoyt
Hudson (New York: Harper and Row, 1960), 46. See also *Critique of Pure Reason*, tr. Norman
Kemp Smith (London: Macmillan, 1953), A548.

11. For analysis of Kant on this point, see Gordon Michalson, *Kant and the Problem of God*
(Oxford: Blackwell, 1999). See also Nicolas Wolterstorff, "Conundrums in Kant's Rational
Religion," 40–53; Denis Savage, "Kant's Rejection of Divine Revelation and His Theory of
Radical Evil," 54–76; and Leslie Mulholland, "Freedom and Providence in Kant's Account of
Religion: The Problem of Expiation," 77–102, in *Kant's Philosophy of Religion Reconsidered*, eds.
Philip Rossi and Michael Wreen (Bloomington: Indiana University Press, 1991).

implies and assumes this. ... This ability is called the natural ability, because it belongs to man as a moral agent, in such a sense that without it he could not be the proper subject of command, of reward or punishment.[12]

By combining biblical imperatives with "ought implies can" to conclude that "the human will is free," Finney's argument is synonymous with the Moral Imperative Argument.

Before Kant and Finney, Erasmus articulated the principle of "ought implies can" in his famous sixteenth century exchange with Luther. Erasmus highlights the patent absurdity (and even the cruelty) of asking someone to do that which they are unable to do, an argument still echoed in support of "ought implies can."[13]

Over a millennium before Erasmus, "ought implies can" was a guiding axiom in the theology of Pelagius.[14] Pelagius found Augustine's prayer "Command what thou wilt and grant what Thou commandest" to be ethically dangerous because it implied that we cannot do what we ought to do. For Pelagius, the denial of moral ability to perform our moral duty justifies a morally lax fatalism, a concern echoed by Erasmus and contemporary libertarians.[15]

Before Kant ushered the notion that "ought implies can" into the canons of secular ethical philosophy (where it still resides[16]), this notion had already been articulated, endorsed, and opposed in the

12. Charles Finney, *Finney's Systematic Theology*, 3rd ed., ed. Dennis Carroll (1878; Minneapolis: Bethany House, 1994), 307.

13. See Erasmus, *Diatribe Concerning Free Will*, cited in Martin Luther, *Bondage of the Will*, tr. J. I. Packer and O. R. Johnston (Westwood, NJ: Revell, 1957), 137; and Clark Pinnock, "From Augustine to Arminius: A Pilgrimage in Theology," in *The Grace of God, the Will of Man*, ed. Clark Pinnock (Grand Rapids: Zondervan, 1989), 22.

14. On the role of "ought implies can" in Pelagian theology, see "Augustine," in *Routledge Encyclopedia of Philosophy*, ed. Edward Craig (New York: Taylor & Francis, 1998), 555.

15. See Erasmus, *Diatribe Concerning Free Will*, preface (cited in Luther, *The Bondage of the Will* [Cambridge: James Clarke/Westwood, NJ: Revell, 1957], 97); and Irving Singer, *The Nature of Love: Plato to Luther*, vol. 1, 2nd ed. (Cambridge, MA: MIT Press, 2009), 293–94.

16. See James Sturba, "Liberalism and the Challenge of Communitarianism," in *The Blackwell Guide to Social and Political Philosophy*, ed. Robert Simon (Oxford: Wiley-Blackwell, 2002), 183.

history of Christian theological reflection. Though several formidable philosophical challenges have emerged in recent years to cast doubt on "ought implies can,"[17] the focal point of this analysis is if this notion has a strong depth capacity when immersed in biblical insight.

JOHANNINE PERSPECTIVES ON "CAN"

In interest of depth over superficiality, our focus on biblical insight will be narrowed largely to John's Gospel. Do John's insights into the human condition exert logical pressure on "ought implies can"?

In John 6, a crowd who witnessed Jesus feed the five thousand in Tiberias follows Him to Capernaum to gratify their physical hunger (John 6:1–13, 22–26). Jesus moves beyond their felt needs to their deeper need to "believe in Him whom [the Father] has sent" (John 6:29). As the "Bread of Life" (John 6:35), Jesus offers Himself for the satisfaction of the crowd's spiritual hunger. As His repeated invitations to believe are met with disbelief (οὐ πιστεύετε; John 6:36), Jesus responds, "No one can come to me, unless the Father who sent me draws him. And I will raise him up on the last day" (John 6:44).

What does John 6:44 tell us about the human ability to respond to divine imperatives? This question is particularly relevant to assessing the depth capacity of "ought implies can" since John 6:44 occurs in the immediate context of invitations to believe (John 6:27a, 29, 35). A positive response to these invitations is a feat that "no one can" perform. The Greek word pair οὐδείς δύναται ("no one can") goes beyond factual-behavioral language (i.e., what one *does not* do; cf. οὐ πιστεύουσιν, μή πιστεύοντες; John 6:64) to the language of moral modalities (i.e., what one *cannot do*). John offers insight not merely on human *action* but on the deeper level of human *ability*.

---

17. See Jonathan Harrison, *God, Freedom and Immortality* (Burlington, VT: Ashgate Publishing, 1999), particularly chapter 17; John Kekes, "The Reflexivity of Evil," in *Social Philosophy and Policy: Virtue and Vice* 15 (Winter 1998): 216–32, 222–32; and Ishtiyaque Haji, *Moral Appraisability: Puzzles, Proposals and Perplexities* (New York: Oxford University Press, 1998), 226.

The phrase "no one can" exposes a universal moral inability by which it is impossible for any human agent operating independently of the Father's drawing to respond positively to Jesus. Since "moral conversion" lies beyond the scope of human ability, John's concept of evil is more radical than Kant's "radical evil." In John 6:44, a moral duty—that people *ought* to believe in Jesus—does not correspond to a moral ability, since people *cannot* believe in Jesus apart from the Father's drawing.[18] Johannine evil is too radical for self-recuperation.

Can the notion that "ought implies can" breathe at the depth of John 6:44? This crucial premise of the Moral Vision Argument could survive at the depth of John 6:44 if we envision the Father's drawing (ἑλκύσῃ) as a universal phenomenon. On this interpretation, the Father draws *all* humans, thereby supplying us with the moral ability to fulfill our moral duty to believe in Jesus. From this perspective, the inability in John 6:44 captures only a hypothetical anthropological insight, i.e., how powerless humans *would be* without the Father's drawing.

Three factors count against such an interpretation and exert additional pressure on the claim that "ought implies can."

1. *The immediate context of John 6:44 treats actual disbelief, not hypothetical inability.* In the antecedent context of John 6:44, Jesus' invitation to believe is met with disbelief (John 6:36). It is precisely this disbelief within the flow of the John's narrative that motivates Jesus to expose their moral inability in John 6:37–66. If the phrase "no one can come to me" expresses only a hypothetical insight into what the crowd *would be* without the Father's drawing (highlighting what they in fact

---

18. Bruce Ware concurs,

> Surely, so the argument goes, these statements must indicate that anyone and everyone can believe. ... The "ought" of believing in Christ to be saved implies the "can" of common human ability to believe. ... [John 6:44] devastates the logic of this position. ... Although all ought to believe in Christ, only those drawn by the Father can believe and be saved ("The Place of Effectual Calling and Grace in a Calvinist Soteriology," in *The Grace of God the Bondage of the Will*, vol. 2, eds. Thomas Schreiner and Bruce Ware [Grand Rapids: Baker Books], 339–63, 349, 351).

are as recipients of this universal drawing), then Jesus has offered no explanation for the actual disbelief in the immediate context.[19]

2. *The Father's drawing is co-extensive with an eschatological raising up.* The strong grammatical connection in John 6:44 between being drawn and being "raised up on the last day," precludes a universal drawing interpretation. James White clarifies,

> The identity of those raised up on the last day to eternal life *is absolutely co-extensive* with the identity of those who are drawn. Obviously, then, it cannot be asserted that Christ, in this context, is saying that the Father is drawing *every single individual human being*.[20]

If all of the drawn will be raised up to eternal life (as John 6:44 affirms), and if all are drawn, then it follows that all will be raised up. A universal drawing interpretation of John 6:44 forces us to affirm a universalism in which "every single individual human being" will be saved. This notion stands at odds with the condemnation motifs throughout John's Gospel.[21]

3. *The broader context of John's Gospel reinforces the reality of a non-hypothetical inability.* Beyond John 6:44, John revisits the theme of human moral inability in unambiguously actual (versus hypothetical) terms. Shortly after expressing imperatives (ποιεῖτε; John 8:38), Jesus offers a pride-leveling assessment of his audience, "Why do you not understand what I say? It is because you *cannot* (οὐ δύνασθε) bear

---

19. The unpalatability of Jesus' words to the crowd reinforce this point. In John 6:65, Jesus reiterates that "no one can come to me unless it is granted him by the Father." As the direct result of this teaching (ἐκ τούτου), many abandon Jesus (John 6:66). If Jesus was teaching a universal drawing, then there seems to be no catalyst for this abandonment. Abandonment would be expected more if Jesus was teaching the far less crowd-appealing message that human moral inability has not been universally negated.

20. James White, *The Potter's Freedom: A Defense of the Reformation and Rebuttal of Norman Geisler's* Chosen But Free (Amityville, NY: Calvary Press, 2000), 160; emphasis original.

21. See John 3:17–20; 12:48; 15:6, 22; 16:8–10 (cf. Dan 12:2; Matt 25:41, 46; Mark 9:43, 48; Luke 16:22–28; Rev 14:9–11).

to hear my word" (John 8:43; emphasis added). Here is an actual inability to respond to a moral imperative, not a hypothetical inability that has been nullified by a universal drawing.

In John 12:36, Jesus commands a crowd, "While you have the light, *believe* (πιστεύετε; imperative) in the light, that you may become sons of light" (emphasis added). However, "they still did not believe in Him" (John 12:37b). In John's commentary on this incident, the apostle adds to the factual-behavioral claim of John 6:37b the modal claim of moral possibility and impossibility: "They *could not* (οὐκ ἠδύναντο) believe" (John 12:39; emphasis added). He reinforces this insight with a citation from Isaiah 6:10, most likely from Massoretic Text sources, given the imperatival verbs (vs. the LXX, which uses the passive): "He has blinded their eyes, and hardened their heart, lest they see with their eyes, and understand with their heart, and turn, and I would heal them" (John 12:40). John follows Jesus' imperative with a strong expression of human moral inability.[22]

In a final Johannine passage relevant to the depth capacity of "ought implies can," Jesus says, "I am the vine; you are the branches. Whoever abides in me and I in him, he it is that bears much fruit, for apart from me *you can do nothing* (οὐ δύνασθε ποιεῖν οὐδέν)" (John 15:5; emphasis added; note the emphatic double negative—οὐ and οὐδέν). If "ought implies can," then it would follow from Jesus' statement that those apart from Him who have no moral *ability* to bear fruit are under no moral *duty* to bear fruit, since they are powerless to do so. Nowhere does John's text warrant this conclusion. It is reasonable to conclude that within the anthropological framework of John's

---

22. In its original context, Isaiah 6:10 serves as another case of "ought" in the absence of "can." Isaiah's message begins with a set of present-tense imperatives (Isa 6:9), followed by God's command to "make the heart of this people dull, and their ears heavy, and blind their eyes." When Isaiah asks, "How long, O Lord?" God responds, "Until cities lie waste without inhabitant, and houses without people, and the land is a desolate waste" (Isa 6:11). The function of the imperatives in this context is less a barometer of moral ability than to expose moral inability in a judgment-incurring fashion. John reiterates the judgment-incurring function of moral imperatives with a Christological emphasis (John 15:22).

Gospel, "ought" is consistent with "cannot," an insight reinforced in the Synoptic,[23] Pauline,[24] and Old Testament literature.[25] These biblical insights move us a considerable distance from Finney's claim that, "the human will is free, therefore men have power or ability to do all their duty." If "ought implies can," and all men "ought" to obey God's every command, then it would follow that all men "can" do so, as Pelagius, Erasmus, Finney, and Geisler taught. Such optimistic conclusions lack depth capacity when submerged in biblical insights concerning a profound moral brokenness at the heart of humanity.

TWO ERASMIAN STRATEGIES

Helpful assessments of depth capacity not only look for biblical pressure exerted on a given notion, but also engage attempts to relieve that pressure. Here we examine two libertarian attempts to salvage "ought implies can" at the depth of John's unflattering anthropological insights. Erasmus develops both of these strategies in his sixteenth century

---

23. Matthew 7:18 adds to the fruit motif of John 15:5: "A healthy tree cannot bear bad fruit, nor can a diseased tree bear good fruit." The indicative-to-infinitive verb shift with respect to the move from what trees actually do in Matthew 7:17 (ποιεῖν) to what they are not able to do in Matthew 7:18 (οὐ δύναται ... ποιεῖν) indicates a synthetic parallelism in which the second statement does not echo the first but deepens it. Bad trees not only produce bad fruit—the factual insight into people's moral behavior—they also cannot produce good fruit—the deeper modal insight into people's moral condition.

24. Romans 8:7 adds, "For the mind that is set on the flesh is hostile to God, for it does not submit to God's law; indeed, it cannot (οὐδέ γάρ δύνανται)" (emphasis added). As in the Gospels, we find strong language of moral inability (ἀδύνατόν; Matt 19:26; Mark 10:27; Luke 18:27). Paul uses a synthetic parallel not unlike Jesus in Matthew 7:18. The fleshly mind "does not submit to God's law"; this is a factual claim on what the mind actually does (οὐχ ὑποτάσσετα; indicative). More deeply, the fleshly mind "cannot" do so; this is the modal claim. Paul reinforces the modal claim in the next phrase: "Those who are in the flesh cannot (οὐ δύνανται) please God" (Rom 8:8; emphasis added).

25. According to Jeremiah 17:9, "The heart is deceitful above all things, and desperately sick." As in the New Testament, Jeremiah adds the modal to the factual. Jeremiah asks if those who are accustomed to doing evil can do good (Jer 13:23). He answers with two images of inability: an Ethiopian's inability to alter his skin color and a leopard's inability to change his spots. Evildoers are no more able to accomplish the moral feats of loving God and breaking their addictions to evil than the Ethiopian or leopard could accomplish those natural feats. This dim assessment of human moral ability is echoed throughout the Hebrew Bible (Gen 8:21; cf. 6:5; Pss 14:3; 52:2–3).

theological exchange with Luther. I will extend Luther's responses into the conversation with contemporary libertarians who adopt these Erasmian strategies.

The first strategy comes from Erasmus' efforts to distance himself from the optimistic anthropology of Pelagius. In Pelagian thought, "human nature is uncorrupted, and the natural will competent to all good ... and salvation is essentially a work of man."[26] For Erasmus by contrast, "The human will after sin is so depraved that it has lost its freedom and is forced to serve sin, and cannot recall itself to a better state ... man without grace cannot will good."[27] Contemporary libertarian, Norman Geisler, echoes Erasmus on this point:

> When we say *"ought* implies *can"* we do not mean that whatever we ought to do we can do by our own strength. This would be contrary to the clear teaching of Christ that "without me you can do nothing" (John 15:5). ... Hence, *"ought* implies *can"* only in the sense that we can *by the grace of God.*[28]

Thus, MIA2—"ought implies can"—undergoes a semantic shift to what we may call MIA2*:

> **MIA2*:** "Ought implies can *only by the grace of God,*" i.e., without God's grace humans cannot do what we ought to do.

Luther responds to this first Erasmian strategy as follows:

> For once it is granted and settled that "free-will" has lost its freedom, and is bound in the service of sin, and can will no

---

26. Philip Schaff, *History of the Christian Church*, vol. 3 (Grand Rapids: Eerdmans, 1985), 815. For similar analysis of Pelagius' thought, see Richard Flathman, *Political Obligation* (London: Taylor & Francis, 1973), 36.

27. Erasmus, *Diatribe Concerning Free Will*, cited by Luther, *Bondage of the Will*, 137, 145.

28. Geisler, *Chosen But Free*, 31. Paul Copan concurs, "Kant's 'ought implies can' should be modified to 'ought implies can, with God's available grace' " ("Original Sin and Christian Philosophy," *Philosophia Christi*, vol. 5, no. 2 [2003]: 519–41, 538). John Hare suggests the same modification in "Naturalism and Morality," in *Naturalism: A Critical Analysis*, eds. W. L. Craig and J. P. Moreland (London: Routledge, 2000), 194; emphasis original.

good. I can gather nothing from these words but that "free-will" is an empty term whose reality is lost.[29]

For Luther, the move from MIA2 to MIA2* is such a drastic semantic shift that "ought implies can" becomes its antithesis, "ought implies cannot." If obedience to divine imperatives lies beyond the scope of autonomous human willpower, then Erasmus loses the libertarian free will that he set out to defend.

To extend Luther's argument, it is clear that the premise "ought implies can *only by the grace of God*" no longer merits the libertarian conclusion. To reach the conclusion of libertarian free will, the Moral Imperative Argument requires a new additional premise. Specifically, the scope of grace must be clarified as a libertarian free will-friendly reality.

Consider a counterexample that brings the need for such an additional premise to the surface. Suppose that God's grace so radically reorients the inner *telos* of a human agent that she not only *can* but also *will* necessarily say "yes" to God. In this case, the premises that humans are subject to divine commands (MIA1) and that grace is required to heed those commands (MIA2*) both hold true, but the libertarian conclusion (MIA3) does not follow. Once we open the door to grace as a prerequisite for human obedience, what is to keep us from defining grace along the lines of such an efficacious reorientation of the human heart? In order to reach the libertarian conclusion, grace must be defined as a divine act that enables us to say "yes" or "no" to God's commands.

What problems arise with completing the induction of the Moral Imperative Argument by defining grace as a libertarian free will-friendly reality? Let us assume that grace makes obedience to divine imperatives possible though not necessary. We can draw a distinction between humanity "apart-from-grace," who cannot respond positively

---

29. Luther, *Bondage of the Will*, 148.

to God's commands, and humanity "under-grace," who gains the ability to respond positively.

Two troublesome conclusions follow from this picture. First, humanity apart-from-grace does not measure up to libertarian standards of moral responsibility. Geisler says, "Praise and blame make no real sense unless those praised or blamed have the ability to do otherwise."[30] Humanity apart-from-grace, therefore, cannot be blamed for failing to obey divine imperatives since they lack the ability to do so. Once grace is extended, humans under-grace gain something new, i.e., "the ability to do otherwise," and therefore incur blame in a way that they did not in their former apart-from-grace state. On this libertarian paradigm, God would not have to bother with the incarnation or crucifixion in order to achieve the goal of declaring humans morally blameless. Rather, He could achieve universal salvation by withholding the grace that renders humanity able to obey and, therefore, blameworthy for not obeying. This leads to a perplexing notion of damning grace—grace that magnifies rather than mitigates blame.

Second, it becomes *obligatory* for God to extend grace if He wishes to issue moral imperatives without being indicted for cruelty. If God issues the command "Love me!" and humans exist apart-from-grace, then they *cannot* love Him. In this case, the imperative would be meaningless and God would be "mocking their misery" (Erasmus). In Erasmus' logic, God *must* move humans from being apart-from-grace to the being under-grace in order to issue meaningful, non-mocking imperatives. Thus, we are led into the enigmatic notion of obligatory grace, grace that *must* be given. In this scenario, God's grace becomes non-obligatory if and only if He withholds all moral imperatives. What then becomes of God's moral vision for His creatures?

This leads to a second libertarian strategy to salvage the depth capacity of "ought implies can." In Erasmus' words,

---

30. Geisler, *Chosen But Free*, 31.

If it is not in the power of every man to keep what is commanded, all the exhortations in the Scriptures ... are of necessity useless. ... Ecclesiasticus, by saying "if thou art willing to
keep," indicates that there is a will in man to keep or not to
keep; otherwise, what is the sense of saying to him who has no
will, "if thou wilt"? Is it not ridiculous to say to a blind man:
"if thou are willing to see, thou wilt find treasure"? or to a deaf
man: "if thou art willing to hear, I will tell a good story"? That
would be mocking their misery.[31]

If humans lack the libertarian power to respond positively to divine
imperatives, then two undesirable conclusions follow for Erasmus.
First, imperatives "are of necessity useless," and second, God would be
"mocking their misery." Just as it would be meaningless and mean-spir-
ited to ask a blind man to behold the Sistine Chapel, so it would be
absurd and sadistic for God to issue imperatives if we lack libertarian
free will to obey them. Contemporary libertarians Norman Geisler
and Clark Pinnock have revived Erasmus on this point.[32]

Luther responds to Erasmus,

If, now, God, as a Father, deals with us as His sons, with a
view to showing us the impotence of which we are ignorant;
or as a faithful physician, with a view to making known to us
our disease. ... He should say: "do," "hear," "keep," or: "if thou
shalt hear," "if thou art willing," if thou shalt do"; can it be fairly
concluded from this that therefore we can do these things freely,
or else God is mocking us? Why should not this conclusion
follow rather: therefore, God is trying us, that by His law He
may bring us to a knowledge of our impotence.[33]

---

31. Erasmus, *Diatribe Concerning Free Will* (cited in Luther, *Bondage of the Will*, 171).

32. See Geisler, *Chosen But Free*, 31; and Pinnock, "From Augustine to Arminius," 22.

33. Luther, *The Bondage of the Will*, 153. In Augustine's words,

   The law was given for this purpose: to make you, being great, little; to show that
   you do not have in yourself the strength to attain righteousness, and for you, thus

For Luther, imperatives do not lead to the libertarian conclusion that "ought implies can," but rather: *Ought exposes cannot, and cannot exposes the need for a radical grace.*

Luther reached this conclusion through the portal of Pauline theology in which "the law" does not serve as a gauge of human moral ability. For Paul, the law *cannot* (ἀδύνατον) solve humanity's moral problem (Rom 8:3) because it cannot be adequately obeyed (Rom 3:20; Gal 2:15–16; 3:10–14).[34] The law does, however, serve a meaningful function in Paul's theology; it reveals and reinforces our moral powerlessness in a way that the cross of Jesus becomes utterly indispensable (Rom 8:3; Gal 2:21; 3:24).[35]

From this "ought exposes cannot" perspective, God is not like a bully commanding a blind man to behold the Sistine Chapel for sadistic pleasure. Rather, the picture of God comes closer to that of a compassionate optometrist who commands a blind patient to behold the Sistine Chapel before restoring his sight. The impossible command serves the vital function of demonstrating who deserves all credit once the patient marvels at the painted ceiling with clear eyes.

In addition to exposing our need and evoking our gratitude for grace, can we expand Luther's case on moral imperatives? Does "ought" serve other important functions in the absence of a libertarian "can"? I briefly offer five points.

1. *"Ought" renders the plea of moral ignorance obsolete.* Independent of libertarian ability, moral imperatives preclude human agents from pleading innocence on the grounds of ignorance. Oughts make us *knowing* violators of God's commands. The Bible frequently connects

---

helpless, unworthy, and destitute, to flee to grace. (Cited by John Calvin, *Institutes of the Christian Religion*, vol. 20, ed. John T. McNeill, [Louisville: Westminster John Knox Press], 357.)

34. See Frank Thielman, *Paul & the Law: A Contextual Approach* (Downers Grove, IL: InterVarsity, 1994), 124–30.

35. On the law as "pedagogue" to drive us to Christ in Galatians 3:24 see Ben Witherington, *Paul's Narrative Thought World: The Tapestry of Tragedy and Triumph* (Louisville: Westminster/John Knox Press, 1994), 54.

the degree of knowledge to the degree of moral culpability (Dan 5:22; cf. Luke 12:47–48; Rom 2:12–16; 3:19–20).[36] In John's Gospel, Jesus says, "If I had not come and spoken to them, they would not have been guilty of sin, but now they have no excuse for their sin" (John 15:22). The function of the imperatives in this context is not to assert human moral ability but to underscore the inexcusability of moral evil.

2. *"Ought" leads to obedience when coupled with the Spirit.* The New Testament frames the gospel message to "repent and believe" as an imperative,[37] which the Holy Spirit makes operative in people's lives.[38] In 3.2 we ask if libertarian free will factors into these motifs. For our present purposes, the crucial point is this: logic does not demand that we possess libertarian free will in order for imperatives to serve as a means through which God brings about obedience.

3. *"Ought" highlights the moral achievements of Jesus.* Jesus transcends "ought implies can" with a superior moral dictum: "ought implies *did*." Luther argued that moral imperatives serve to "bring us to a knowledge of our impotence." We may move deeper to the conclusion that moral imperatives help bring us to a realization of Jesus' unique moral *omnipotence*.[39]

4. *"Ought" offers a glimpse into the character of the Ought-Giver.* Imperatives against idolatry reveal God to be the supreme object of worship; imperatives against lying reveal truth-telling and relational

---

36. See R. K. McGregor Wright, *No Place for Sovereignty: What's Wrong with Freewill Theism* (Downers Grove, IL: InterVarsity Press, 1996), 56–58.

37. See John 14:11; 20:27 (cf. Mark 1:15; Acts 15:7 and 16:31).

38. See John 3:5–8; 6:37, 44 (cf. Acts 13:48; 16:4; 18:27; Phil 1:29 and 2:13).

39. Jesus fulfilled His Father's imperatives not in a mythic realm, but in a real time-space-cultural context, complete with I-Other relations, economic inequities, bodily limitations, and social pressures. It is one thing to command "love your enemy." It is quite another to command love of enemies from someone sleep-deprived with an inflated ego in a vengeful society whose enemy is a lot richer than him. The crucial point is that Jesus obeyed His Father's imperatives amidst the forces that frequently seduce the rest of us into moral evil.

authenticity to be core values within God's character; imperatives against slavery reveal the profound value God places on His image-bearers, etc.[40] Independent of libertarian free will, "ought" says something significant about the heart of the God.

5. *"Ought" reflects a supreme moral reference point.* Divine imperatives are disclosed as a transcendent code to help us avoid elevating our own artificial moralizations to the level of absolutes. They offer an axiological framework for seeing ourselves as we are.[41]

This brief inventory reinforces Luther's point that moral imperatives do not require libertarian free will to maintain "usefulness" or to clear God of mockery charges. A meaningful account of "ought" can be formulated in the absence of a libertarian "can." I conclude that Erasmian strategies in their original and contemporary forms do not relieve the pressure exerted by the biblical insight against "ought implies can."

ANTHROPOLOGICAL OPTIMISM

The final step gauging depth capacity is to ask: Does the notion represent true insight into the human condition or does it miss the mark and thereby carry negative existential implications? The presupposition of this question is that ideas are not epiphenomena devoid of causal power. Bad ideas have bad consequences. More specifically, bad ideas *about people* have bad consequences *on people*. This rings

---

40. The way in which the God of the Bible does not fall victim to Plato's famous Euthyphro dilemma highlights this function of "ought." Moral imperatives come neither from a God-transcending code nor an arbitrary divine willing, but from His nature: "Good and upright is the LORD; therefore He instructs sinners in the way" (Ps 25:8; emphasis added). "*Be holy* (imp.) for *I am* holy" (Lev 11:44; emphasis added; cf. 20:26; Ps 99:9). "Beloved, let us *love one another* (imp.), for love is from God. ... God *is* love" (1 John 4:7a, 8b; emphasis added). See William Alston, "What Euthyphro Should Have Said," in *Philosophy of Religion: A Reader and Guide*, ed. William Lane Craig (New Brunswick, NJ: Rutgers University Press, 2002), 283–98.

41. Pascal observed, "Men never do evil so completely and cheerfully as when they do it from a religious conviction." How many divine missions turn out to be egocentric ambitions marked with a forged signature of God's approval? Divine imperatives aid us in the process of deciphering between morals born in our own imaginations and moral truths that transcend our creative powers.

particularly true if the bad idea is unrealistically optimistic. An unrealistically optimistic diagnosis of chronic fatigue syndrome for a man suffering from cancer will have dismal consequences for that man, despite the naïve peace of mind he may temporarily enjoy from the less harsh diagnosis.

To illustrate this point further, consider the optimistic diagnosis of humanity's moral condition from the French revolutionary, Marquis de Condorcet, "The moral goodness of man … is capable of indefinite perfection like all his other faculties."[42] Condorcet continues,

> Is there any vicious habit, any practice contrary to good faith, any crime, whose origin and first cause cannot be traced back to the legislation, the institutions, the prejudices of the country wherein this habit, this practice, this crime can be observed?[43]

Humanity's problem is not internal, but external according to Condorcet (e.g., "legislation, the institutions, the prejudices of the country").

This optimistic portrait of "the moral goodness of man" was typical of the French Revolution.[44] Despite this widespread anthropological optimism, the French Revolution became one of the bloodiest revolutions in the history of Western culture. We may count Condorcet's notion of "the moral goodness of man" among the over ten thousand casualties of the French guillotines.[45]

The utopian dreams of the French revolutionaries failed to materialize in large part because their anthropological critique did not go deep enough. They did not consider the internal moral corruption that

---

42. Marquis de Condorcet, "Sketch for a Historical Picture of the Progress of the Human Mind," in *Readings on Human Nature*, ed. Peter Loptson (Petersborough, Ontario: Broadview Press, 1998), 127.

43. Condorcet, "Sketch for a Historical Picture," 127.

44. This optimism is evidenced by the French revolutionaries declaring 1790 year 1, hiring young actresses to play the goddess of reason, and celebrating them in French cathedrals as living statues to the omnicompetence of a humanity freed by reason from religious and political corruption. See Paul Copan, "Original Sin and Christian Philosophy," 521; and Gillian Evans, Alister McGrath, and Alan Galloway, *The Science of Theology*, vol. 1 (Grand Rapids: Eerdmans, 1986), 224.

45. Condorcet died in prison while awaiting his own turn at the guillotine.

hinders the progress of all people, no matter how scientifically enlightened, politically unfettered, or unrepressed by religious authoritarianism they may be. While properly recoiling at institutionalized evils
(e.g., political tyranny, religious authoritarianism, economic exploitation), they failed to recognize the deeper anthropological roots of
evil. Since all evils were located externally, there was no reason to
probe internally, no category of corruption within the heart to warrant self-critique.

Anthropological optimism remains an entrenched idea in Western
culture. Our most fundamental problem is external—too little government, too much government, too much religion, not enough religion, too much materialism, not enough prosperity, etc.[46] The mantra
becomes, "Change the soil around the tree and the tree will grow and
produce fruit." What if the tree itself is sick at its very root, and this
deeper disease explains why no matter what soil we find ourselves
in politically, religiously, or economically, bad fruit persists, spreads,
and mutates into new forms? A bad tree cannot produce good fruit
(Matt 7:18).[47]

It is here that the Moral Imperative Argument's crucial premise
that "ought implies can" falls short of true insight into the human
condition. It represents an unrealistically optimistic view of humanity.
Recall Finney's claim that "men have power or ability to do all their
duty." For Erasmus, it is "in the power of every man to keep what is
commanded." We "can" overcome egocentrism and exhibit constant,
universal love because we "ought" to do so. We "can" end all war,
greed, economic exploitation, religious scandal, and interpersonal
strife because we "ought" to end them. We "can" solve all concrete
problems of evil, whether personal, cultural, or spiritual, through the

---

46. Governmental, economic, and religious reform are not intrinsically bad projects. They
simply fail as cure-all remedies when they are elevated as such by those who define all of
humanity's problems exclusively in external terms. Hendrik Vroom says, "Blessings like technology and medical care cannot undo the brokenness of the world" ("Sin and a Decent Society,"
International Journal of Public Theology 1 [2007]: 471–88, 477).

47. For more passages that cast doubt on anthropological optimism see Genesis 8:21 (cf. 6:5;
Pss 14:3; 52:2–3; Jer 13:23; 17:9; Matt 19:26; Mark 10:27; Luke 18:27; John 15:5; and Rom 8:7–8).

power of libertarian free will. Whether this libertarian power of "can" is ours because of a universally bestowed grace (Erasmus and Geisler), or without such grace (Pelagius), humans are a race of staggering moral competence.[48] In the spirit of Condorcet, we underestimate a deep moral incompetence in the human heart and set the stage for the resurgence of more failed utopias. In this way, the anthropological ingredients of the Relational Free Will Defense to solve the abstract problems of evil may ironically intensify the concrete problems of evil.

In church contexts this downplaying of depravity takes many shapes. The emphasis gradually shifts from dealing with internal propensities to evil by *becoming* the right kind of person by God's grace to *doing* the right actions of which *I* am already capable, an entry point for religious legalism and an unhealthy emphasis on rule-keeping. My need for community—others to spur me on toward love—is overshadowed by the ability of the competent *I* to do what it ought to do. The critical social dimensions of virtue formation are lost. Beginning with an unrealistically optimistic diagnosis, our churches begin to look as successful as the French Revolution or communism.[49]

---

48. The moral omnicompetence implicit in "ought implies can" would be a sound anthropological insight for heaven's citizens who find themselves relieved of evil propensities. In the state of glory, love will flow with an ease and spontaneity that are a far cry from present experience. Therefore, the principle "ought implies can" is not so much false as it is ahead of the times. The premature application of "ought implies can" to humans as we are now represents an unrealistically optimistic appraisal of our present moral state, unrealistic precisely on account of its prematurity.

49. According to Harry Schaffer,

> Socialists and Communists of all shades and leanings believe in the perfectibility of all mankind. Man is basically good and capable of being master of his own destiny. Only the economic, social, and political environment (with the stress on "economic") has prevented man from realizing the utmost limits of his capabilities both as a productive and social being" (*The Soviet System on Theory and Practice* [New York: Appleton-Century-Crofts, 1965], 30).

The utopian dreams of Russian communism turned into a nightmare with staggering human casualties. Failure to wrestle with the internal anthropological problem in a narrow focus on externals is perhaps the main downfall of communism, Islamo-fascism, and virtually all other normative systems of human progress with a utopian edge. See Vroom, "Sin and a Decent Society," 477.

The foregoing critique not only exposes the negative existential consequences of the idea that "ought implies can." It also highlights the insightfulness of the biblical alternative. Vroom observes, "The more we perceive society to be perfectible, the more we consider the idea of sin to be an old-fashioned and depressing category."[50] The historic failures of the "man is basically good" anthropology ought to give us pause and open us to a fresh assessment of biblical insights into the human condition. With the guillotines of the French Revolution, the massive death tolls of communism, two world wars, and other historical travesties that we may all too easily enumerate, which view into the human condition carries more insight: that we "can" do all that we "ought" to do, or that "the heart is deceitful above all things, and desperately sick" (Jer 17:9)?

An answer to this question comes from an unlikely source. Michael Ruse, whose commitment to metaphysical naturalism drives him to the conclusion that ethics are illusory,[51] acknowledges:

> I think Christianity is spot on about original sin. How could one think otherwise, when the world's most civilized and advanced people (the people of Beethoven, Goethe, Kant) embraced that slime-ball Hitler and participated in the Holocaust? I think Saint Paul and the great Christian philosophers had real insights into sin and freedom and responsibility, and I want to build on this rather than turn from it.[52]

When we supplement the list of egregious historical evils with an honest survey of our own moral incompetence, we have proof enough

---

50. Vroom, "Sin and a Decent Society," 471.

51. Ruse says, "Ethics as we know it is an illusion fobbed on us by our genes" ("The Evolution of Ethics," in *Religion and the Natural Sciences,* ed. J. E. Huchingson [Orlando: Harcourt Brace, 1993], 308–11, 310).

52. Michael Ruse, "Darwinism and Christianity Redux: A Response to My Critics," *Philosophia Christi* 4 (2002): 189–94, 192. Alvin Plantinga concurs, "The doctrine of original sin has been verified in the wars, cruelty, and general hatefulness that have characterized human history from its very inception to the present" (*Warranted Christian Belief* [Oxford: Oxford University Press, 2000], 207).

for the biblical assessment of humanity under the bondage of sin. "Ought implies can" does not withstand the depth of biblical insight, cannot survive this depth through two Erasmian strategies, and contains an unrealistic optimism that paves the way for more doomed projects toward human perfection. Since the crucial middle premise of the Moral Imperative Argument does not enter deep enough into the human *aversio a Deo* and corresponding *conversio ad creaturam* (Rom 1:21–25), the libertarian conclusion does not follow.

2.2

The Grievous Resistance Argument

Does Divine Grief Imply Human Autonomy?

God does look down on his world and weep. But its twistedness did not catch Him by surprise.

—*Joni Eareckson-Tada,* When God Weeps

RESISTANCE AND AUTONOMY

Although moral imperatives do not warrant the conclusion of libertarian free will, perhaps we can reach the libertarian conclusion through evidence that the human will can shun these imperatives. Scripture portrays humans at war against God's will, disobeying His commands, shirking His invitations, and resisting divine calls. We turn to the second attempt to find biblical warrant for libertarian free will—the Grievous Resistance Argument.

We approach the depth capacity of this second attempt by first clarifying its logical structure. What is the motivating logic behind the Grievous Resistance Argument? Consider a story of the kind of moral resistance that motivates the argument. At the age of fourteen, Siri was coerced into The Always Prospering brothel in the Thai city of Ubon Ratchitani.[1] Her age and youthful appearance attract high profits for her pimp. If Siri shares the fate of many young girls ensnared in the global sex slavery industry, then she will likely contract HIV. Then, no longer useful for generating profits, she will be thrown to the street like an irreparably broken factory machine. Siri's pimp and clientele resist God's imperative to "love" your neighbor as yourself with grievous consequences.

If we sense the tragedy and twistedness of Siri's situation, then we move toward what the New Testament calls σπλαγχνίζομαι.[2] This verb expresses a deep internal compassion that evokes suffering-alleviating action. Does God's heart convulse with such compassion for Siri, or is He rather like Epicurus' Zeus whose "blessed and immortal nature knows no trouble"?[3]

From these questions we are able to see the logic motivating the Grievous Resistance Argument. Libertarian free will seems like a glowing prospect for upholding the sanity of God, a Being who shudders with us at moral evil and its consequences. In the words of Clark Pinnock:

> According to the Bible, human beings are creatures who have rejected God's will for them and turned aside from his plan. This is another strong piece of evidence that God made them truly free. Humans are evidently not puppets on a string. They are free even to pit their wills against God's. ... Obviously we

---

1. See chapter 2 of Kevin Bales, *Disposable People: New Slavery in the Global Economy* (Berkeley: University of California Press, 2000).

2. See Matthew 9:36; 14:14; 15:32; 20:34 (cf. Luke 7:13; 10:33; Eph 4:32; and 1 Pet 3:8).

3. Epicurus, *Principal Doctrines*, I, in *Epicurus: The Extant Remains*, tr. Cyril Bailey (Oxford: Clarendon Press, 1926).

are free because we are acting as a race in a way disruptive of God's will and destructive to the values God holds dear for us. It is surely not possible to believe that God secretly planned our rebelling against him. Certainly our rebellion is proof that our actions are not determined but significantly free.[4]

For Pinnock, God cannot determine His creatures to trample one another and at the same time be truly broken up when they do so. If Siri's pimp and clientele are marionettes on God's strings, then the divine string-holder could not shed sincere tears over their actions. This reveals an additional premise required to complete the induction from grievous resistance to the libertarian conclusion. The Grievous Resistance Argument takes the following logical form:

GRA1 (The Biblical Premise): According to biblical insights, humans resist God's will and He is genuinely grieved when they do so.

GRA2 (The Additional Premise): Divine grief implies human autonomy, i.e., grievous resistance must emerge from choices that occur independently of and contrary to the will of God.

GRA3 (The Libertarian Conclusion): Therefore, humans must have libertarian free will to embrace or resist God's will.

Libertarian free will—our autonomous ability to say "no" to God's will without divine action determining our decision—is a necessary condition of authentic divine grief. Does the Bible exert pressure on the Grievous Resistance Argument's crucial premise that "divine grief implies human autonomy" (GRA2)?

---

4. Clark Pinnock, "God Limits His Knowledge," in *Predestination and Free Will: Four Views of Divine Sovereignty and Human Responsibility*, ed. David Basinger and Randall Basinger (Downers Grove, IL: InterVarsity, 1986), 149. See also Terry Miethe, "The Universal Power of the Atonement," in *The Grace of God, the Will of Man*, ed. Clark Pinnock (Grand Rapids: Zondervan, 1989), 74; John Sanders, *The God Who Risks: A Theology of Providence* (Downers Grove, IL: InterVarsity Press, 1998), 222; and Gregory Boyd, *Satan and the Problem of Evil* (Downers Grove, IL: InterVarsity, 2001), 53–54.

A DIVINE TENSION

Consider, along with Siri, another victim of grievous resistance to God's commands. Jesus endured murder by crucifixion. Does the Father take some sadistic pleasure in watching His beloved Son endure the betrayal, false indictment, beating, mockery, and execution at the hands of His creatures? Surely not. " 'For I have *no pleasure* in the death of anyone,' declares the LORD GOD" (Ezek 18:32; emphasis added). How much more so the death of His beloved Son!

The theologian John Frame does not stray from the biblical picture when he affirms, "Certainly the Father empathized, agonized, and grieved over the death of his Son."[5] Jürgen Moltmann also remains true to text when identifying the suffering of God in the suffering of Jesus.[6] Alvin Plantinga expounds:

> God can and does suffer; His capacity for suffering exceeds ours in the same measure that His knowledge exceeds ours. Christ's suffering was no charade. ... God the Father was prepared to endure the anguish of seeing His Son, the second person of the Trinity, consigned to the bitterly cruel and shameful death of the cross.[7]

The Father's anguish at the cross stands in proper balance with the full weight of its heinousness.[8]

At this depth, the claim that "divine grief implies human autonomy" breathes. When we push deeper into the text, however, Isaiah 53:10 adds, "It *pleased* the LORD to bruise Him; He has put Him to grief" (emphasis added; cf. Isa 53:4b, 6b). It both "*pleased* (Hebrew: *haphez*) the LORD to bruise Him" and He has "no *pleasure* (Hebrew: *haphez*)

---

5. John Frame, *No Other God: A Response to Open Theism* (Phillipsburg, NJ: P&R Publishing, 2001), 188.

6. Jürgen Moltmann, *The Crucified God* (San Francisco: Harper San Francisco, 1990).

7. Plantinga, *Warranted Christian Belief* (Oxford: Oxford University Press, 2000), 319.

8. In the same way, God's response to Siri exceeds our own in its intensity and correspondence to her loss.

in the death of anyone who dies."[9] There is tension here. At times it pleases God to do that which, in another sense, displeases Him. On this duality, D. A. Carson comments, "precisely how both operate in one sovereign God is extremely difficult to understand."[10] This extreme difficulty should not surprise us, given the sheer magnitude of God. We behold through a mirror dimly.

To exhibit strong depth capacity, a notion must sustain both the Isaiah 53:10 "pleasure" aspect of God *and* the Ezekiel 18:32 "no pleasure" aspect of God. Otherwise, we artificially resolve a fundamental tension within the text, resulting in a theological oversimplification of God. If, for example, we focus exclusively on "pleasure" texts, then our concept of God merges with ancient Greek philosophy. For the Epicureans and Stoics, grief represents the kind of weakness and reactivity that are unbecoming of a perfect being. The God of the Bible, by contrast, is "hurt to His heart" by the moral resistance of His creatures (Gen 6:6).[11]

If, on the other hand, we fixate only on "no pleasure" passages, then we reach an opposite (though equally artificial) resolution of the biblical tension. God grieves over evil if and only if He plays no active role in bringing evil about. This tension-relieving tactic offers a God whose feelings resonate strongly with our human experience of grief. We grievously watch news coverage and otherwise behold evils in which we play no active role.

Are God's feelings the same as ours as we watch the news? According to Plantinga, God's capacity for suffering exceeds ours as does His knowledge. We may extend this point to include a wider

---

9. The cross is not an exclusive case of this divine tension. The God who takes no pleasure in anyone's death also desired (*haphez*) to put Eli's sons to death through their spurning of their father's wise counsel (2 Sam 2:22–25). He took "delight" (*yasis*, a stronger emotional verb than *haphez*) in bringing ruin and destruction upon Israel (Deut 28:63).

10. D. A. Carson, *Divine Sovereignty & Human Responsibility: Biblical Perspectives in Tension* (Eugene, OR: Wipf and Stock, 1994), 214.

11. The Hebrew term for "hurt" in Genesis 6:6 is used throughout the Old Testament, referring to the emotional state of a deserted wife, brothers hearing of their sisters' rape, and of Jonathan upon hearing his father's intention to murder David. On the reality of divine grief see also Isaiah 1:11–14, 24; 59:15 (cf. Ezek 23:18; 36:17; and Eph 4:30).

range of feelings.[12] A woman, whose longtime friend has recently lost
a parent to an unexpected heart attack, receives news that another
dear friend has just celebrated the birth of a healthy baby. She may
find either her grief for one friend mitigated by the happy news of
the other or her elation over new life curbed by her other friend's
terrible loss. Unlike us, God can feel the weight of the cumulative
travails and triumphs of billions of people, weeping with those who
weep *and* rejoicing with those who rejoice. His heart is incalculably
more adept at complex feeling than our own.

At the cross there is not only a divine grief that transcends our
finite capacities; there is also a divine grief over suffering that was
predetermined by the Griever. Those who crucified Jesus did "whatever [God's] hand and [His] plan had predestined to take place"
(Acts 4:28). We return to this important text for analysis in the next
section. For our present purposes, the point is this: If God can truly
grieve over an event that He Himself determines to happen, then
the Bible exerts significant pressure against the notion that "divine
grief implies human autonomy." This crucial premise of the Grievous
Resistance Argument rests on the pre-exegetical assumption that God
cannot have *both* an evil-determining "pleasure" *and* an evil-grieving
"no pleasure" outlook on moral evil.

In gauging the depth capacity of the claim that "divine grief implies
human autonomy," we encounter a God who

> *both* desires all of humanity to "fear [Him] and keep His com-
> mandments" (Eccl 12:13) *and* who can "make [the Israelites]
> wander from [His] ways and harden [their] heart, so that
> [they] fear [Him] not" (Isa 63:17);

---

12. Building on Plantinga's insight (*Warranted Christian Belief,* 319), divine grief exceeds
our own, at least in part, *because* His knowledge exceeds our own. He knows the full extent of
the evil He grieves, seeing not only evil actions but also the full scope of vile intentions prior
to them and hurtful consequences after them. Through the cross, He has a reference point of
infinite pain by which to grasp it experientially. The best we can do is experience snapshots of
the evil and relate them to our own finite experiences of pain.

both "desires all people to be saved and to come to the knowledge of the truth" (1 Tim 2:4) *and* "sends [some] a strong delusion, so that they may believe what is false" (2 Thess 2:11;[13] cf. John 12:40; Rom 9:18, 22);

both desires that His creatures "shall not bear false witness" (Exod 20:16) *and* "has put a lying spirit in the mouth of all these your prophets" (1 Kgs 22:23);

both wants everyone to "love our neighbor" (Matt 22:39) *and* "turned [Israel's enemy's] hearts to hate his people, to deal craftily with his servants" (Ps 105:25; cf. Judg 9:23; Josh 11:20; Gen 50:20; Exod 4:21; Deut 2:30).

Libertarians might object that these biblical both-ands do not occur at the same moment within God. Rather, His response may vacillate dynamically between pleasure and grief relative to the unfolding free responses of His creatures.

However, each biblical case above features a divine imperative. God commands people to fear Him, know the truth, tell the truth, and love their neighbors. Is there ever a time that God does not endorse His commands with divine feeling? God grieves when His creatures shun Him, tell lies, believe lies, and trample their neighbors. Did He temporarily suspend such grief when He made the Israelites wander from His ways, sent a powerful delusion, instilled a lying spirit in prophets' mouths, or turned Israel's enemies' hearts to hatred? Because God is holy without exception (Deut 32:4–5; Isa 6:3; Jas 1:13), there is no biblical reason to think that such temporary suspensions of God's anti-sin posture ever occurred. We cannot resolve the biblical tension by superimposing the time dimension on God's feelings.

---

13. In Boyd's interpretation of this passage God only sends some a powerful delusion once those individuals have already exercised their libertarian free will to refuse belief in Jesus. Even on this interpretation, we do not escape the tension since God continues to will the salvation of every individual person and in another sense he wills that certain individuals who have persistently refused His salvation offer should be further deluded into believing what is false.

There is a reason why theologians have always posited two wills
in God (e.g., *voluntas beneplaciti* and *voluntas signi*).[14] These theologians were not trying to construct an artificial tension but to do justice
to the complexities that confronted them in the biblical text. While
these complexities are palpable in many biblical narratives on moral
evil,[15] there is one biblical case in which these complexities reach
their sharpest expression. We now turn to the crucifixion of Jesus as
understood in Acts 4:28 and the pressure it exerts against the notion
that "divine grief implies human autonomy."

AN EXEGESIS OF ACTS 4:28

This crucifixion passage occurs in the context of a prayer of the early
Jerusalem church that spans Acts 4:24–30. The catalyst for this ancient
prayer is the aggressive attempts of the Jewish leadership in Jerusalem
to silence Peter and John (Acts 4:17–18, 21a). Significantly, the cast
of those who arrest Peter and John in Acts 4:5–6 overlaps with the
perpetrators of Jesus' trials and execution in Luke's Gospel.[16] Annas,
the "high priest" (who retained his prestige and title among the Jewish
populace in Jerusalem despite being deposed by the Romans in AD 15),
and his son-in-law, Caiaphas, are named at both the trial of Peter and
John and the trial of Jesus (John 18:13–14, 19–24, 28; cf. Luke 22:54).

The Jerusalem church faces the possible elimination of two of
their most formative leaders by the same religious aristocracy whose
threats had only a few months earlier materialized in the (temporary) elimination of Jesus. Peter and John did not stand alone in

---

14. See John Piper, "Are There Two Wills in God?" in *Still Sovereign: Contemporary
Perspectives on Election, Foreknowledge, and Grace*, eds. Thomas Schreiner and Bruce Ware
(Grand Rapids: Baker Books, 2000).

15. These include Zedekiah's rebellion (Jer 52:3; cf. 2 Kgs 24:19), the dealing of Shechem's
men against Abimelech (Judg 9:23ff), Saul's spear attack on David (1 Sam 18:10), David's num-
bering of his troops (2 Sam 24; cf. 1 Chron 21:1–7), the human trafficking of Joseph by his
brothers (Gen 45:5–8; 50:14; cf. Ps 105:16–25), the destruction of Sihon (Duet 2:30ff; cf. Judg
11:19ff), and the war atrocities of Assyria (Isa 10:5ff; cf. Isa 14:24–27). For exegetical analysis
see Carson, *Divine Sovereignty & Human Responsibility*, 9–44.

16. τοὺς ἄρχοντας, τοὺς πρεσβυτέρους (cf. Luke 22:52, 66); τοὺς γραμματεῖς (cf. Luke 22:66);
and ὁ ἀρχιερεύς (cf. Luke 22:54).

the crosshairs of this threat. The members of the Jerusalem church believed that their new identity was fundamentally missional and that speaking out about Jesus as the Christ was, therefore, essential. By implication, the aristocracy's threats would have affected the entire believing community within their jurisdiction.

Within the context of this threat, the church opens their prayer by addressing God as "Sovereign Lord" (δεσπότης; Acts 4:24). This rare liturgical title for God occurs sporadically in the Bible (Exod 20:11; Ps 146:6; Job 5:8 [LXX]; Luke 2:29; Jude 4; Rev 6:10), with some usage in Jewish prayers (Josephus, *Jewish Wars* 7.323; 3 Macc 2:2; Wis 6:7; 3 Sir 36:1) and greater attestation in Greek political literature (Aelius Aristides, *Works* 37:1; Xenophon, *Anabasis* 3:2, 13). In the context of Acts 4, the term "Sovereign Lord" signals a power-hierarchy in the minds of the early church. The author surrounds this divine title on all sides by impressive titles of human authority, e.g., priests, temple captains, Sadducees (Acts 4:1), rulers, elders, scribes (4:5, 8, 23), the high priest and all who were of high priestly descent (4:6), the Council (4:15), kings and rulers (4:26), Herod and Pontius Pilate (4:27). Only God, however, merits the title "Sovereign Lord."[17] The church may be under these assembled human authorities, but these finite deputies of human behavior are all under God's supreme authority as δεσπότης. The praying church reinforces God's supreme authority by reiterating both His unique role as Creator (Acts 4:24b) and the futility of all human attempts to thwart His redemptive plans (with a *pesher* interpretation of Psalm 2 in Acts 4:25–27).[18]

---

17. For an interesting parallel to the prayer of Acts 4:24–30 see Josephus, *Antiquities of the Jews*, in *Josephus: Complete Works*, tr. William Whiston (Grand Rapids: Kregel, 1981), 40–50, 87. Josephus has Moses praying, "Do thou at this time demonstrate that all things are administered by thy providence, and that nothing happens by chance, but is governed by thy will, and thereby attains its end."

18. There is a *pesher* correspondence between Herod Antipas and Psalm 2's "kings of the earth" (Acts 4:26a), Pilate and the gathered "rulers" (4:26b), Gentile soldiers to raging "Gentiles" (4:25b), and the people of Israel to the futility-devising "peoples" (4:25c).

Having hailed God in terms of "a ruler of unchallengeable power,"[19] the Jerusalem Christians identify divine power as operative behind the moral evil perpetrated in their own city against Jesus:

> For in this city, in fact, Herod and Pontius Pilate, with the Gentiles and the peoples of Israel, gathered together against your holy servant Jesus, whom you anointed, to do whatever your hand and your plan had predestined to take place. (Acts 4:27–28)

This passage offers an assorted list of evil human agents who conspired against Jesus. It is significant that the praying church does not envision these human agents as either automatons acting against *their* will or autonomous acting against *God's* will. In the terms of our analysis in 1.2, the conspirators behind Jesus' death were not forced by either Necessity of the Machine or that of the Gunman.[20] As human agents, they *willfully* killed Jesus, and as willful killing agents they were also morally responsible for their evil actions. This point finds heavy emphasis throughout the two-volume Luke-Acts narrative.[21]

While morally responsible agents, the church's prayer clarifies that Jesus' executioners were not autonomous agents in the libertarian sense of autonomy. They did not meet the libertarian requirement of non-hypothetical two-way power, but did what the "hand" (ἡ χείρ) and "plan" (ἡ βουλή) of the "Sovereign Lord" "predestined" (προώρισεν) for them to do (Acts 4:28). What is the significance of these consecutive terms of divine action?

---

19. John Stott, *The Message of Acts: The Spirit, the Church, and the World* (Downers Grove, IL: InterVarsity Press, 1994), 99.

20. For further support of this claim see F. F. Bruce, *Acts of the Apostles: The Book of Acts*, New London Commentary (Grand Rapids: Eerdmans, 1951), 70; and Joseph Fitzmeyer, *The Acts of the Apostles* (New Haven, CT: Yale University Press, 1998), 274.

21. See Acts 2:23, 38; 3:13–15, 19; 4:10; 5:30; 10:39; 13:27–29 (cf. Luke 23:5, 20–23, 25, and 51). See also John Polhill, *Acts,* The New American Commentary, vol. 26 (Nashville: Broadman & Holman, 1992), 112.

God's "hand" (χείρ) is an "image of His power ... to denote sovereign control."[22] It is common in the LXX. God's "hand" liberated the Israelites from Egyptian slavery (Exod 13:3, 14, 16; cf. Ps 55:21). Nebuchadnezzar acknowledges that "no one can hinder [God's] hand" (οὐκ ἔστιν ὃς ἀντιποιήσεται τῇ χειρί; Dan 4:32, LXX). In addition to God's "hand," His "plan" (βουλή) was also active in the death of Jesus. As Acts uses this term, God's "plan" cannot be overthrown by human power (οὐ δυνήσεσθε καταλῦσαι; Acts 5:38–39). In Acts 2:23, the parallel of Acts 4:28, it is by God's ὡρισμένη βουλή, i.e., His "determined" and "clearly defined plan" that Jesus was delivered over to His executioners.[23] While "the notion of a divine plan is ... typically Lukan,"[24] it is certainly not *exclusively* Lukan, particularly as this plan relates to redemptive suffering. From the *protoevangalium* of Genesis 3:15 in which a seed of woman would be bruised while crushing the serpent's head[25] to the suffering servant whom it *pleased* (βούλεται [LXX]) the LORD to bruise (Isa 53:10), the Old Testament previews a divine plan that was in motion towards a supreme act of redemptive suffering. The Luke-Acts narrative acknowledges the Old Testament precedent for a suffering messiah (Luke 24:25, 46; Acts 17:3; 26:23). This ancient Hebrew motif underscores the claim in Acts 4:28 that God's "plan" was active in the sufferings of Jesus.

This leads us to the third key term of divine action used by the praying Jerusalem church in Acts 4:28. The verb "predestined" (προώρισεν), expresses the action performed by God's hand and plan. The prefix προ, from which English derives the prefix "pre" and the

---

22. Fitzmeyer, *The Acts of the Apostles*, 310.

23. According to Simon Kistemaker, "The expression *set purpose* [ὡρισμένη βουλή] denotes a plan that has been determined and is clearly defined. The author of this purpose is God himself" (*Acts*, New Testament Commentary [Grand Rapids: Baker Books, 1991], 93). See also Ernst Haenchen, *The Acts of the Apostles: A Commentary* (Louisville: Westminster/John Knox Press, 1971), 180; and I. Howard Marshall, *The Acts of the Apostles* (Grand Rapids: Eerdmans, 1980), 75.

24. Hans Conzelmann, *Acts of the Apostles* (Minneapolis: Fortress Press, 1987) 20. See also Conzelmann, *Theology of St. Luke* (New York: HarperCollins, 1961), 151–54, 173–84, and James Dunn, *The Acts of the Apostles* (Harrisburg, PA: Trinity Press International, 1997), 57.

25. See Walter C. Kaiser's scholarly analysis in *The Messiah in the Old Testament*, Studies in Old Testament Biblical Theology (Grand Rapids: Zondervan, 1995), 37–42.

word "prior," modifies the verb ὁρίζω, "meaning determine, establish, appoint."[26] Divine action in the execution of Jesus transcends mere foresight to include God's active *predetermination*.

Acts 2:23, a parallel passage of 4:28, uses the related term— πρόγνωσις—to denote God's foreknowledge. This term is placed in the instrumental dative case to express the means by which Jesus was "delivered up" (ἔκδοτον, *hapax legomenon*) by God to His executioners. "Yet," MacArthur observes, "mere knowledge cannot perform such an act. Foreordination can act, however, and that is the NT meaning of *prognosis*."[27] This idea stands in contrast to passive advance knowledge of future events as we find in Euripides (*Hippolytus*, 1072) and NT references to *human* foreknowledge (Acts 26:5; 2 Pet 3:17). This renders any interpretation of the death of Jesus that limits God's role to passive foresight semantically untenable.[28]

These insights do not diminish the involved human agent's moral responsibility or dispel God's authentic grief at what these agents did to His Son. Acts 4:28 does, however, exert strong logical pressure against the crucial premise of the Grievous Resistance Argument. Divine grief does not imply human autonomy, because the "Sovereign Lord" authentically grieved the crucifixion that His "hand" and "plan" "predestined."

---

26. G. Dulon, "ὁρίζω," in *The New International Dictionary of New Testament Theology*, vol. 1, ed. Colin Brown (Grand Rapids: Zondervan, 1971), 472.

27. John MacArthur, *Acts 1–12*, The MacArthur New Testament Commentary (Chicago: Moody, 1994), 63. For other examples of πρόγνωσις and its verb form in the NT, further highlighting its role as more than passive advance knowledge, see Acts 26:5; Romans 8:29; 11:2; and 1 Peter 1:2, 20.

28. See Everett Harrison, *The Expositor's Bible Commentary*, vol. 10: Romans-Galatians, ed. Frank E. Gaebelein (Grand Rapids: Zondervan, 1976), 98; John Feinberg, *No One Like Him: The Doctrine of God* (Wheaton, IL: Crossway, 2001), 519–26; and Ben Witherington, *Acts of the Apostles: A Socio-Rhetorical Commentary* (Grand Rapids: Eerdmans, 1998), 202–3.

GREGORY BOYD ON A
PREDETERMINED CRUCIFIXION

Boyd offers three innovative attempts to relieve the pressure exerted by Acts 4:28 against the libertarian notion of autonomy. First, Boyd argues, "[Acts 2:23 and 4:28] only affirm that it was preordained and foreknown that the messiah would be crucified. *That* Jesus would be killed was predetermined. *Who* would do it was not."[29] God predetermined the crime, not the particular criminals. We will call this the "That Without Who Argument."

Second, Boyd argues that God can predetermine *who* will carry out an evil action without indicting His goodness if the chosen evil agents have previously exercised libertarian power to "resolve" their own evil characters toward that evil action. Boyd expounds,

> Traditionally theologians have distinguished the character a person receives from God (*habitus infusus*) from the character they freely acquire (*habitus acquirus*) [sic]. There is no contradiction in the claim that a person is morally responsible for an act even though they could not have done otherwise, so long as the character that now rendered their action certain flowed from a character they themselves acquired. It was not "infused" into them by God. ... Hence, if God decides that it fits his providential plan to use a person whose choices have solidified his character as wicked, God is not responsible for this person's wickedness.[30]

We will call this the "Auto-Corruption Argument."

Third, Boyd suggests that the cross is such a pivotal moment in God's plan that His powers of predetermination were more active in this case than normally. From such an exceptional case we can draw

---

29. Boyd, *Satan and the Problem of Evil*, 121; emphasis in original.
30. Boyd, *Satan and the Problem of Evil*, 122. The Latin should read *habitus acquisitus*.

no general conclusions about the relation between God's will and moral evil.[31] We will call this the "Exception Argument."

1. *The That Without Who Argument.* Three problems emerge from Boyd's first argument. First, if libertarian power was active in every *who* facing the prospect of involvement in the crucifixion, then it was metaphysically possible (though perhaps improbable in Boyd's estimation) for every *who* to refrain freely from bringing about this climactic event in God's redemptive plan. It was possible (in the absence of any participating *whos*) for the *that* of Jesus' murder never to take place. In what sense can an event be meaningfully described as "predetermined" if it was *possible* for that event never to transpire? "Predetermined" does not mean "highly probable." In this paradigm, the only reason that God's predetermined redemptive plan was not thwarted is that some *whos* did choose to participate in the crucifixion event.

Second, there are several specifics of the crucifixion event that render the That Without Who Argument untenable. There is the *how* to consider. Boyd recognizes that *crucifixion* was the method that God determined for Jesus' death.[32] Given the political power structures in which the crucifixion occurred, certain government officials would have had to dirty their hands in His death. The Jews had lost their legal authority to exercise capital punishment prior to Jesus' death (Jerusalem Talmud, *Sanhedrin*, 1:1, 7:2; Babylonian Talmud, *Sanhedrin* 12a, 41a; cf. John 18:31). Roman corroboration was essential to a predetermined *crucifixion*. The *how* of Christ's death (i.e., crucifixion) required certain *whos*. Certain Roman leaders, notably Pilate, formed vital links in the chain of command to authorize such an execution within the locale of Jerusalem. Without specified Roman

---

31. Boyd, *Satan and the Problem of Evil*, 423; and *God of the Possible* (Grand Rapids: Baker Books, 2000), 44–45.

32. See Boyd, *Satan and the Problem of Evil*, 121. The language of piercing in the Hebrew prophetic literature reinforces this particular execution method (Zech 12:10, Ps 22:16; cf. Matt 27:35; John 20:25).

corroboration, Jesus could have more likely endured exile or fallen victim to the traditional Jewish execution method, i.e., stoning.[33]

Third, Scripture is explicit about the predetermined involvement of at least two *whos* in the crucifixion event, namely, Judas (Luke 22:21–22) and Satan (Gen 3:15; cf. Luke 22:3).

2. *The Auto-Corruption Argument.* The role of Judas as a predetermined conspirator in the crucifixion moves us to Boyd's second argument. For Boyd, Judas "freely resolved [his] own character" toward evil; God directed the course of Judas' chosen evil path so that it would intersect with His redemptive strategy.

What if we rewind our analysis to earlier chapters in the story of Judas' character resolution? What moves the pre-auto-corrupted Judas when he makes his first character shaping choice for or against Jesus? If we grant libertarian agent causation, then *Judas* moves Judas to make that first choice. He acts as a self-mover. We must remember, however, that at this point Judas' "self" does not yet possess a "resolved character." There is nothing in Judas' character to tip the scales of action decisively one way over another. What then moves him if not his character?

To appreciate the scope of this problem, let us analyze Judas at his first character-shaping choice against Christ. At this important moment, t^1, the rejection of Christ becomes a new acquisition of Judas' character (*habitus acquisitus*). Immediately following t^1, Judas' acquired character is devoid of Christ-accepting propensities and has a Christ-rejecting propensity that is one-decision strong. The next time Judas faces a Christ-accepting or rejecting crossroads, t^2, this asymmetry in his acquired character will either tilt the scales of action decisively in favor of rejecting Christ again or it will not. I do

---

33. Predetermining a *when* without the *whos* casts further doubt on Boyd's hypothesis. Perhaps by the time each required *who* had made the requisite libertarian choices to bring the *that* of crucifixion to pass, it would fall on some prophetically irrelevant Tuesday rather than Passover. Or perhaps they would have made libertarian choices at different timeframes from one another, precluding the corroboration necessary to the crucifixion.

not think that Boyd would want to defend the proposition that this asymmetry tilts the scales of action decisively. A snowball effect in Judas' character in which his every decision from t^2 to t^{1000} is the determined aftereffect of his decision at t^1 seems like a severely atrophied version of libertarian free will.

If we say instead that the asymmetry does not tilt the scales decisively, such that Judas still has choosing power to make a Christ-accepting decision at t^2, then something important about the nature of the libertarian agent comes to light. In a thorough libertarian account of agency, the choosing self is not identical with his or her acquired character. Whatever the "self" is, it is capable of acting contrary to all that is within that *habitus acquisitus* (since opposition to Christ is all that is within Judas' acquired character when approaching t^2). The self somehow *transcends* character so that it retains the power to choose in harmony or discord with it. This leads us back to Leibniz's indifferent queen, a poor candidate for morally significant choice-making power (see 1.3). Boyd has left us without a coherent libertarian account of auto-corruption.[34]

The Bible does not portray human agents as Leibnizian queens, transcending either infused or acquired characters. All agents in the moral drama of the Old and New Testaments have teleological propensities at the core of their being. John Frame observes,

> Libertarianism violates the biblical teaching concerning the unity of human personality … we are fallen and renewed as whole persons. This integrity of human personality is not possible in a libertarian construction, for on that view the will must always be independent of the heart and all our other faculties.[35]

---

34. For more on this problem, see Galen Strawson's argument for the impossibility of libertarian "self-creation" expounded in Saul Smilansky, *Free Will and Illusion* (Oxford: Oxford University Press, 2000), 65.

35. Frame, *No Other God*, 127.

Where in the Bible do we meet the character-transcending agents required by Boyd's Auto-Corruption Argument?

3. *The Exception Argument.* Lastly, Boyd argues, "At times [God] exercises unilateral control over what transpires in history ... even predetermining some events long before they come to pass (e.g., Acts 4:28)."[36] Boyd suggests that we err in drawing comprehensive conclusions about God's relation to human resistance from isolated cases of divine control, like the crucifixion.[37] Perhaps the cross is an *exception* rather than the *rule* of how God controls evil.

Did the praying church in first-century Jerusalem interpret the cross as an isolated case of divine control over evil? As clarified in 2.2.3, the catalyst for the prayer in Acts 4:24–30 was the religious aristocrats' silencing tactics against the missional church of Jerusalem. These same aristocrats did what God "predestined" them to do when they condemned Jesus to execution. "Having done their worst, they merely succeeded in fulfilling God's eternal plan."[38] The church drew on this insight to shed a more hopeful perspective on their predicament. The transitional phrase, "And now" (καί τὰ νῦν; Acts 4:29a), signals a shift from God's control over the cross to "the present distress of the community."[39] As William Larkin observes, "The believers declare the scope of God's omnipotence. So they encourage themselves through praise that even the threatening Sanhedrin is not outside God's sovereign control."[40]

If the Jerusalem church saw the cross as an isolated case of God predetermining evil, then such an exception to God's typical rule would not be a source of boldness as they faced a new threat. If,

---

36. Boyd, *Satan and the Problem of Evil*, 11.

37. Boyd, *Satan and the Problem of Evil*, 186, 423.

38. Louis Berkhof, *Systematic Theology* (Grand Rapids: Eerdmans, 1938), 141.

39. Gerd Lüdemann, *Early Christianity According to the Traditions in Acts: A Commentary* (London: SCM Press, 1989), 58.

40. William Larkin, *Acts*, The IVP New Testament Commentary Series, ed. Grant Osborne (Downers Grove, IL: InterVarsity, 1995), 78–79. See also Polhill, *Acts*, 149.

however, they understood the cross as the archetype for how God controls evil, then there are compelling grounds for the "boldness" experienced in Acts 4:29–31.

Appealing to the cross as an archetype of divine control serves an overarching goal of the book of Acts. This first-century narrative of the expanding church was composed not only to educate but also to embolden,[41] not only to see what God did in a narrow sliver of history but also to glimpse what God does regularly on behalf of His suffering servants. Like Jesus and the Jerusalem Christians, the readership of Acts throughout the centuries would encounter the menace of moral evil. Nero disingenuously credited Rome's devastating fires (AD 64) to Christian arson, motivating the arrest of many followers of Jesus. Would these Christians have understood the crucifixion as an isolated case of divine control, irrelevant to their own trouble as they faced crucifixion, dismemberment, and the gruesome public spectacle of being burned alive in Nero's garden?

In the decades and centuries after Nero, the church faced more systematic and widespread extermination attempts.[42] As Tertullian noted in his *Apology*,

> If the Tiber floods the city, or if the Nile refuses to rise, or if the sky withholds its rain, if there is an earthquake, a famine, a pestilence, at once the cry is raised: Christians to the lion.

Christians threatened by such an imposing array of moral evils would not have read Acts as a record of merely historical relevance. Infused within that historical record are insights with far-reaching

---

41. See Ernst Haenchen, "The Book of Acts as Source Material for the History of Earliest Christianity," in *Studies in Luke-Acts*, ed. Leander E. Keck and J. Louis Martyn (Nashville: Abingdon, 1966), 258–78; and I. Howard Marshall, *The Acts of the Apostles*, 20–21.

42. In AD 95 Domitian unleashed a massive wave of anti-Christian brutality. Christian death sentences were frequently dispensed under Trajan and Marcus Aurelius in the second and third centuries. More widespread persecution came from Decius, Valerian, and Diocletian in the latter third and early fourth centuries.

implications into God's sovereign action on behalf of His church.[43] We sustain this broader church-emboldening purpose of Acts if we interpret the crucifixion not as an exception but as God's rule over moral evil.

SOLIDARITY AND STABILITY IN SUFFERING

How does the notion that "divine grief implies human autonomy" fare at the existential level? When evil meets us not as an abstraction but with concrete force through suffering, there are two common fear responses. First, we may find our suffering compounded by a fear of cosmic alienation, fear that God is aloof and unmoved by our traumas. "Sound of human sorrow [never] mounts to mar His sacred, everlasting calm."[44] In *A Grief Observed*, C. S. Lewis recalls seeking God in desperation only to find, "a door slammed in your face, and a sound of bolting and double-bolting on the inside. After that, silence."[45] In the song "Knights of Cydonia," lyricist Matthew Bellamy laments that God "falls asleep on the job." In short, there is the fear that God does not grieve with us.

Second, we may fear that although God may grieve with us, He does not control our suffering. It is the panicked sensation that our travails are beyond the scope of divine action, that our suffering is meaningless, and that our lives are, therefore, on an erratic course

---

43. This insight finds support in the experiences of contemporary Christians who see the gospel progress in countries of harsh opposition. According world missions researcher, Patrick Johnstone,

> It is estimated that 20 million Chinese lost their lives during Mao's Cultural Revolution. Christians stood firm in what was probably the most widespread and harsh persecution the Church has ever experienced. The persecution purified and indigenized the Church. Since 1977 the growth of the Church in China has no parallels in history. Researchers estimate that there were 30–75 million Christians by 1990. Mao Zedong unwittingly became the greatest evangelist in history. (*Operation World* [Grand Rapids: Zondervan, 1993], 164)

44. These are the words of B. B. Warfield to which he adds emphatically, "Let us bless God that it is not true. God can feel; God does love" (cited in Frame, *No Other God*, 190).

45. Lewis, *A Grief Observed* (San Francisco: HarperCollins, 2000), 6.

toward some unforeseen doom. This is not the fear of cosmic alienation but of cosmic absurdity. God may be with us in our suffering,
but He has no purpose behind our suffering, which makes it absurd.
In the words of John Sanders, many evils "are gratuitous or pointless. ...
Given our libertarian freedom, God cannot guarantee that a greater
good will arise out of each and every occurrence of evil."[46] Thus, our
encounters with concrete evil may evoke the fear that either God is
in control but disturbingly apathetic or that He grieves with us but
is not fully in control.

The God we encounter at the crucifixion speaks to both of these
fears. To the suffering who fear that God does not grieve, there is
the God who wept at the cross and takes "*no pleasure* in the death of
anyone who dies." On this side of the tension, God genuinely grieves
with us at the pains induced by moral evil: "In all their distresses He
too was distressed" (Isa 63:9a). To the suffering who fear that God is
not fully in control, leaving many particular pains without purpose,
there is the "Sovereign Lord" who "predestined" the crucifixion. John
Piper speaks to this side of the tension:

> When a person settles it biblically, intellectually and emotionally,
> that God has ultimate control of all things, including evil ... then
> a marvelous stability and depth come into that person's life.[47]

Sustaining the biblical tension at the cross between a God who *both*
predetermines *and* grieves evil replaces fears of cosmic alienation
and absurdity with a sense of solidarity (because God authentically
feels our suffering) and stability (because God authoritatively purposes our suffering).

Keeping this tension intact has been crucial to the suffering
church's response to concrete evils throughout history. In April of

---

46. John Sanders, "Divine Providence and the Openness of God," in *Perspectives on the
Doctrine of God: Four Views*, ed. Bruce Ware (Nashville: B&H, 2008), 213.

47. John Piper, *Desiring God* (Colorado Springs, CO: Multnomah, 2011), 354.

1567 during the Spanish Inquisition, Guido de Brès penned the following letter to his wife prior to his public execution:

> I am writing this for the consolation of both of us, and espe-
> cially for your consolation. ... Remember that I did not fall
> into the hands of my enemies by mere chance, but through
> the providence of my God who controls and governs all things,
> the least as well as the greatest. ... How then can harm come
> to me without the command and providence of God? It could
> not happen unless one should say that God is no longer God. ...
> That is why the Evangelists write so carefully of the suffer-
> ings and of the death of our Lord Jesus Christ, adding, "And
> this was done that that which was written of Him might be
> accomplished." The same should be said of all the members
> of Christ.[48]

Having located his own suffering within the scope of God's predetermining power, de Brès turns to the emotional implications:

> It is very true that human reason rebels against this doctrine
> and resists it as much as possible and I have very strongly
> experienced this myself. When I was arrested, I would say to
> myself, "... We ought not to have been arrested." With such
> thoughts I became overwhelmed, until my spirits were raised
> by meditation on the providence of God. Then my heart began
> to feel a great repose. I began then to say, "My God ... may your
> will be done. I cannot escape from your hands. And if I could,
> I would not, since it is happiness for me to conform to your
> will." These thoughts made my heart cheerful again. ... I pray
> you, my dear and faithful companion, to join me in thanking
> God for what he has done.

---

48. Guido de Brès, personal letter reprinted in *Bibliotheca Reformatoria Neerlandica*, tr. W. L.
Bredenhof, 7 (1903): 624–28.

Did de Brès' sense of stability from interpreting his suffering as God's sovereign will lead him to conclude that God is aloof on His throne rather than involved in de Brès' cell? On the contrary,

> I am held in a very strong prison, very bleak, obscure and dark. The prison is known by the obscure name "Brunain" (Black Hole). The air is poor and it stinks. On my feet and hands I have irons, big and heavy. ... But for all that, my God does not take away his promises, consoling my heart, giving me very much contentment. ... I have found by experience that he will never leave those who have trusted in him. ... He fortifies me and consoles me in an unbelievable way. ... Since such things have happened, my dear sister and faithful wife, I implore you to find comfort from the Lord in your afflictions and to place your troubles with him. He is the husband of believing widows and the father of poor orphans. ... Farewell, Catherine, my dearly beloved. I pray my God that he will comfort you and give you contentment in his good will.

In the alienation of the "Black Hole," de Brès' belief in a God who genuinely feels our suffering prevented him from succumbing to the fear of cosmic alienation. In his cell, de Brès knew solidarity with a God who takes "no pleasure" in death. In the absurdity of facing execution for writing the Belgic Confession, de Brès' belief in a God who authoritatively purposes suffering relieved him of the fear of cosmic absurdity. He knew stability in a God who was "pleased" to bruise Christ.

By defining divine grief in a way that excludes divine predetermination, the notion that "divine grief implies human autonomy" upholds our solidarity with God at the expense of our stability in God. This notion artificially resolves a tension reinforced in the biblical story of the crucifixion. There is an existential price to pay for relieving this tension. In letting go of God's predetermining power in an effort to vindicate a libertarian solution to abstract problems of evil, we lose an insight that has emboldened the suffering church throughout its ongoing confrontation with concrete problems of evil.

I conclude that the Grievous Resistance Argument with its crucial premise that "divine grief implies human autonomy" lacks depth capacity. It survives at the depth of a God who grieves, but cannot breathe at the depth of a "Sovereign Lord" whose "hand" and "plan" "predestined" the crucifixion, and who exerts that same stabilizing sovereignty over our suffering.

2.3

The Relational Vision Argument

Can One Guarantee Another's Love?

With man it is impossible, but not with God.

—*Jesus, in Mark 10:27*

RELATIONSHIP IMPLIES RESISTIBILITY

The God of the Bible is not the relationally disinterested deity of deism. God is deeply and even painfully involved in realizing His relational vision for His creatures. Clark Pinnock moves from this premise to the libertarian conclusion:

> According to the Bible, it is not only possible for God to create a world with significantly free finite agents. God actually did exactly that. This is evident from ... a central biblical assertion about human beings that ... they are historical agents who can respond to God in love. ... By its very nature this covenant

relationship cannot be coerced but is something which both parties enter into voluntarily. In light of this possibility we must conclude that human freedom is significant and real. The response of faith and love cannot be forced.[1]

What is the basic logical structure of this third argument for libertarian free will? The Relational Vision Argument takes the following shape:

RVA1 (The Biblical Premise): According to biblical insights, God has a relational vision for His creatures, desiring humans to exist in an authentic love relationship with Him.

RVA2 (The Additional Premise): Relationship implies resistibility, i.e. in authentic love relationships neither party can exert any action that renders a love response of the other necessary.

RVA3 (The Libertarian Conclusion): Therefore, humans must have the libertarian free will to say "yes" or "no" to an authentic love relationship with God.

Given my analysis up to this point, it may come as a surprise that I find the additional premise that "relationship implies resistibility" (RVA2) to be a true insight into the nature of love relationships. Why then do I not join my libertarian brothers and sisters in walking the logical line from RVA1 and RVA2 to the libertarian conclusion?

The answer becomes clear when we add depth to our portrait of love with the following question: Does the claim that "relationship implies resistibility" represent a relative or an absolute insight into love relationships? *Relative to human-to-human love connections*, it rings true that we cannot act over another agent to necessitate their

---

1. Clark Pinnock, "God Limits His Knowledge," in *Predestination and Free Will: Four Views of Divine Sovereignty and Human Responsibility*, ed. David Basinger and Randall Basinger (Downers Grove, IL: InterVarsity, 1986), 147–48. See also John Sanders, *The God Who Risks: A Theology of Providence* (Downers Grove, IL: InterVarsity Press, 1998), 222; and Gregory Boyd, *Satan and the Problem of Evil* (Downers Grove, IL: InterVarsity, 2001), 53–54.

love response without stripping love of authenticity. Does this relative insight into human relationships warrant absolute conclusions about God's ability to render our human-to-God love both necessary and authentic?

In approaching this question, it is vital to see that many libertarian theologians already embrace a distinction between human and divine ability. Any theology that does not merely create God in our own image upholds the Creator's ability to act in ways that transcend the creature's abilities. This distinction does not function as a *deus ex machina*, swooping in to save us from the libertarian conclusion of the Relational Vision Argument. Rather, a distinction between the Creator and the creature's abilities is axiomatic to theology, uniting libertarians and non-libertarians alike. God can create a universe *ex nihilo*; we cannot. God can raise the dead; we cannot. God can respond to billions of simultaneous needs; we cannot. Given this distinction, the question becomes: Does the insight that "relationship implies resistibility" hold true for both the creature and the Creator (i.e., an absolute insight into love relationships)? Or does it only apply at the level of the creature (i.e., a relative insight into love relationships)?

In order for the Relational Vision Argument to reach its libertarian conclusion with logical success, the premise "relationship implies resistibility" must be read as an absolute insight. It must be assumed that God's reciprocal love-seeking capacities are largely co-extensive with our own. If "relationship implies resistibility" is only true relative to creatures seeking love, then the Creator, acting beyond the scope of our love-seeking abilities, can render our love both necessary and authentic. In this relative reading of "relationship implies resistibility," the libertarian conclusion does not follow.

LOVE RELATIONSHIPS AND
CREATURELY FINITUDE

To assess the depth capacity of the claim that "relationship requires resistibility" we must further crystallize the distinction between an absolute versus a relative reading of this claim. Consider a thought experiment in which a human agent is substituted for God in the logic of the Relational Vision Argument. In place of the Creator, a creature named Jim has a relational vision that his neighbor, Claudia, would love him. How could Jim draw Claudia into reciprocating his love? He could practice acts of love towards her, affectionately celebrating her best qualities and unconditionally embracing her in her worst. For all of Jim's winsome efforts, however, the lingering risk that Claudia will resist remains. It is beyond Jim's scope of creaturely ability to *guarantee* her love. The libertarian claim that love relationships entail an inescapable risk of resistance rings true in this human-to-human context.

What if Jim cannot tolerate the prospect of Claudia's resistance and sets to the task of *guaranteeing* her love response? What means are at Jim's disposal as a finite creature? Since all of his most valiant efforts to evoke her love carry the risk of resistance, there are only two available means to eliminate the risk. First, he could resort to Necessity of the Machine (see 1.2). He could exploit a brain-regulating technology akin to Boyd's "sophisticated chip" to necessitate Claudia's "love" behavior. Second, without requiring fictitious will-overriding technologies, Jim could resort to Necessity of the Gunman, employing scare tactics, emotional manipulation, violence, or other coercive means to evoke "love" behavior from Claudia.

The moment Jim crosses the line into either Necessity of the Machine or Gunman, he ceases to love her as a person. He has violated the Axiom of Unforced Love (see 1.2), thereby trampling what Brümmer calls her "personal integrity," and reducing Claudia to a "paper doll." Any "love" expressed by Claudia as the result of Jim's use of Necessity of the Machine or Gunman is stripped of moral value. Artificial affection is all that remains, and a dim, love-less picture emerges of a dehumanizing Jim and a dehumanized Claudia. The claim that "relationship requires resistibility" holds true given the unavoidable implication of Jim's creaturely finitude: he cannot guarantee Claudia's love without nullifying her heart.

Jim's limitation is our limitation. Bound by creaturely limitations, we cannot guarantee the love of other finite creatures, no matter how tireless our love-seeking efforts. The moment we resort to the only humanly available means to guarantee reciprocated love is the moment that we cease to love. As Sartre observed, "If the beloved is transformed into an automaton, the lover finds himself alone." The only guarantee remaining in this picture is that any "love" resulting from such means falls short of true love. For finite people bound by such limitations, relationship *does* imply resistibility.

What if God is not bound by the limitations that bind us? From the perspective of creaturely finitude, establishing a pulse after a person has flatlined requires CPR or a charged defribulater. "Walking" on water requires a Jet Ski or some other hydro-propulsion technology. Parting a sea requires massive pumps and concrete barricades. Likewise, receiving authentic love requires us to allow a degree of autonomy from our influence over our sought-after beloved, and all the risk and vulnerability that emerge from the relative autonomy of the other. Is it possible that just as God could raise the dead, walk on water, and part seas without resorting to difribulators, jet skis, and barricades, so He has a unique ability to guarantee authentic love without resorting to either Necessity of the Machine or Gunman?

Francis Turretin captures this possibility,

> [God exercises] an omnipotent and most friendly power. ... Strength powerful that it may not be frustrated; sweet that it may not be forced. ... The supernatural power of grace and the divine and ineffable motion of God, which so sweetly and at the same time powerfully affects the man that he cannot (thus called) help following God.[2]

Elsewhere Turretin adds, "[God] does not compel, but draws and influences by a friendly necessity."[3] From within this theological paradigm,

---

2. Francis Turretin, *Institutes of Elenctic Theology*, vol. 2, tr. George Musgrave Giger, ed. James Dennison (Phillipsburg, NJ: P&R Publishing, [1696] 1994), 521, 525.

3. Turretin, *Institutes of Elenctic Theology*, vol. 2, 550.

Augustine could describe God as the "Delightful Conqueror,"[4] and Luther could speak of the

> will changed under the sweet influence of the Spirit of God [so that it] desires and acts, not of compulsion, but of its own desire and spontaneous inclination.[5]

Is Luther's "sweet influence of the Spirit" that changes the will without compulsion a contradiction in terms? Is Augustine's "Delightful Conqueror" an oxymoron? Is Turretin's God who exerts strength "powerful that it may not be frustrated [and] sweet that it may not be forced" a manifest irrationality?

ABSOLUTE AND
CREATURE-RELATIVE IMPOSSIBILITIES

To approach these questions, we must develop the distinction between an "absolute impossibility" and a "creature-relative impossibility." An absolute impossibility obtains for any possible agent, such as the impossibility of creating a square circle or making the sum of one and one equal three. The impossibility is, therefore, a priori and logical in nature (i.e., it cannot be instantiated in any possible world). By contrast, a creature-relative impossibility represents something that, though an a priori possibility, lies beyond the scope of the cumulative abilities of a given class of creatures due to their ontological limitations (e.g., the impossibility of humans to jump to the Andromeda Galaxy).

To nuance this distinction further, consider a possible world made up of creatures called Spuds that stand no more than four feet tall and can jump no higher than six inches. They stumble on a regulation size basketball hoop in their world, and a debate breaks out on the possibility of slam-dunking on a ten-foot high hoop. Certain skeptical Spuds contend that a slam-dunk is impossible because four and a

---

4. Augustine, *On the Forgiveness of Sins and Baptism*, 2.32 (cited in Turretin, *Institutes of Elenctic Theology*, vol. 2, 524).

5. Martin Luther, *Bondage of the Will*, tr. J. I. Packer and O. R. Johnston (Westwood, NJ: Revell, 1957), 102–3.

half feet (plus the maximum Spud overhead arm length of six inches) leave even the best of Spud jumpers a discouraging five feet from the rim. Certain innovative Spuds respond that a dunk may be possible with the assistance of Spud stairs or standing on the shoulders of a fellow Spud. Skeptical Spuds respond that any dunk resulting from such artificial means does not count as an authentic dunk.

A third group of Spuds believe in the existence of some higher being in this world, whom they call Kobe. He stands nearly seven feet tall and has a vertical jump several feet high, such that a slam-dunk is effortless for him. Kobe transcends the creaturely height and jumping limitations that apply to Spuds. These Spuds forward a more nuanced view of the impossibility of a slam-dunk. They agree with the skeptical Spuds that dunking is impossible for a Spud, and that any dunk resulting from artificial means, like stairs or a boost, is less than authentic. They add a distinction between a creature-relative and an absolute impossibility, contending that a slam-dunk is impossible only in a creature-relative sense. Relative to the limitations of height and jumping ability that go with Spud creatureliness, a dunk is impossible.

They argue that dunking is not an absolute impossibility. There is no logical contradiction in affirming the existence of some higher being, not bound by Spud limitations, who can dunk without resorting to artificial means. Furthermore, they present evidence of Kobe's existence and dunking ability, concluding that dunking is not only a possibility but also an actuality for this higher being. Many Spuds remain unconvinced and retain their belief that a dunk is an absolute impossibility.

What does this possible world scenario reveal? It reveals a close connection between the ontological limitations that circumscribe a creature and how that limited creature conceptually interprets the modalities of possibility and impossibility. Our ontology colors our modal concepts. Spuds, with their own ontological limitations as the conceptual starting point, conceive of a slam-dunk as impossible, and, therefore, rule out the existence of Kobe as a dunking entity. If they retain belief in Kobe at all, given the strong role they have allowed their own ontological limitations to play in their modal concepts, they would likely conceive of him as a being not far removed from their own size and jumping ability. They have confused a creature-relative impossibility with an absolute impossibility. Their concept of Kobe, therefore, fails to capture the higher reality of Kobe's abilities.

Wayne Grudem offers two illustrations that further crystallize this distinction between a creature-relative and an absolute impossibility. First, he envisions plants, endowed with sentience, debating the possibility of the existence of mobile, living beings.[6] From the vantage point of a plant's creaturely limitations, a mobile *and* living being is impossible because mobility requires freedom from roots and living requires grounded roots. Plants starting from their own creaturely limitations conclude that the existence of mobile, living beings (e.g., humans) is impossible. In drawing this conclusion, they have confused a creature-relative impossibility with an absolute impossibility. Their ontology has overcolored their modal concepts.

Second, Grudem offers an example of rational dogs debating the possibility of beings communicating through the mail.[7] From the perspective of a dog's ontological limitations, mail communication is impossible because communication requires that the communicator be seen, heard, and often smelled. If Grudem's dogs disavow the possibility of mail communication then, once again, a creature-relative impossibility has been mistaken for an absolute impossibility.

What importance do Grudem's examples have for us when attempting to conceptualize God? As with Grudem's fictional plants and canines, problems emerge for people when we draw theological conclusions about what is impossible for God with creature-relative impossibilities as our conceptual starting point. Grudem warns that we can

---

6. Wayne Grudem, *Systematic Theology* (Grand Rapids: Zondervan, 1994), 346.

7. Grudem, *Systematic Theology*, 346.

wrongly [take] information from our situation as human beings and then [use] that information to place limitations on what God can and cannot do ... [failing] to recognize that God is far greater than our limited human abilities. ... [We must beware of] limiting God based merely on observation of finite human experience.[8]

I. HOWARD MARSHALL ON PREDETERMINATION

Does the notion that "relationship implies resistibility" obtain for the Creator as it does the creature? Consider an argument forwarded by I. Howard Marshall:

[Concerning] the possibility of *my* predetermining a course of action involving *myself* and another subject ... on the level of free agents it is *impossible*.[9]

Marshall's starting point for determining what is and is not possible for God in His relational dealings with humans is what it would be like for *him*, I. Howard Marshall, to predetermine a course of action with another subject. I share Marshall's limitations in being unable to predetermine a course of action involving myself and another subject without abolishing the humanity of the other. Should this shared limitation, however, become the modal paradigm from which we draw final conclusions about what God can and cannot do in dealing with us as His subjects?

Marshall continues, "When we try to think of a person foreordaining the course of a relationship between himself and another person ... this concept is logically contradictory."[10] Note well Marshall's recommended starting points for forming our modal conceptions: "When *we* try to think of *a person*" (emphasis added). Starting from the premise

---

8. Grudem, *Systematic Theology*, 346, 347.

9. I. Howard Marshall, "Predestination in the New Testament," in *Grace Unlimited*, ed. Clark Pinnock (Minneapolis: Bethany House, 1975), 132; emphasis added.

10. Marshall, "Predestination in the New Testament," 135.

that *human* foreordination undermines a relationship, Marshall draws conclusions about what *God* can and cannot do in relationships. God cannot foreordain the course of a relationship with another person because this concept is "logically contradictory." However, it is only when we inject human persons as the foreordinators in the formula that the logical contradiction occurs. Marshall elevates creature-relative impossibilities to the status of absolute impossibilities that define the scope of divine action. Marshall's analysis of divine action could be significantly strengthened by his own advice:

> The basic difficulty is that of attempting to explain the nature of the relationship between an infinite God and finite creatures. Our temptation is to think of divine causation in much the same way as human causation, and this produces difficulties as soon as we try to relate divine causation and human freedom. It is beyond our ability to explain how God can cause us to do certain things (or to cause the universe to come into being or behave as it does).[11]

The case of Boyd's "sophisticated chip" analyzed in 1.2.4 demonstrates how we may succumb to the "temptation to think of divine causation in much the same way as human causation." Boyd reasons from the premise that *he* cannot guarantee his wife's love without abolishing her willpower to the conclusion that *God* cannot guarantee human love without abolishing our willpower.[12]

Another case of confusing creature-relative with absolute impossibilities comes from John Eldredge:

> Any parent or lover knows this: love is chosen. ... You cannot, in the end, force anyone to love you. ... You have to allow freedom. You cannot force love. God gives us the dignity of freedom, to choose for or against him.[13]

---

11. Marshall, "Predestination in the New Testament," 138.

12. Boyd, *Satan and the Problem of Evil*, 55.

13. John Eldredge, *Epic: The Story God Is Telling* (Nashville: Thomas Nelson, 2004), 52.

Eldredge's starting points for conceptualizing God's abilities are the finite human paradigms of parent and lover *as we experience these roles*. "Forced love" represents an oxymoron within these human paradigms, as Eldredge clarifies. Eldredge then steps from the premise of our finite interpersonal capacities to conclusions about God's interpersonal capacities. Thus, we bypass the crucial question: Can God, as the original Parent and Lover, bring about love in others in a way that we cannot in our finite reflections of these relational roles?

We may clarify this question with a biblical parallel. In Exodus 15:3 we read of God's anthropomorphic self-disclosure as Warrior (cf. Isa 42:13a). Since a guarantee of military success lies beyond the human scope of warrior-power, we may conclude that this same limitation circumscribes God's abilities as Warrior. Such a conclusion, however, inverts the type-archetype relation in the biblical anthropomorphism.[14] This inversion strips something away from our theological picture of "the One who gives victory to kings" (Ps 144:10[15]). The Creator can ensure military victory in a way that the creature cannot.

A similar anthropomorphic inversion may occur when we seek to understand God as Parent and Lover. For all the energy exerted by human parents and lovers, we possess two-way power to reciprocate or resist their love. Human parents and lovers cannot guarantee reciprocated love any more than human warriors can guarantee

---

14. In A. B. Caneday's words,

> Here is the essence of anthropomorphism. God reveals himself to us in human terms, yet we must not compare God to us as if we were the ultimate reference point. ... God is the original; we are the organic image, the living copy ("Veiled Glory: God's Self-Revelation in Human Likeness—A Biblical Theology of God's Anthropomorphic Self-Disclosure," in *Beyond the Bounds: Open Theism and the Undermining of Biblical Christianity*, eds. John Piper, Justin Taylor, and Paul Kjoss Helseth [Wheaton, IL: Crossway, 2003], 149–99, 163).

See also Cornelius Van Til, "The Nature of Scripture," in *The Infallible Word*, ed. N. B. Stonehouse and Paul Woolley (Philadelphia: Presbyterian & Reformed, 1947), 273; and Herman Bavinck, *The Doctrine of God*, tr. William Hendrickson (Grand Rapids: Eerdmans, 1951), 85–86.

15. On God's unique warrior-power to ensure military victory, see Judges 6:16, 12:3 (cf. 1 Sam 17:47; 2 Sam 8:14; 1 Chron 5:22; 11:14; 2 Chron 20:15; Ps 44:7; Isa 42:13; 43:13; and Job 12:16).

military victory. Perhaps God, as the archetypal Parent and Lover of whom our parent and lover relations are but an "organic image," can ensure the love of finite humans in a way that we cannot. A. B. Caneday echoes,

> Imagine the difference between God and us. When we carry out our plans, especially plans that encompass humans, because we are creatures we are restricted to two options: we may do so by persuasion or resort to coercion. Neither is necessarily effective. God is unlike us. Because God is the sovereign creator, and not a creature, he does not relate to his creatures as one creature relates to another. As one who made us, he has his own divine ways to move us to do his bidding without violating our wills. God does not coerce his creatures.[16]

IMPOSSIBILITY AND THE SYNOPTIC VIEW OF FAITH

Does the Bible speak to the phenomenon of elevating creature-relative impossibilities to the level of absolute impossibilities? In the Synoptic Gospels, Jesus frequently measures "faith" (πίστις) as the capacity to conceptualize God accurately and rely on Him relationally as acting outside the boxes of human ability.

Mark 5:25–34 relates a story about a woman suffering from a chronic bleeding disorder whose physicians could not heal her. She believed that Jesus was not bound by the creaturely limitations of first-century doctors. The ability to heal by having your clothes touched represents a creature-relative impossibility for mere humans. She did not believe Jesus to be a mere human confined by this impossibility, touched his clothes, and received the healing that her doctors were unable to perform. Jesus commends her "faith" (πίστις; Mark 5:34). Multiple synoptic contexts support this interconnection

---

16. Caneday, "Veiled Glory," 179.

between "faith" and seeing Jesus as unbound by creature-relative impossibilities.[17]

Reinforcing faith as an awareness of God at work beyond the scope of human ability, Jesus uses the terms "little faith" (ὀλιγόπιστις) and the more forceful "no faith" or "unbelief" (ἀπιστίαν). These terms describe people who shaped their notions of what He could and could not do based of their own creaturely colored imaginative scopes.[18] The term "no faith" describes those in Nazareth who rejected Jesus' messianic identity in Mark 6:6. Their rationale for rejecting Jesus is replete with modal projections of creature-relative impossibilities into the realm of absolute impossibility. "Is not this the carpenter, the son of Mary and brother of James and Joseph and Judas and Simon, and are not his sisters here with us" (Mark 6:3a)? From their finite frame of reference, carpenters were not messiahs. Sons and brothers, in their own experience, held no titles to deity. Jesus, unbound by creature-relative impossibilities, could simultaneously be the Messiah and a carpenter, son, and brother from a small town in the ancient Near East. Jesus marveled at their absence of faith (ἀπιστίαν; Mark 6:6) and refrained from doing many deeds that displayed His transcendence over creature-relative impossibilities in Nazareth (cf. Matt 13:58).

To summarize this element of synoptic insight into the nature of faith: Jesus commends faith as the capacity to see Him unbound

---

17. In Matthew 9:27–30, Jesus heals two blind men with a touch and commends their "faith" for believing He could do so. Restoring sight with a touch represents a creature-relative impossibility. In Mark 2:3–7, caring friends lower a bedridden paralytic through a roof to Jesus in Capernaum. Their "faith" is recognized, and their friend is healed. Successfully commanding a paralytic to walk represents a creature-relative impossibility. In this context, Jesus' unique authority to forgive sins is also highlighted. It is precisely Jesus' claim to have actualized a creature-relative impossibility (i.e., forgiving the paralytic's sins) that prompts the charge of blasphemy from the Jewish leadership. In Luke 7:36–50, a weeping woman anoints Jesus' feet in the house of a Pharisee. Her sins are forgiven and her "faith" lauded. The divine authority to bestow forgiveness represents a creature-relative impossibility (cf. Mark 2:6–7). See also the case of the Canaanite woman with a demon-possessed daughter (μεγάλη σου ἡ πίστις; Matt 15:28), the Samaritan leper (ἡ πίστις σου; Luke 17:19), and the Roman centurion (πίστις; Matt 8:10).

18. Cases include the disciples in storm on the Sea of Galilee (οὔπω ἔχετε πίστιν; Mark 4:40; cf. ὀλιγόπιστοι; Matt 8:26; Luke 8:22–25), Peter sinking into the Sea of Galilee (ὀλιγόπιστε; Matt 14:31), and those worried about material needs (ὀλιγόπιστοι; Matt 6:30).

by creature-relative impossibilities. He criticizes absent faith when people limit their concepts of what He can and cannot do on the basis of their own ontological limitations.

From this synoptic concept of faith we return to the crucial premise of the Relational Vision Argument. The claim that "relationship implies resistibility" encapsulates our human experience in which it is impossible to guarantee authentic love from another agent. Could guaranteeing authentic love from another agent be something to which the words of Jesus may apply when He said, "With man this is impossible, but not with God" (Mark 10:27)?

There are essentially four ways to avoid an affirmative answer to this question. First, we could argue that the very notion of an agent who guarantees love without abolishing personhood is no more possible than an agent who creates round squares. This argument confuses a creature-relative impossibility with an absolute impossibility. There is a possible world in which Augustine's "Delightful Conqueror" exists. Second, we could argue that any love resulting from such divine action cannot count as authentic love because love requires the freedom to resist. This argument begs the question by assuming libertarian free will as a necessary condition of true love. Third, we could argue that the theological concept of a God who can guarantee authentic love conflicts with the biblical picture in which humans repeatedly and grievously resist God's relational vision. This response has been handled at length in 2.2. Fourth, we could argue that God may possess such a unique ability but refrains from exercising it, much like His power to supernova every star in the universe instantly (a power that He possesses but thankfully refrains from exercising).

The success of these libertarian responses rests on the following question: Does the Bible credit God with the unique ability to guarantee authentic love? A serious drawback of the Relational Vision Argument is that its logic *requires* a negative answer to this question. Any biblical text that speaks of the scope of divine action in human love *must* be interpreted in a way that preserves resistibility, or the libertarian conclusion is lost. If, however, the Bible credits God with love-guaranteeing ability, then the claim "relationship requires resist-ibility" lacks depth capacity when submerged in biblical insight. We will examine the biblical scope of divine action in human love in part 3. For now, I conclude that the Relational Vision Argument gains its persuasive force by moving from the premise "*we* cannot guarantee authentic love" to the conclusion "*God* cannot guarantee authentic love." Libertarians must justify the leap from "we cannot" to "God cannot."

Part 2:
Freedom and the Enslaved Heart

Summary and Conclusions

Part 2 began with the question of whether or not three attempts to reach the libertarian conclusion from biblical premises are successful. Success was analyzed in terms of depth capacity, i.e., the ability of a given theological notion to be integrated through successive levels of biblical insight without the force of biblical insight exerting fatal logical pressure on that notion.

The Moral Imperative Argument of Pelagius, Erasmus, Charles Finney, and Norman Geisler rests on the additional premise that "ought implies can" (MIA2). Biblical insights into the compatibility of moral duty and moral inability exert pressure in this premise. In particular, "ought implies can" drastically underestimates the lethal moral corruption internal to the human heart as expressed in John's Gospel. Two Erasmian strategies revived by contemporary libertarians do not relieve this pressure. Moreover, "ought implies can" represents an anthropological optimism in which we "can" do all that we "ought" to do, an optimism that has been refuted by all utopian efforts marred by humanity's moral incompetence throughout history.

The Grievous Resistance Argument of Gregory Boyd, Clark Pinnock, and John Sanders rests on the premise that "divine grief implies human autonomy" (GRA2). This crucial second premise artificially resolves a fundamental biblical tension within a God who both grieved and predetermined the crucifixion. Given this tension as highlighted in such passages as Acts 4:28, the claim that "divine grief implies human autonomy" lacks depth capacity. We examined Greg Boyd's three attempts to reconcile Acts 4:28 with libertarian free will. The claim that "divine grief implies human autonomy" has an existential price tag. When suffering the effects of concrete evil, it grants us solidarity with a God who grieves evil but robs us of stability in a God who sovereignly purposes evil. If "divine grief implies human autonomy," then suffering can only access half of God's available resources when meeting concrete problems of evil in their emotional form.

The Relational Vision Argument posited by Clark Pinnock, I. Howard Marshall, and John Eldredge requires the premise that "relationship implies resistibility." This premise captures a true insight into the nature of love relationships if those relationships are construed horizontally in the human-to-human context. No finite human can guarantee love from another finite human without obliterating the essence of love and treading on the personhood of the beloved. This is a basic insight from the Relational Vision Argument that rings true. There is a strong tendency to project our horizontal human-to-human limitation vertically as a modal paradigm into which God must fit. If biblical insight reveals the Creator as transcending our interpersonal abilities, then the claim that "relationship implies resistibility" lacks depth capacity when applied to God. The core question emerges: Does the Creator have the unique ability to guarantee authentic love from His creatures without trampling our personhood?

PART 3

Love and the Reformed Heart

The Scope of Divine Action in Human Love

3.1

Five Models of Divine Action in Human Love

Batter my heart, three person'd God; for, you
As yet but knock, breathe, shine and seek to mend;
That I may rise, and stand, o'erthrow me, and bend
Your force, to break, blow, burn and make me new.
I, like an usurpt town, to another due,
Labour to admit you, but Oh, to no end,
Reason your viceroy in me, me should defend,
But is captiv'd, and proves weak or untrue.
Yet dearly "I love you," and would be loved fain,
But am betrothed unto your enemy:
Divorce me, untie, or break that knot again,
Take me to you, imprison me, for
Except you enthrall me, shall never be free,
Nor ever chaste, except you ravish me.

—*John Donne, "Holy Sonnets," no. 14*

GOD AND THE HEART

Does the Creator share our creaturely limitation of being unable to guarantee love without trampling the personhood of the beloved? Without distinguishing the major theological possibilities for answering this question, we succumb to a common blunder. Any passage that speaks of divine action is taken as proof positive that all libertarian theologies are fatally flawed. Conversely, passages that emphasize human responsibility are interpreted as a death knell for any non-libertarian theology. In this way, we trivialize the opponent's views, ignore important middle-of-the-road perspectives, and reduce the Bible to a "nose of wax" (Albert Pighius), which may be custom molded to fit virtually any theological profile.

This chapter lays the conceptual groundwork for the biblical analysis to follow by mapping the theological landscape around the question of divine action in human love. The literature on divine action in human love is both historically wide-ranging and highly nuanced. I aim to clarify the possibilities that have been the primary voices on God's role in human love through the history of theological dialogue. I do not aim at a full-scale, historical analysis but state each theological possibility, briefly reconstruct its underlying logic, and expose its core anthropological dimensions.

Beginning with the most emphatically libertarian views and ending with non-libertarian perspectives, I label these five theological possibilities: Heart Persuasion, Heart Cooperation, Heart Activation, Heart Reformation, and Heart Circumvention. Consider these five possibilities in the heart of Claudia:[1]

> **1. Heart Persuasion:** God's role in Claudia's choice to love Him is that of "Heart Persuasion" if God acts in some external way to display who He is, His saving intentions, and His moral requirements to Claudia's heart.

---

1. The analysis that follows is heavily indebted to the historical-theological work of R. C. Sproul in *Willing to Believe: The Controversy over Free Will* (Grand Rapids: Baker Books, 1998).

2. Heart Cooperation: God's role in Claudia's choice to love Him is that of "Heart Cooperation" if God acts in some internal way to reinforce and strengthen any weak motion toward Him within her heart.

3. Heart Activation: God's role in Claudia's choice to love Him is that of "Heart Activation" if God acts in some internal way to counteract forces of moral depravity within her heart, bestowing a new ability to respond positively to Him in love.

4. Heart Reformation: God's role in Claudia's choice to love Him is that of "Heart Reformation" if God acts in some internal way that effectively changes the moral orientation of her heart so that she willingly chooses to love Him and cannot ultimately choose otherwise.

5. Heart Circumvention: God's role in Claudia's "choice" to "love" Him is that of "Heart Circumvention" if God acts in some internal way that coercively bypasses her heart such that any "love" for God is not an expression of her desires but of divine force.

These five possibilities can be thought of as a freeway, with each mode of divine action serving as an off-ramp at which we may exit, continue no farther, and call our theological home.

PELAGIUS AND CASSIAN
ON DIVINE ACTION

1. *Pelagia.* If we maintain that the scope of divine action in human love goes no farther than Heart Persuasion, then we have exited the theological freeway and entered what might be called "Pelagia." Within the theological metropolis of Pelagia (and within contemporary Christianity, we may accurately envision Pelagianism as a heavily

populated metropolis[2]) we encounter a highly optimistic anthropology. In the analysis of Adolph Harnack, "[Pelagius] preached that God commanded nothing impossible, that man possessed the power of doing the good if only he willed."[3]

Within this anthropological framework, God need only offer salvation to humans because our hearts are morally intact enough to exercise libertarian free will to embrace salvation *without the internal aid of divine grace*. Philip Schaff expounds:

> [According to Pelagius] freedom is the supreme good, the honor and glory of man, the *bonum naturae* that cannot be lost. It is the sole basis of the ethical relation of man to God, who would have no unwilling service. It consists ... essentially in the *liberum arbitrium*, or the *possibilitas boni et mali*; the freedom of choice, and the absolutely equal ability at every moment to do good or evil.[4]

Schaff clarifies the scope of divine action that follows logically from this Pelagian anthropology,

> If human nature is uncorrupted, and the natural will competent to all good, we need no Redeemer to create in us a new will and a new life, but merely an improver and ennobler; and salvation is essentially a work of man.[5]

---

2. On the widespread influence of Pelagianism in contemporary Christianity, see R. C. Sproul, "The Pelagian Captivity of the Church," *Modern Reformation* 10, no. 3 (2001): 22–29.

3. Adolph Harnack, *History of Dogma*, part 2, book 2, tr. James Millar [1898; New York: Dover, 1961], 174. For a more recent assessment of Pelagian thought that reinforces Harnack's analysis, see Alister McGrath, *Christian Theology* (Hoboken, NJ: John Wiley & Sons, 2010), 352–55.

4. Philip Schaff, *History of the Christian Church*, vol. 3 (1907–1910; Grand Rapids: Eerdmans, 1952–53), 802–3. Schaff's analysis, "The Pelagian Controversy—A Historical Essay" (*Bibliotecha Sacra and Theological Review*, 5 no. 18 [1848] 205–43) remains a landmark exposition of Pelagian thought. More recent works reinforcing Schaff's analysis include: Frederick Teggart, *The Processes of History* (Charleston, NC: BiblioLife, 2009), 125–27; and Rebecca Harden Weaver, *Divine Grace and Human Agency: A Study of the Semi-Pelagian Controversy* (Mercer, GA: Mercer University Press, 1998), 122.

5. Schaff, *History of the Christian Church*, vol. 3, 815.

The optimistic anthropology of Pelagius and his corresponding view of divine action clearly preserve the agent's libertarian power to love God or refrain.

The church councils of Carthage (418), Ephesus (431), and Orange (529) uniformly declared Pelagianism a heresy. Their verdicts were heavily influenced by the rigorous theological rebuttals set forth by Augustine, who defended two overarching points. First, there is a stark contrast between Pelagius' optimistic assessment of humanity's moral competence and the effacement of our moral abilities described in the Bible. Second, there is vast distance between Pelagius' minimalistic view of God's grace and a biblical picture of the magnitude of God's grace in saving sinners.[6]

2. *Cassiana.* The theological traveler could move past Pelagia, driven by a conviction that divine action transcends Heart Persuasion and entails Heart Cooperation as well. If we proceed no farther than Heart Cooperation then we have entered the theological city of Cassiana. Reinhold Seeberg clarifies the thinking of the fourth century abbot, John Cassian:

> The idea of Cassian is, that the human will has indeed been crippled by sin, but that a certain freedom has yet remained to it. By virtue of this, [the human will] is able to turn to God, and, just as though God had first turned to it, it is able, with the assistance of divine grace, setting before it the law [i.e., Heart Persuasion] and infusing the needed power [i.e., Heart Cooperation], to will and to do that which is good. Hence the sinner is not dead, but wounded. Grace comes to view, not as *operans*, but as *cooperans*; to [God's grace] is attributed not alone-activity, but synergy.[7]

---

6. For a compilation of Augustine's anti-Pelagian writings, see *The Nicene and Post-Nicene Fathers*, vol. 5, ed. Philip Schaff.

7. Reinhold Seeberg, *History of Doctrines in the Ancient Church*, vol. 1, tr. Charles Hay (1905; Grand Rapids: Baker, 1977), 371–72. For more recent analysis of Cassian's position that supports Seeberg, see Weaver, *Divine Grace and Human Agency*.

In the synergistic thought of Cassian, humanity has not escaped the fall of Genesis 3 without suffering debilitating moral damage. The fall has rendered our hearts wounded in our moral capacity to love. The wound, however, has not proven fatal to our freedom. Our power to love God remains fundamentally intact, though it is admittedly handicapped.

When creatures make good use of their wounded abilities, God responds by supplying them with additional strength. He cooperates synergistically with His creatures to bring about their love response. In Cassiana, God's power does not only take external forms (e.g., calls, invitations, commands, etc.) as in Pelagia. He also exercises power internally to work cooperatively with our wounded hearts. Like Pelagianism, Cassian's view sustains humanity's libertarian power to say "yes" or "no" to God.

ARMINIUS AND AUGUSTINE
ON DIVINE ACTION

3. *Arminia.* The theological traveler could go still farther and enter the next city, Arminia, in which divine action also includes Heart Activation. In this city, humanity is not viewed as morally unscathed by the fall of Genesis 3 (as in Pelagia), or as wounded yet capable of some Godward motion (as in Cassiana). Rather, in the words of Arminius,

> The mind of man, in this state, is dark, destitute of the saving knowledge of God, and, according to the Apostle, incapable of those things which belong to the Spirit of God. … Exactly correspondent to this Darkness of Mind and Perverseness of Heart, is the utter Weakness [*impotentia*] of all the Powers to perform that which is truly good.[8]

---

8. James Arminius, *The Public Disputations of James Arminius, D. D.,* in James Arminius, *The Works of James Arminius: The London Edition,* tr. James and Williams Nichols, vol. 2 (1825–75; Grand Rapids: Baker, 1986), 192–95.

John Wesley echoes, "Since the fall, no child of man has a natural power to choose anything that is truly good."[9]

What must God do to be loved by creatures of such profound moral powerlessness? The seventeenth-century followers of Arminius, known as the Remonstrants, answer:

> Man does not have saving faith of himself nor by the power of his own free will, since he is in a state of apostasy and sin cannot of and through himself think, will or do any good which is truly good. ... But it is necessary that he be regenerated by God, in Christ, through his Holy Spirit, and renewed in understanding, affections or will, and all powers, in order that he *may* [note: the subjunctive to convey possibility, versus the future indicative "will"] rightly understand, meditate upon, will, and perform that which is truly good.[10]

God, if He is to be loved by humans, must actively extend grace that counteracts the morally fatal effects of the fall on human nature. He activates hearts otherwise plagued by moral *impotentia,* so that they *may potentially* (versus *will actually*) love Him. The Remonstrants add,

> With respect to the mode of this grace ... it is not irresistible. ... Man is able of himself to despise that grace and not to believe, and therefore to perish through his own fault.[11]

God activates otherwise powerless hearts, graciously lifting them to a place where their libertarian free will, the *possibilitas boni et mali,* may be exercised to love or refrain. As in Pelagia and Cassiana, libertarian free will is at home within Arminia. The human agent's power of saying "yes" or "no" to God remains intact, though it is a graciously

---

9. John Wesley, *The Works of John Wesley,* ed. T. Jimson, vol. 10 (Grand Rapids: Baker, 1979), 350.

10. "The Remonstrance of 1610," Appendix C, in *Crisis in the Reformed Churches: Essays in Commemoration of the Great Synod of Dort, 1618–1619,* ed. Peter De Jong (Grand Rapids: Reformed Fellowship, 1968), 208–9, cited in Sproul, *Willing to Believe,* 135–36; emphasis added.

11. "The Remonstrance of 1610," 208–9.

restored power rather than the undamaged power we find in Pelagia or the wounded power in Cassiana.

This notion of a restored power to love God sheds light on the anthropology found in Arminia. Although humans, in our natural state, are "incapable of those things which belong to the Spirit of God," the divine work of Heart Activation renders us capable of those things that belong to God's Spirit. A dual anthropology emerges: There are *humans as we would be* if Heart Activation were never extended to us, and *humans as we really are* since Heart Activation has been extended to us.

To highlight this distinction, it is important to see that Heart Activation is *universally* bestowed according to this view. Wesley writes, "There is a measure of free will supernaturally restored to *every man*" (emphasis added).[12] Humanity is no longer bound to anti-God propensities. Through universal Heart Activation, such bondage has been banished to the realm of the hypothetical. The hypothetical anthropology—humanity incapable of saying "yes" to God—distinguishes this view from both Pelagianism and Cassianism. The actual anthropology—humanity capable of saying "yes" to God because He has activated our hearts—distinguishes this view from the next theology we will explore.

4. *Augustinia.* If we press on farther, then we enter the theological city of Augustinia. Augustine attributes to God not only the power of Persuasion, Cooperation, and Activation, but also Heart Reformation. In this view, humans are *actually,* not hypothetically, in a state of moral *impotentia.* In Francis Turretin's words,

> Scriptures teach ... [that men exist in a state of] total and absolute impotence for good. ... [The Scriptures] call them

---

12. Wesley, *The Works of John Wesley*, vol. 10, 229–30. See Robert Rakestraw, "John Wesley as a Theologian of Grace," *Journal of the Evangelical Theological Society* 27 (1984): 196–99; and J. Weldon Smith III, "Some Notes on Wesley's Doctrine of Prevenient Grace," *Religion and Life* 34 (1964–65): 70–75.

not only sick and weak, but "dead in sins," Eph 2:1, 2; "blind,"
nay even "darkness" itself, Eph 4:18; 5:8; "who do not receive
and cannot receive the things of the Spirit of God," 1 Cor 2:14;
"the servants of sin," John 8:34; Rom 6:19; "the enemies of
God," Col 1:21; "who are not and cannot be subject to his law,"
Rom 8:7; in one word "who can neither think nor do anything
good of themselves," John 15:5; 2 Cor 3:5. ... For why should
[Scripture] so often propose to us the sinner as wholly weak
(*asthene*) and destitute of strength (who can neither know anything true nor do anything good), if this was always in his own
power and truly from himself (*ek ton eph hemin*)?[13]

In this anthropological framework, loving God lies beyond the capacity of the human heart. Humanity's moral *impotentia* has not been
undone by a universally bestowed grace,[14] rendering the hypothetical
anthropology of Arminia the actual anthropology of Augustinia.[15] We
are in bondage to sin, suffering from the *liberum arbitrium captivatum*
("the captive free will," Augustine). In this bondage, humanity is not
like a prisoner who curses the chains that prevent him from reaching
out to God in love. Humanity in bondage does not *want* to love God.
We are like a prisoner who "kisses his chains and refuses deliverance."[16]

---

13. Turretin, *Institutes of Elenctic Theology*, vol. 2, tr. George Musgrave Giger, ed. James
Dennison (Phillipsburg, NJ: P&R Publishing, [1696] 1994), 530–31.

14. Within Augustinia, there is a notion of "common grace" that resembles Heart Activation.
Both common grace and Heart Activation are universally bestowed, both contribute to a
measure of moral behavior among the unbelieving people, both curb the full expression of
evil in society, etc. Common grace is distinct from Heart Activation in that it does not bring
the human heart to a place where it can make a saving decision to embrace God. See Thomas
Schreiner, "Does Scripture Teach Prevenient Grace in the Wesleyan Sense?" in *The Grace of
God the Bondage of the Will*, vol. 2 (Grand Rapids: Baker Books, 1995), 371.

15. On points of contact between these two anthropologies, see M. Elton Hendricks, "John
Wesley and Natural Theology," *Wesley Theological Journal* 18 (1983): 9; and J. Weldon Smith III,
"Some Notes on Wesley's Doctrine of Prevenient Grace," 70–74. H. Orton Wiley adds helpful
qualifications on the extent of anthropological agreement in *Christian Theology*, vol. 2 (Kansas
City: Beacon Hill, 1952), 353.

16. Turretin, *Institutes of Elenctic Theology*, vol. 1, 671.

In this affectionate enslavement to evil, more than Heart Persuasion, Cooperation, and Activation is needed for us to turn our love toward God. God must extend the grace of Heart Reformation to liberate humans from captivity to self-centeredness and infuse us with new efficacious desires to love. Turretin expounds,

> [God infuses] his vivifying Spirit, who, gliding into the inmost recesses of the soul, reforms the mind itself, healing its depraved inclinations and prejudices. ... [God] so sweetly and at the same time powerfully affects the man that he cannot (thus called) help following God.[17]

In contrast to Arminia, God does not alter hearts so that humans *may* love Him. If God reforms a human heart, then the human *will* love Him. In his exposition of Ephesians 2:8–10, John Calvin clarifies:

> The Apostle does not say that we are assisted by God. He does not say that the will is prepared, and has then to proceed in its own strength. He does not say that the power of choosing aright is bestowed upon us, and that we have afterwards to make our own choice. ... But he says that we are God's work, and that everything good in us is His creation. ...It is not mere power of choosing aright, or some indefinable preparation, or assistance, but *the right will itself, which is His workmanship.*[18]

The "right will," the will *actually* engaged in love for God, and not merely an neutral will *potentially* engaged in love for God, is the product of divine workmanship within Augustinia.

---

17. Turretin, *Institutes of Elenctic Theology*, vol. 2, 523, 521.

18. John Calvin, *The Epistles of Paul the Apostle to the Galatians, Ephesians, Philippians and Colossians*, tr. T. H. L. Parker, Calvin's Commentaries, eds. David Torrance and Thomas Torrance (Grand Rapids: Eerdmans, 1965), 145–46; emphasis added. Elsewhere Calvin adds, "The willingness with which men follow God is what they already have from Himself, who has formed their hearts to obey Him" (*Commentary on the Gospel According to John*, tr. William Pringle, vol. 1 [Grand Rapids: Baker, 1979], 257).

DIVINE ACTION IN NO MAN'S LAND

5. *No Man's Land.* In this final destination, God does not extend Heart Persuasion, Cooperation, Activation, or Reformation, but Heart Circumvention. He bypasses the human will in such a way that morally relevant human agency is lost. Such a theology becomes a "modified pantheism"[19] in which God remains the only active agent in existence. Here we enter a "No Man's Land" in a literal sense of the terms. There can be no "man" if God practices Heart Circumvention. With human desires, aversions, reasons, and intentions voided by an exercise of divine force, man reduces to the level of a machine.

Libertarian and compatibilist theologians throughout history are united in their rejection of this mechanistic view of humanity. Turretin offers clarity from a compatibilistic perspective,

> With respect to the actual [conversion], the principle cause is indeed God, but the proximate and immediate cause is man, who (excited by the Holy Spirit and imbued with the habits of faith and love) believes and loves. ... Hence it appears that man is not like a log and a trunk in his regeneration as our opponents falsely charge upon us. ... The Spirit does not force the will and carry it on unwillingly to conversion, but glides most sweetly into the soul ... and operates by an infusion of supernatural habits by which it is freed little by little from its innate depravity, so as to become willing from unwilling. ... The will so renewed and acted upon immediately acts, converting itself to God and believing.[20]

For Turretin, there is a qualitative distinction between Heart Reformation and Heart Circumvention (though the two are often conflated in the contemporary literature). When God reforms a heart, the human creature is left intact as a morally relevant agent with

---

19. See Irving Singer, *The Nature of Love: Plato to Luther*, vol. 1, 2nd ed. (Cambridge, MA: MIT Press, 2009), 293–94.

20. Turretin, *Institutes of Elenctic Theology*, vol. 2, 523–24.

active power. Our center of choice-making power is not circumvented, but infused with new supernatural habits (*habitus supernaturalis sive spiritualis*).[21] Augustine says, "It is not words that God wants of you, but your hearts. ... It is with the heart that we ask; with the heart we seek; and it is to the voice of the heart that the door is opened."[22] God desires authentic, from-the-heart love from His creatures, not contrived affection from a being with a circumvented heart.

We have mapped five theological cities, Pelagia, Cassiana, Arminia, Augustinia, and No Man's Land, including their distinct views of divine action and corresponding anthropologies:

- In Pelagia, humanity is naturally competent at loving God. To be loved by such people, God must do nothing more than externally persuade their hearts through moral education. With divine action proceeding no farther than Heart Persuasion, the Assertion of Libertarian Love finds a home.

- In Cassiana, humanity is morally wounded, capable of only faint efforts at loving God. To be loved by such people, God cooperates with their hearts by internally strengthening their moral resolves. With divine action moving no farther than Heart Cooperation, the Assertion is again welcomed.

- In Arminia, humanity is morally dead, incapable of loving God. To be loved by such people, God activates

---

21. Richard Muller offers a definition,

  "A supernatural or spiritual habit; a disposition, capacity, or aptitude that does not belong to the natural capacities of man but which rests upon the divine work of grace in us and is therefore both of the Spirit (*spiritualis*) and from beyond our nature (*supernaturalis*)." (*Dictionary of Latin and Greek Theological Terms Drawn Principally from Protestant Scholastic Theology* [Grand Rapids: Baker, 1985], 135)

22. Augustine, "Sermon 91," 3 (cited in Thomas Hand, *Augustine on Prayer* [New York: Catholic Book Publishing, 1986], 20). Hand comments, "In these texts, of course, the term 'heart' is used in the scriptural sense, in which it indicates our whole interior life and spiritual life and all its faculties" (*Augustine on Prayer*, 20).

the hearts of every human agent so that we may exercise our restored free power to say "yes" to Him. With divine action terminating at Heart Activation, the Assertion again finds welcome.

- In Augustinia, humanity is morally dead, actually incapable of loving God. To be loved by such people, God must reform the human heart, which entails that the reformed agent cannot ultimately say "no" to Him. Love may remain authentic even in the absence of the power to resist love. With divine action including this Heart Reformation, there exists no room for the Assertion of Libertarian Love (although the Axiom of Unforced Love [see 1.2.5] is at home in this city).

- In No Man's Land, humanity is morally vacuous, incapable of loving God. God does not persuade, cooperate with, activate, or reform human hearts but circumvents them in order to evoke a "love" response. Heart Circumvention violates both the Assertion of Libertarian Love and the Axiom of Unforced Love.

OBSERVATIONS ON THE
THEOLOGICAL LANDSCAPE

From these theological options, three points crucial to the coming biblical analysis emerge. First, we are in a better place to discern a fourth relative freedom (in addition to Freedom from the Machine, Gunman, and Heart) that libertarian free will requires. To see the need for this fourth freedom, imagine a case in which Claudia can love God or refrain relative to the cumulative forces of the physical world, coercive agents, and the propensities of her heart. This two-way power is essential to libertarian free will (see 1.2.2). However, what if God extends Heart Reformation to Claudia so that she cannot ultimately refrain from loving Him? In this case, libertarian free will is lost because there is no longer two-way power. Therefore, libertarian free will includes what we may call "Freedom from the Reformer."

> Claudia has "Freedom from the Reformer" to love God or refrain from loving God if *relative to all divine action extended on her heart*, she can still love God or refrain from loving God.

With this fourth freedom essential to libertarian free will, the Assertion takes a more refined form:

> Any agent, A, must possess Freedom from the Machine, the Gunman, the Heart, *and the Reformer* to love or refrain from loving another agent, B, if A's love for B is to count as authentic.

3.2 examines whether or not the Bible endorses Freedom from the Reformer as a condition of authentic love.

Second, it is clear that a commitment to libertarian free will does not require the theologian to give up all meaningful divine action in human love. Libertarian free will does not logically force us to the embrace the relationally disengaged deity of Epicurus, Thomas Paine, or Francois Voltaire. God may be actively engaged in Heart Persuasion, Cooperation, and Activation without excluding the human agent's non-hypothetical two-way power. This two-way power is lost only if we include Heart Reformation in the scope of divine action (i.e., Heart Reformation violates the libertarian requirement of Freedom from the Reformer).

Third, a rejection of libertarian free will does not require the theologian to give up all meaningful human action. Rejecting libertarian free will does not logically force us to embrace a coercive deity who circumvents human hearts. God may engage in Heart Reformation so that humans lack the libertarian ability to say "no" to loving Him, while we remain active agents in the expression of that love. This view features a compatibilistic rather than libertarian account of human free will. In this compatibilistic account developed in 1.2, the agent is free when her actions express her own heart (rather than physical or coercive forces). If God reforms an agent's heart so that she cannot ultimately reject Him, then she is still free (and perhaps *more* free) since *her* ego-liberated heart is expressed in the act of loving. This is qualitatively different from saying that God exercises Heart Circumvention. Augustinia occupies altogether different terrain than No Man's Land.

3.2

Heart Reformation
and the Bible

*The Holy Spirit produces knowledge in the believer; in
sealing this knowledge to our hearts, however, [he] also
produces the right affections. Chief among these right
affections is love of God—desire for God, desire to know
him, to have a personal relationship with him, as well
as delight in him, relishing his beauty, greatness, holiness,
and the like. ...The Holy Spirit does more than produce
in us the belief that this or that proposition is true. As
Aquinas repeats four times in five passages, "the Holy
Spirit makes us lovers of God."*

—*Alvin Plantinga,* Warranted Christian Belief

Heart Persuasion, Cooperation, Activation, Reformation, and
Circumvention represent the basic theological possibilities for understanding God's role in human love. Do any of these theological possibilities represent biblical actualities? By and large, biblical insights
into the scope of God's role in the actualization of human love have

not been seriously reckoned with in the Relational Free Will Defense literature. It is the aim of 3.2 to exposit some relevant texts, narrowed primarily (though not exclusively) to John's Gospel, welcoming biblical insight into the scholarly dialogue surrounding abstract problems of evil.

The following analysis will be structured around three questions posed by Paul Gauguin's painting, *Whence Come We? What Are We? Whither Go We?* (1897). Hanging in Boston's Museum of Fine Arts, Gauguin's canvas tells a tragic gospel of our natural origins, reach for meaning, and final demise. In Gauguin's words, "I have finished a philosophical work … comparable to the gospel." Like the modern visual gospel of Gauguin, the ancient literary Gospel of John speaks to the same three questions: "Whence Come We? What Are We? Whither Go We?" To what extent do John's answers to these origin, identity, and destiny questions feature divine action in the actualization of human love?

AN ANCIENT HEBREW TENSION

Before attempting to discern John's answers to the origin, identity, and destiny questions, it is important to sketch some basic features of the Old Testament perspectives that form the primary backdrop of the Fourth Gospel. Of particular relevance is an ancient Hebrew tension that John reiterates and deepens. This tension is palpable in Deuteronomy 30:6:

> And the LORD your God will circumcise your heart and the heart of your offspring, so that you will love the LORD your God with all your heart and with all your soul, that you may live.

This promise of a circumcised heart falls within the context of Moses' speech at Moab. A tension emerges within the Moab covenant that any viable interpretation must leave intact. Israel's responsibility to exercise their hearts in the choice to love God (Deut 30:15–20) is sustained alongside God's active role in circumcising hearts to bring about their love for Him (Deut 30:6). Patrick Miller recognizes the tension,

In this juxtaposition of human act commanded and divine act promised there is a fundamental and appropriate tension that is characteristic of the covenantal relationship in the biblical context. ... On the one hand, conversion is a human decision and commitment to direct oneself toward the will of God; on the other hand, its actuality is always accomplished by the gracious power of God.[1]

Failure to appreciate this tension generates two theological extremes. A first extreme focuses only on God's heart-circumcising action. Singer pinpoints the problem with this narrow focus:

There seems to be no point in exhorting human beings to *anything*. ... [They] can only wait quietly for *agape* to descend. Such patience may be admirable, but it hardly counts as love.[2]

He criticizes the attitude that says, "If God must actively circumcise our hearts, then we wait passively for Him to do so, disengaging our hearts from all efforts to love." The Mosaic imperative—"choose life"— prevents the Israelites from drawing such laxity-justifying conclusions (Deut 30:19b; cf. 11, 16a). In Deuteronomy 10:16, Moses again places the onus squarely on the Israelites, urging them to "circumcise, therefore, the foreskin of your heart." Such commands become incoherent within the Heart Circumvention model of divine action.

An opposite extreme focuses exclusively on the "human act commanded." "Choose life" is interpreted as proof positive that humans possess a power to say "yes" or "no" to God that operates independently of divine control and may even frustrate God's love-actualizing efforts.[3] On such a libertarian free will-friendly interpretation, heart circumcision is best understood in terms of Heart Persuasion,

---

1. Patrick Miller, *Deuteronomy* (Philadelphia: Westminster Press, 1990), 207–8.

2. Irving Singer, *The Nature of Love: Plato to Luther*, vol. 1, 2nd ed. (Cambridge, MA: MIT Press, 2009), 293–94; emphasis original.

3. See Ian Cairns, *Word and Presence: A Commentary on the Book of Deuteronomy* (Grand Rapids: Eerdmans, 1992), 264.

Cooperation, or Activation. Let us examine these libertarian interpretive options in order.

1. *Circumcision as Heart Persuasion.* In the prologue to the Moab covenant, Moses informs the Israelites, "But to this day the LORD has
not given you a heart to understand or eyes to see or ears to hear"
(Deut 29:4). The optimistic anthropology of Pelagia in which "man
possessed the power of doing the good if only he willed" (Schaff) is
foreign to the Moab covenant. In the anthropology of Deuteronomy
29:4, humans are not the competent moral agents that Pelagius envi-
sioned but morally dull-hearted, blind, and deaf apart from the internal activity of God. While God extends Heart Persuasion throughout
the Moab covenant (Deut 29:10–28; 30:11–20), the circumcision
metaphor goes beyond these external persuasions to signal divine
action *within* the Israelites' hearts. This pushes the metaphor of
Deuteronomy 30:6 beyond (while still including) Heart Persuasion.

2. *Circumcision as Heart Cooperation.* As Ian Cairns interprets heart
circumcision, "When a person seeks to purify himself, he receives
help in doing so."[4] In this interpretation, Israel obeys God through an
exercise of libertarian free will, and God responds by circumcising
their hearts. On this view, Deuteronomy 30:6 is best understood in
a conditional if-then relation—*if* you do x, y, and z, *then* you will be
rewarded with circumcised hearts.[5]

There are exegetical reasons for viewing heart circumcision as
moving beyond a conditional if-then relation.[6] This becomes clear
when we juxtapose the promise of a circumcised heart with the
conditions of the Moab covenant. These conditions include loving

---

4. Cairns, *Word and Presence*, 264.

5. Norman Geisler forwards such an interpretation (*Chosen But Free* [Minneapolis: Bethany
House, 1999], 63). Geisler correctly interprets "restoration," in the sense of regained fortunes
and gathering from dispersion, as conditional on Israel's repentance. Geisler then equivocates
"restoration" with God changing the Israelites' hearts in order to make heart circumcision conditional on Israel's libertarian choices, a semantic switch for which he offers no textual support.

6. See Walter Brueggemann, *Deuteronomy* (Nashville: Abingdon Press, 2001), 267.

God "with all your heart and with all your soul" (Deut 30:2, 10). In Deuteronomy 30:6, God circumcises the Israelites' hearts, "to love Him *with all your heart and with all your soul*" (emphasis added), the same Hebrew expression used to express the covenant conditions. If whole-hearted love for God is a condition that Israel had to meet in order to receive the reward of whole-hearted love for God, then the blessing of circumcised hearts becomes redundant.

Moreover, circumcision, in the metaphorical sense applied to the human heart, stands for the removal of inner dullness toward God and the resulting disobedience to His commands.[7] Like the presence of physical foreskin, spiritual foreskin marks one as being in a state of extra-covenantal disobedience. If Israel had met the requirements of the Moab covenant—namely, loving God with all their hearts (Deut 30:2, 16, 20)—then they would have already stood in a positive covenantal connection with God. A heart circumcision would be as superfluous as subjecting a grown male Israelite to a second cut of the *izmel*. The promised blessing of a circumcised heart, however, retains its force if Deuteronomy 30:6 is read not as a consequence resulting *from* covenantal obedience but as the divine condition resulting *in* covenantal obedience.

3. *Circumcision as Heart Activation.* A third interpretation of Deuteronomy 30:6 locates libertarian free will not before the heart circumcision but after it. In the words of Jeffrey Tagay, "The removal of the 'foreskin' implies only that God would remove impediments that prevent Israel from voluntarily following God's teachings."[8] Through the divine act of Heart Activation, God moves humans from a state

---

7. The *Targum Onkelos*, with its tendency to replace metaphor with concrete language, renders Deuteronomy 30:6: "The LORD your God will remove the *obduracy* of your heart and the *obduracy* of the heart of your children" (emphasis added).

8. Jeffrey Tagay, *The JPS Torah Commentary: Deuteronomy*, ed. Nahum Sarna (Philadelphia: The Jewish Publication Society, 1996), 285. Tagay does, however, see Hosea 2:21; Jeremiah 24:7; 31:31–34; 32:38–41; Ezekiel 11:19–20; and 36:25–28 as clear cases of God's decisive action to cause Israel's obedience. Abravanel argues that God will only remove wrongful appetites from Israel, not their freedom of choice (*The JPS Torah Commentary*, 285).

where they can only say "no" to God to a new state from which they can say "yes" or "no" to Him.

There are at least three problems with interpreting heart circumcision as Heart Activation. First, there are no indicators in the text that heart circumcision will have any result other than actualized love.[9] Second, the promise of Deuteronomy 30:8—that Israel "shall again obey the voice of the LORD keep all His commandments"—loses meaning if Israel can use circumcised hearts to say "no" to Him. The promise reduces to a predilection that may prove falsified by the libertarian resistance of activated hearts. Third, heart circumcision is an internal sign of a positive covenantal relationship with God. If the circumcised heart is merely an activated heart that can say "no" to God, then we face an enigmatic prospect: It becomes possible to exist in positive covenantal relationship with God *vis-à-vis* having a circumcised heart, while simultaneously existing outside of a positive covenantal relation by saying "no" to God. The text knows no such contradiction.

The best interpretation of the heart circumcision metaphor is as *both* a "human act commanded" *and* a "divine act promised." The text sustains what we may call a Mosaic Circumcision Tension:

MCT1: God promises a heart circumcision, a divine action extended to humans that results in authentic human-to-God love.

MCT2: Humans receive the circumcise-imperative, making them morally responsible to circumcise their own hearts and love God.

By limiting divine action to Heart Persuasion, Cooperation, and Activation, Pelagia, Cassiana, and Arminia fail to uphold the "divine

---

9. The love resulting from heart circumcision appears as a complementary infinitive. The text, therefore, is properly rendered "to love" rather than conveying subjunctive possibility (e.g., "may love" or "might love").

act promised" side of the tension (MCT1). No Man's Land, with its responsibility-eliminating notion of Heart Circumvention, fails to sustain the "human act commanded" side of this tension (MCT2). Augustinia, by forwarding Heart Reformation as a model of God's role in human love, sustains both sides of the tension. From this perspective, Moses' covenantal challenge becomes: Love God! But love in a radically dependent way, recognizing that any success in loving God originates not in your autonomous power, but in His heart-reforming grace.[10] Says Augustine, "O holy God ... when your commands are obeyed, it is from you that we receive the power to obey them."[11]

The tension of the Moab covenant is preserved in the new covenant motifs of later Hebrew literature. Ezekiel urges the Israelites to "get yourselves a new heart and a new spirit" (Ezek 18:31) in one breath while emphasizing divine action in the next,

> And I will give you a new heart, and a new spirit I will put within you. And I will remove the heart of stone from your flesh and give you a heart of flesh. And I will put my Spirit within you, and cause you to walk in my statutes and be careful to obey my rules. (Ezek 36:26–27)

What, in the ancient Hebrew mindset, was the *summum bonum* of God's "statutes" and "rules"? Deuteronomy 6:5 affirms, "You shall love the LORD your God with all your heart and with all your soul and with all your might."[12] Divine action brings about authentic love in human hearts (cf. Ezek 11:19–20). Here we encounter Ezekiel's Transplant Tension:

---

10. See J. Gary Millar, *Now Choose Life: Theology and Ethics in Deuteronomy* (Grand Rapids: Eerdmans, 1998), 93.

11. Augustine, *Confessions*, tr. R. S. Pine-Coffin (New York: Penguin, 1961), 181 (IX.1).

12. Note the parallel noun pairings of *hoq* and *mispat* between Deuteronomy 6:1 and Ezekiel 36:27.

ETT1: God promises a heart transplant, a divine action extended to humans that results in authentic human-to-God love.

ETT2: Humans receive the transplant-imperative, making them morally responsible to get a new heart that loves God.

A common theological thread runs through Moses' heart circumcision metaphor and Ezekiel's picture of a stone-to-flesh heart transplant. It is the shared affirmation that God extends grace to transform hearts so that people love Him, without relieving people of the responsibility to love Him.[13] The metaphor undergoes alteration and new emphases emerge,[14] but the tension remains fundamentally intact.

Jeremiah borrows the imagery of Deuteronomy 10:12: "Circumcise yourselves to the Lord; remove the foreskin of your hearts, O men of Judah and inhabitants of Jerusalem" (Jer 4:4a). To this "human act commanded," Jeremiah adds,

> But this is the covenant that I will make with the house of Israel after those days, declares the Lord: I will put my law within them, and I will write it on their hearts. And I will be their God, and they shall be my people. (Jer 31:33; cf. Jer 33:18)

The metaphor of divine action shifts from heart circumcision (Moses) and heart transplantation (Ezekiel) to heart transcription. Here we encounter Jeremiah's Transcription Tension:

---

13. Paul Joyce views this heart transplant as Heart Activation, "the gift of a renewed capacity to respond ... in obedience." ("Divine Initiative and Human Response in Ezekiel," Journal for the Study of the Old Testament Supplemental Series [Sheffield Academic Press, 1989], 111. Baruch Schwartz views Joyce's interpretation as "certainly short of the mark (since in Ezekiel's view Israel never had this capacity to begin with)" ("Ezekiel's Dim View of Israel's Restoration," in *The Book of Ezekiel: Theological and Anthropological Perspectives*, ed. Margaret Odell and John Strong, Symposium [Atlanta: Society of Biblical Literature, 2000], 47). The possibility of this gracious heart transplant resulting in anything other than loving obedience is closed by the formula of covenantal intimacy—"I will be your God and you shall be my people" (Ezek 36:28). See Schwartz, "Ezekiel's Dim View of Israel's Restoration," 51, 61, n. 49.

14. See Schwartz, "Ezekiel's Dim View of Israel's Restoration," 43–67; and M. Goshen-Gottstein, "The Theocentric Trend in Ezekiel's Prophecies," Interpretation 38 (1984): 181–208.

JTT1: God promises a heart transcription, a divine action of writing His law on human hearts that results in authentic human-to-God love.

JTT2: Humans receive the circumcise-imperative, making them morally responsible to circumcise their own hearts and love God.

God writes the *torah*, which has love as its *summum bonum* (Deut 6:5), not only through human authors on papyri but also directly on the hearts of His people. The relational effects of this divine action are still more explicit in Jeremiah 32:39–40:

> I will give them one heart and one way, that they may fear me forever, for their own good and the good of their children after them. I will make with them an everlasting covenant, that I will not turn away from doing good to them. And I will put the fear of me in their hearts, that they may not turn from me.

Note the recurrent emphasis on the heart (*leb*) within these ancient Jewish formulations of the tension (cf. Jer 24:7). This emphasis on the heart captures one of the core convictions of proponents of the Assertion—the conviction that any "love" that is rendered necessary by nullifying human hearts is not worthy of that word. This insight, captured in the Axiom of Unforced Love (see 1.2.5), rings true to the Hebrew portrait in which God desires from-the-heart love from His creatures. In Isaiah 29:13, God laments the fact that "this people draw near with their mouth and honor me with their lips, *while their hearts are far from me*" (emphasis added). We are true to the text when we say that love requires a willing heart;[15] we veer from the text

---

15. Thus, Schwartz veers from the text when he affirms,

> This spiritual regeneration is conceived by Ezekiel as being YHWH's doing alone, *against—indeed nullifying—the will* of his recalcitrant people. Instead of a new covenant, Ezekiel envisions YHWH bringing about *forced compliance* with the old one (11:19–20; 36:25–27), since willing compliance proved utterly unrealizable. ("Ezekiel's Dim View of Israel's Restoration," 60; emphasis added)

when we fail to recognize that, just as love must come from a willing heart (MCT2, ETT2, JTT2), so a willing heart must come from God (MCT1, ETT1, JTT1).

DIVINE GIVING AND HUMAN COMING

John's Gospel both echoes and expands this ancient Hebrew tension between "human act commanded" and "divine act promised." As John answers Gauguin's first question—"Whence Come We?"—the tension takes unique form as the Johannine Origin Tension:

JOT1: The Father loves the Son, and, therefore, "gives" the Son a believing people whose belief follows from divine giving and drawing.

JOT2: The Son issues the believe-imperative, and those given and drawn by the Father do in fact "come" to the Son.

JOT1. John, more than any other biblical author, emphasizes the "divine act promised" side of the tension within the profound context of intratrinitarian love. The precosmic ("You *loved* [aorist] me before the creation of the world" [John 17:24b]) and ongoing ("I *love* [present] the Father" [John 14:31a]) relationship between the Father and Son pervades Johannine thought.[16] The Father-Son relationship occurs with explicit "love" terminology in nine verses[17] and forms the theological substratum of multiple pericopes throughout the Fourth Gospel.[18]

For John, the Father-Son relationship is not passive and complacent but active and expressive. The act of *obeying* (τηρέω) is the primary medium of the Son expressing love for His Father (John

---

16. In analyzing Trinitarian dimensions within the Fourth Gospel, I will limit myself primarily to the Father-Son love relation as emphasized by John without entering into the broader, theological complexities of Trinitarian theology (e.g., Social Trinitarianism versus Latin Trinitarianism). Such theological analysis lies beyond the scope of this work, and the points I develop do not rest exclusively on any single Trinitarian model.

17. See John 3:35; 5:20; 10:17; 14:31; 15:9, 10; and 17:23–26.

18. See John 6:37–46; 10:14–38; 12:23–30; and 16:17–32.

15:10; cf. John 12:49–50; 14:31; 15:10, 17:4), whereas the act of *giving* (δίδωμι) recurs as the dominant medium of the Father expressing love for His Son. The Father gives the Son "life in himself" (John 5:27a), "authority to judge" (5:27b; cf. 5:22), "work" (5:36), "sheep" (10:29); "authority over all people" (17:2); "those ... out of the world" (17:6; cf. 17:24), "words" (17:8), "the name" (17:11–12); "glory" (17:22, 24; cf. 13:31–32), and "the cup" (18:11). Our analysis of JOT1 narrows the focus to the specific gift of John 6:37, namely, the Father's expression of love to the Son by giving Him a believing people (πᾶν ὃ δίδωσιν).

In John 6:37, this Father-to-Son giving takes on the force of a divine promise: "All that the Father gives me will come to me." Carson, among other interpreters, equates coming to (ἐλθεῖν) Jesus with the positive expression of faith in Jesus, a conclusion unambiguously warranted by the immediate literary context (ὁ πιστεύων [John 6:35; cf. John 6:29, 36]).[19] Who will come to/believe in Jesus? The logic of John 6:37 is that the cumulative sum ("all"—πᾶν: neuter singular) of those given by the Father will be those who believe in the Son.[20] There is a chronology intrinsic to John's logic: Jesus' gifts of love are not such because they first came to the Son, but they come to the Son because they are first the Father's gifts of love to the Son.

The positive promise of John 6:37 finds reinforcement in the sweeping negative terms of John 6:44: "*No one* (οὐδεὶς contrasted with πᾶν in John 6:37) can *come* (ἐλθεῖν) to me unless the Father who sent me draws him. And I will raise him up on the last day" (John 6:44; emphasis added). All are powerless (οὐδεὶς δύναται) to believe in the Son, except those whom the Father draws. All those whom the Father draws believe in the Son and are subsequently raised up.[21] The

19. D. A. Carson, *Divine Sovereignty & Human Responsibility: Biblical Perspectives in Tension* (Eugene, OR: Wipf and Stock, 1994) 184. See also Bruce Ware, "The Place of Effectual Calling and Grace in a Calvinist Soteriology," in *The Grace of God the Bondage of the Will*, vol. 2 (Grand Rapids: Baker Books, 1995).

20. For an extended defense, see O. Hofius, "Erwählung und Bewahrung. Zur Auslegung von Joh. 6, 37," *Theologische Beiträge* 8 (1977): 24–29.

21. These considerations lead Adolf Schlatter to conclude that "faith is God's work" (*Der Evangelist Johannes: Wie er spricht, denkt und glaubt: Ein Kommentar* [Stuttgart: Calwer, 1948], 175).

believers' origin as believers runs deeper than human initiative; it flows from the love-motivated act of the Father's giving and drawing.

Does libertarian free will fit into John's picture of divine giving and drawing? A standard libertarian interpretation runs as follows: Indeed, the Father must draw a human before that human can come to the Son. Nevertheless, the Father draws *all* of humanity. Those drawn individuals who exercise libertarian power to come to the Son are, in turn, given to the Son.[22]

Three divine actions undermine this libertarian interpretation: the Father's giving (John 6:37), His drawing (John 6:44), and His teaching (John 6:45). We will examine these divine actions in the above order.

1. *Divine giving precedes human coming.* On the libertarian interpretation, the Father's *giving* to the Son is premised on the human agent's prior *coming* to the Son. The grammar of John 6:37 inverts this picture. The Father "gives" (ὃ δίδωσιν) in the present tense, whereas people "will come" (ἥξει) in the future tense. The present-tense-followed-by-a-future-tense structure of John 6:37 is grammatically equivalent to the statement: "All whom the governor *pardons* (present tense verb), *will enjoy* (future tense verb) freedom from death row." The governor's pardoning is the basis of the prisoner's enjoyment, just as the Father's giving is the basis of the believers' coming. This grammatical structure occurs in other Johannine contexts with the same implication.[23]

The libertarian interpretation of John 6:37 would require the reversed verb order (e.g., all who *come* [present] to me, the Father *will give* [future] to me). In John's logic, people do not believe in order to

---

22. J. H. Charlesworth forwards a variation of this libertarian interpretation that features not only a universal drawing but also a universal giving (*John and Qumran* [London: Geoffrey Chapman Publishers, 1972], 95). This interpretation falters for the same reasons developed in this section.

23. John 16:13 reads, "But when He, the Spirit of truth, *comes* (present: ἔλθῃ), *He will guide* (future: ὁδηγήσει) you into all truth." The Spirit's guiding is conditioned on the Spirit's prior coming. In John 14:15 the believers' obeying (future: τηρήσετε) is premised on a prior loving (present: ἀγαπᾶτή).

become gifts of love, as libertarianism requires. Rather, people believe *because* they are gifts, precluding the possibility of being given by the Father without subsequently coming to the Son. This single grammatical factor counts strongly against any view that limits the scope of divine action in John 6 to mere Heart Persuasion, Cooperation, or Activation.[24]

2. *Divine drawing precedes divine raising.* A second problem for the libertarian interpretation is the strong identity relation in John 6:44 between being drawn by the Father and being raised up to heaven by the Son. If the Father's drawing is synonymous with Heart Persuasion, Cooperation, and/or Activation, then it is possible to participate in this universal drawing without participating in the Son's raising up. By exerting our libertarian power to refuse to "come" to the Son, we break the identity relationship between the drawn and the raised. John 6:44 closes this possibility. All those drawn will be raised up. If the divine drawing is universal in scope,[25] then the divine raising is universal in scope. This moves us into an all-roads-eventually-lead-to-heaven

---

24. A counterargument could appeal to John 14:21b: "He who loves me (present: ἀγαπῶν) will be loved (future: ἀγαπηθήσεται) by my Father." Carson tackles this problem in the parallel context of John 16:27:

> Does this mean that the believer's love precedes the Father's love and is in some way the ground of it? The suggestion runs counter to the entire johannine [*sic*] emphasis. ... The preceding two verses (16.25ff.) show that the point at issue is not the difference between the believer and the unbeliever, as if the evangelist were trying to assign to the believer's love the ultimate credit for this distinction; but rather ... John is making a distinction between the disciples' relation to the Father now and in that day." (*Divine Sovereignty & Human Responsibility*, 171)

In John 14:21b, the same distinction between "now" and "in that day" is present. The context of the future tense love of John 14:21b is "on that day" defined in terms of Jesus' return and the believer's resurrection (John 14:18–19). The believer who loves Jesus in the present tense can be assured that, at the final resurrection, the Father and Son will share a loving posture toward him. The broader context of John's Gospel clarifies that the believer's loving obedience is based on prior divine action.

25. Libertarians commonly appeal to the drawing of "all men" in John 12:32 to substantiate a universal ἑλκύσῃ in John 6:44. This appeal is dubious for at least two reasons. First, the Son, not the Father, is the subject of the drawing in John 12:32. Second, the drawing of John 12:32 occurs through Jesus' death (John 12:33), whereas the drawing of John 6:44 occurs through "being taught by the Father" (John 6:45; cf. Isa 54:13). Carson adds,

perspective that runs contrary to both John's Gospel and the broader eschatological tenor of the Bible.[26]

3. *Divine teaching precedes human learning.* A third problem for a libertarian interpretation of John 6 is Jesus' clarification of what the Father's drawing entails. Jesus equates this drawing with the realization of Isaiah's ancient promise, which Jesus paraphrases, "They will all be taught by God" (John 6:45a; cf. Isa 54:13). Divine teaching is the means through which the Father draws; and this teaching is so effectual that its students come to Jesus (John 6:45b). The libertarian may respond, "Yes, everyone who learns from the Father's teaching comes to Jesus; but whether or not we learn rests on our two-way power." Such a response only pushes the problem back one step. If being drawn by the Father means that we are taught by the Father, and the success or failure of the Father's teaching rests on our libertarian power, then it becomes possible to be drawn by the Father and not raised up. This violates the clear affirmation of John 6:44.[27]

The verb [ἐλκύσῃ] is not determinative. John 12:32 ... occurs in a context where the arrival of the "hour" and the request of the Greeks are evoking statements about the universal significance of Jesus' death/exaltation. Jesus draws all men, not just Jews; his stance toward the "world" is a salvific one, one that draws. (*Divine Sovereignty & Human Responsibility*, 185)

Carson concludes, "The context shows rather clearly ... that 12:32 refers to 'all men without distinction' (i.e., not just Jews) rather than 'to all men without exception' " (*The Gospel According to John* [Grand Rapids: Eerdmans, 1991], 293)." There are no grounds for reading the universal scope of the drawing in John 12:32 backwards into the drawing of John 6:44, especially given the distinct emphases of these separate contexts.

26. See John 3:17–20; 12:48; 15:6, 22; 16:8–10 (cf. Dan 12:2; Matt 25:41, 46, Mark 9:43; Luke 16:22–28; and Rev 14:9–11).

27. As a related problem, libertarian free will requires that human agents determine whether they will be hearers and listeners or turn a deaf ear to the Father's teaching. Human agents determine whether they will be sheep or goats (John 10:25–26), God's children or the devil's (John 8:43–47), gifts of love drawn by the Father or unbelievers (John 6:37). However, in each of these contexts we do not find the libertarian formula, "What we choose determines who we are," but its antithesis, "Who we are determines what we choose." In John 8, certain Jews did not reject Jesus to *become* the devil's children. They chose not to believe Jesus *because* they were the devil's children. See C. K. Barrett, *The Gospel According to St. John* (Oxford: Oxford University Press, 1971), 182; and R. Schnackenberg, *Das Johannesevangelium*, vol. 1 (Freiburg: Herder, 1976), 406–10.

Whether the divine action is construed in terms of giving, drawing, or teaching, John precludes the prospect of being given, drawn, or taught by the Father without, in turn, coming to the Son. Thus, John's picture of divine action excludes libertarian power, pushing God's role in the origination of a believing people beyond Heart Persuasion, Cooperation, and Activation.

JOT2. John counterbalances the reality of divine giving (JOT1) with that of human coming (JOT2). John 6:37 occurs in the immediate context of Jesus' invitation to come to Him as the "bread of life" (John 6:35). Those invited by the Son and given by the Father *come* to Jesus; they are not dragged kicking and screaming against their wills.[28] In C. K. Barrett's words, "The coming is real coming, the believing real believing ... man's coming, man's believing."[29] Carson echoes, "Men are not unthinking puppets in the Fourth Gospel."[30] From John's perspective, humans are the proper objects of divine imperatives who make morally significant choices.[31] Indeed, what value would the Father's gift to His Son retain if the gift is merely a collection of "unthinking puppets" incapable of meaningful belief, love, and worship? Divine giving does not obliterate significant human coming.

The theology of No Man's Land artificially resolves the tension in John. It sacrifices human coming on the altar of divine giving. Pelagia, Cassiana, and Arminia undermine divine giving to sustain human coming. Augustinia preserves both sides of the Johannine Origin Tension. In this theological city, God extends the grace of Heart Reformation, a divine action by which the human heart is so deeply altered that it actively says "yes" to the Son, cannot do otherwise, and yet remains quintessentially human. Augustine says, "It is certain that it is we that act when we act; but it is He who makes us

---

28. See John 1:7; 3:15–18, 36; 7:39; and 11:25.

29. C. K. Barrett, *New Testament Essays* (London: SPCK, 1974), 64.

30. Carson, *Divine Sovereignty & Human Responsibility*, 167; cf. 167–73.

31. See John 3:36; 12:24–26; 7:37; 13:18; 14:15, 21, 23; and 15:10.

act by applying efficacious powers to our will."[32] If God gives, then the given will come.

The believers' origin in the Fourth Gospel, therefore, is not mere natural birth as in Gauguin's gospel. Rather, the believers' origin is traced to supernatural action motivated by the vast love between the Father and the Son. Our coming to the Son originates in the Father having given us to the Son whom He has loved since before the world began. It is difficult to imagine a more profound answer to the question, "Whence Come We?"

3.2.3 DIVINE UNIFYING
AND HUMAN LOVING

John's answer to Gauguin's second question, "What Are We?" morphs the tension between the "divine act promised" and the "human act commanded" into a new form, the Johannine Identity Tension:

JIT1: The Son prays for His gift, specifically for His Father to bring about unity.

JIT2: The Son reveals the love-imperative to His gift, commanding unity.

JIT1. The first pole of the Johannine Identity Tension emerges from the prayer of Jesus just prior to His crucifixion in John 17. Jesus prays not only for His first-century disciples (John 17:1–19), but also for all future believers (i.e., "those who will believe in me through their word [John 17:20])."[33] In John 17:24, Jesus refers to the cumulative

32. Augustine, *On Grace and Free-Will*, 32, in *The Nicene and Post-Nicene Fathers*, vol. 5, ed. Philip Schaff (Grand Rapids: Eerdmans, 1980), 457.

33. This phrase "assumes the success of the disciples" mission (alluded to in v. 18)" (George Beasley-Murray, *John*, Word Biblical Commentary, vol. 36 [Waco, TX: Word Publishing, 1987], 302). The guarantee of a plurality of people who "will believe" forms a logical premise of John 17:20–26. If libertarian free will is granted then a disturbing possibility emerges. It remained within the sphere of possibility at the time of the prayer that Jesus was praying for the unity of no one. It was metaphysically possible for each individual to exert his or her libertarian power to refrain from belief. This conflicts with the certitude in Jesus' prayer that a believing group

sum of present and future tense believers with the Father-Son gift terminology introduced in John 6:37: "those given to me" (ὅ δέδωκάς).
Of direct importance to the question "What are we?" is the specific
content of Jesus' request for His gift, namely, their "oneness" (John
17:21, 22, 23).

What is the precise nature of this oneness? E. L. Wenger argues
in favor of a visible institutional unity such as the elusive ecumeni-
cal oneness sought by the World Council of Churches for over sixty
years. T. E. Pollard argues against such an interpretation,[34] joining
D. A. Carson and Raymond Brown in forwarding a non-institutional
though visible unity.[35] Despite different and occasionally competing nuances in the vast litany of proposals,[36] Brown observes that
"sooner or later most authors say that it is a union of love," and cites
Käsemann: "We usually bypass the question at this point with edifying language by reducing unity to what we call love."[37]

To avoid the common reduction of love to sentimental rhetoric,
what more may be said about the "union of love" in John 17? Following
the landmark analysis of Robert Joly, the common Greek term for
"love" (ἀγάπη) is not determinative.[38] The contextual clues inherent
to Jesus' prayer are a more enlightening path toward clarifying the
nature of the "union of love" that He requests for His believers. I will
limit myself to a few contextual observations salient to our analysis.

---

would exist, a certitude that finds reinforcement in John's previous claim that all the given will
come to the Son (John 6:37).

34. See Raymond Brown, *The Gospel According to John XIII-XXI*, The Anchor Bible, vol.
29A (New York: Doubleday, 1970), 775.

35. See Carson, *The Gospel According to John* (Grand Rapids: Eerdmans, 1991), 568; and
Brown, *The Gospel According to John*, 775–79.

36. See Brown, *The Gospel According to John*, 775–76.

37. Brown, *The Gospel According to John*, 776.

38. The LXX uses "love" (ἀγάπάω) to describe Amnon's incestuous love for his half-sister
Tamar (2 Sam 13:1). John's Gospel uses the love term—φιλέω—interchangeably with ἀγάπάω
when describing the Father's love for the Son (John 3:35; 5:20; 17:26), evidencing the semantic
flexibility of these terms. See Robert Joly, *Le vocabulaire chretien de l'amour est-il original? Phlein
et Agapen dans le grec antique* (Brussels: Presses Universitaires, 1968).

The first-century Qumran community had adopted for itself the title of "unity" (*yahad*), expressing their presumed communion with angels. The unity prayed for by Jesus is of a more profound pedigree.[39] The union of love that existed "before the foundation of the world" (John 17:26) between Father and Son is the supernatural reality in which the requested unity of believers subsists. The prayer of John 17 hinges on a distinction between what may be called the "original union of love," the love expressed between Father and Son *before* the world, and the "expanded union of love," the love between Father and Son as it overflows into the human realm, making believers the visible embodiment of the love between Father and Son *to* the world (ἵνα γινώσκῃ ὁ κόσμος [John 17:23]).[40]

John 17 defines the original union in terms of the mutual indwelling of the Father *in* the Son and Son *in* the Father (John 17:21). The expanded union consists of the Father-indwelt Son indwelling believers (John 17:23a). This transitive indwelling of the Father-in-the-Son and the Son-in-believers brings about the miraculous inclusion of believers in the infinite relational intimacy enjoyed between Father and Son. Believers are to be "in" the Father and Son, "so identified with God and dependent upon Him for life and fruitfulness, that they themselves become the locus of the Father's life and work *in them* (cf. 14:12; 15:7)."[41]

Furthermore, John traces the genesis of this expanded union not to human effort but to divine action pouring forth from the original union. Jesus is *praying*, i.e., appealing to His Father's power, for the expansion of the love between the Father and the Son into the realm of human expression. This prayer rests on the crucial premise that the Father can actualize an expanded union. It lies within the scope

---

39. On points of contact and contrast between *yahad* and the Johannine concept of unity, see Brown, *The Gospel According to John*, 777.

40. Anders Nygren writes, "Agape in man is an outflow of Divine Agape" (*Agape and Eros*, vol. 1 [Philadelphia: Westminster, 1953], 115).

41. Carson, *The Gospel According to John*, 568 (emphasis in original).

of divine action to cause the love enjoyed between Father and Son to become a visible reality within believers. Brown concludes,

> Any approach that places the essence of unity in the solidarity of human endeavor is not really faithful to John's insistence that unity has its origins in divine action. The very fact that Jesus prays to the Father for this unity indicates that the key to it lies within God's power.[42]

Can libertarian models of divine action sustain this side of the Johannine Identity Tension? Libertarian free will requires that we possess Freedom from the Reformer, the ability to shun divine action with our two-way power. A significant problem surfaces in this paradigm. It remains possible for libertarian free will to undermine the Son's request for the unification of His gift.[43] The Father may answer the Son's prayer positively but find the realization of that answer beyond His reach as libertarian agents resist divine action.[44]

Jesus promises His disciples, "Whatever you ask the Father in my name, He may give it to you" (John 15:16b; cf. 1 John 3:21–22). If libertarian agents resist the Father's cumulative actions to spur love, then the Son would not receive the expanded union of love that He requests. In such a scenario, there is a promise and a privilege attached to the disciples' prayers that not even the Father's beloved

---

42. Brown, *The Gospel According to John*, 776.

43. This critique could be further sharpened: Given libertarian free will, it is not only *possible* for the Father's answer to the Son's prayer to fail to reach realization, it is highly *probable*. Jesus requests unity for "those who will believe in me" (John 17:20), which presumably entails no small number of human agents through the echelons of time. If each of these human agents has libertarian power to resist the Father's Heart Persuasion, Cooperation, and Activation, then it is reasonable to assume that at least some human agents would resist. All it takes is a single libertarian agent to resist and the requested unity is lost.

44. A further line of evidence that counts against a Heart Activation reading of John 17:20–26 is Jesus' explicit narrowing of the scope of His prayer. The prayer rests on a distinction between His and "the world," requesting the Father's act of unifying not universally but for the gift: "I am not praying for the world but for those whom you have given me" (John 17:9). Moreover, Heart Activation, as a divine act that renders acceptance of the Son *possible*, would be superfluous for the gift. By virtue of their identity as the gift, they are distinguished from "the world" by their *actual* acceptance of the Son. Jesus prays for believers who will need unification, not the morally impotent in need of Heart Activation.

Son enjoyed. Such conclusions are altogether foreign to Johannine thought. John's emphasis on the love between the Father and the Son warrants the conclusion that the Father answers His Son's request for the unification of the gift without human power sabotaging this act of intratrinitarian love.

This conclusion finds reinforcement in the broader continuum of Johannine thought. Being simultaneously a believer and devoid of love is beyond John's concept of possibility. The true believer loves, whereas the absence of love corresponds to the absence of true belief (1 John 2:9–11; 3:10, 14–15). If libertarian free will cannot derail the Father's answer to His Son's request for an expanded union among "those who will believe" (John 17:20), then John's necessary connection between believing and loving makes sense. In short, all believers will exhibit love *precisely because* the Father cannot fail to answer His beloved Son's request in John 17:20–26.

JIT2. If our analysis were to terminate here we may find ourselves haunted once again by the concern of Irving Singer that "there seems to be no point in exhorting human beings to *anything*: either to love or to have faith in Jesus Christ" (emphasis in original).[45] Counteracting such concerns, Brown adds, "None of this need imply passivity on the part of the believers in the question of unity, but their action is not the primary source of unity."[46] In line with Brown's insight, we must balance John's emphasis on divine action with the fact that Jesus' prayer for an expanded union occurs in the farewell discourses of the Fourth Gospel. Jesus' imperatives to love form a central theme throughout these discourses.[47]

No Man's Land cannot sustain this "human act commanded" side of John's tension. Pelagia, Cassiana, and Arminia sustain the "human act commanded" at the expense of the "divine act promised."

---

45. Irving Singer, *The Nature of Love*, 1:293–4.

46. Brown, *The Gospel According to John*, 776.

47. See John 13:34; 14:15–21, 23–24; and 15:9–17.

Augustinia is able to preserve both Jesus' commands to love *and* His prayer that His gift obey those commands with a depth and unity that reflects the original union He enjoys with the Father. This Johannine Identity Tension bears significant resemblance to Augustine's famous prayer that so profoundly offended Pelagius: "Grant what thou commandest, and command what thou dost desire." Jesus commands love as His Father desires (John 14:24; cf. 14:15–21) in one moment, and in the next asks His Father to grant what He commands (John 17:20–26), a request for the love commands to be visibly obeyed. With the unique power of Heart Reformation, the Father answers His beloved Son's request in such a way that the divine will is neither thwarted nor the human will trampled.

The believer's identity is not rooted in anything as transient as economic status, emotional togetherness, religious performance, the successful use of libertarian power, or any other answers we may offer to Gauguin's question of "What Are We?" The believer's identity rests beyond these particulars of status, personality, performance, and personal failures; it rests in the loving solidarity actualized by the active expression of the love between the Father and the Son that existed before the world's creation. Again, a more profound answer to Gauguin's question is hard to imagine.

DIVINE RAISING AND
HUMAN REMAINING

We come to Gauguin's third question—"Whither Go We?" The artist answers on the far left of his canvas with the image of a dim elderly woman on the brink of death. Gauguin comments, "Whither? Close to the death of an old woman, a strange stupid bird concludes: What? O sorrow, thou art my master. Fate how cruel thou art, and always vanquished. I revolt."[48] John's Gospel paints a significantly less grim picture of the believers' destiny with the Johannine Destiny Tension:

---

48. Quoted in Francis Schaeffer, *How Shall We Then Live? The Rise and Decline of Western Culture* (Wheaton, IL: Crossway, 1983), 159.

JDT1: The Son and Father fulfill each other's wills for the "raising up" of the gift.

JDT2: The Son issues the remain-imperative, commanding ongoing connection to Him.

JDT1. In the prayer in John 17, Jesus secures the destiny of His gifts by expressing His "will" (θέλω) to the Father that they may behold His glory (John 17:24). Whether or not believers reach this destiny rests on the ability of the Father to fulfill the beloved Son's will. John 6 reinforces the gift's divinely secured destiny, but from the opposite end of the Father-Son relationship. The Father's "will" (θέλημα) is that the Son lose none of all whom He has given the Son but will raise up the undiminished sum of this gift on the last day (John 6:38–40). Jesus offers assurance that He will successfully carry out His Father's will regarding the destiny of His gift (John 6:38–40, 44; cf. 17:12), just as the assurance of the Father's carrying out of the Son's will forms the premise of John 17:24. The believers' destiny, therefore, rests on the reciprocal love between Father and Son, expressed in John 6:38–40 and 17:24 as the mutual execution of the will of the divine Other.

Both of these elements, the Son fulfilling His beloved Father's will and the Father fulfilling His beloved Son's will, converge in John 10:27–30. In this context, the gift is identified as the Son's "sheep" (τὰ πρόβατα). The sheep are given "eternal life" and "will never perish" because they cannot be snatched from *both* "the Son's hand" (τῆς χειρός μου) *and* "the Father's hand" (ῆς χειρὸς τοῦ πατρός).[49] The idea that either Father or Son could fail in fulfilling each other's will for the destiny of the gifts is altogether alien to Johannine thought.

Can libertarian models of divine action sustain this side of the tension? I offer two points. First, if the destiny of the gift rests on the mutual will-fulfillment of Father and Son, then it follows that the gift does not possess the libertarian power to resist the Son decisively. If these humans exercised power to say with self-condemning finality, "I

---

49. See Carson, *Divine Sovereignty & Human Responsibility*, 194.

refrain from loving Jesus," then humans would have thwarted the will of both the Father and the Son. Since the love between the Father and the Son is expressed as mutual will-fulfillment, it follows from a libertarian premise that the finite human will has the astounding power to impair God's capacity to express love for Himself within the Trinity.

Historically, the theological debate has been focused on whether the human will can interfere with God's will as a Being of infinite *power*. John moves us deeper. Can the human will interfere with God's will as a Being of infinite intratrinitarian *love*? Libertarian free will answers "yes." In John's Gospel, the human will cannot tarnish the full, radiant expression of love between the Father and Son. The efficacy of divine *power* flows from the intimacy of divine *love* within the Trinity.

Second, the perfection of the love-union requested by Jesus (John 17:23–24) precludes the possibility of human resistance. When the Father and Son bring one another's will for the destiny of the gifts to full realization, the gifts will be free from all anti-love propensities that currently haunt them. This divine ability to actualize love fully in a human agent is most at home within the Augustinian framework of Heart Reformation. Augustine says, "The commandment of love shall be perfectly fulfilled in the life to come."[50] If God merely exerts Heart Persuasion, Cooperation, and/or Activation when the believer enters the eternal state, then the libertarian power to resist love remains intact. Human agency becomes a Trojan horse for smuggling anti-love possibilities into the eternal *civitas Dei*. Stanley Grenz counters,

> The experience of glorification will encompass our complete existence. ... We can anticipate that the Spirit will root out our fallen sinful nature. Because we will no longer be susceptible to temptation and sin, we will be totally free to obey God perfectly.[51]

---

50. Augustine, *On Man's Perfection in Righteousness*, 8.19, in *The Nicene and Post-Nicene Fathers*, vol. 5, 165.

51. Stanley Grenz, *Theology for the Community of God* (Nashville: Broadman & Holman, 1994), 583.

In the libertarian scheme, such total freedom is tantamount to the death of freedom because the agent loses the power to resist God. Morally significant choice-making becomes a relic of the past. Is freedom perfected or eliminated in eternity? A libertarian definition of freedom requires the latter.

JDT2. John counterbalances the emphasis on mutual divine will-fulfillment by putting the onus of responsibility on believers with the imperative to "remain" in the Son (μείνατε; John 15:4; cf. John 15:9; 5:38; 8:31, 51; 12:35; 16:1).[52] In John 15:9–12, believers "remain" by obeying and, in turn, "obey" by keeping the love-imperative. Failure to remain identifies one not as a branch connected to Christ, the "true vine" through whom fruit-bearing vitality flows, but as a branch thrown away and finally burned (John 15:1–6), where "fire symbolizes judgment" (cf. Ezek 15:1–8).[53] The text does not entertain the theoretical possibility of a believer failing to remain and, thereby, burning contrary to the will of the Father and the Son. Such a possibility is precluded by John 6:38–40, 44, and 17:23 and their convergence in John 10:28–30. It is exegetically more plausible that John 15:6 forms a concrete warning call to assess whether one is a branch that remains in the Son (and thus a gift that will be raised) or dead wood devoid of love that will be burned.[54] This interpretation comports well with the broader Johannine corpus (1 John 2:19, 24–25, and 28). Carson comments,

> Men must hold themselves responsible to persevere, but if they do so, it is God's grace upholding them; while if they fall away they demonstrate that they were not true disciples in the first place. ... John's maintenance of this tension provides stable balance.[55]

---

52. See Brown, *The Gospel According to John*, 681.

53. Carson, *The Gospel According to John*, 517.

54. See Carson, *Divine Sovereignty & Human Responsibility*, 192–95.

55. Carson, *Divine Sovereignty & Human Responsibility*, 195.

I offer three summary points to highlight how John innovates on the ancient Hebrew tension within the context of intratrinitarian love:

1. *Where do we come from?* The origin of believers rests in the tension between divine giving and human coming. The Father loves the Son so profoundly that He "gives" people to the Son, "all" of whom "will come" to the Son. Divine giving precedes human believing. There is no possibility in John's text of a human agent exerting two-way power to say "no" to Jesus, marring God's expression of intratrinitarian love. Yet, those given are not stripped of personhood. They "come" to Jesus in response to His believe-imperative. If God exercises Heart Reformation, then this tension is preserved.

2. *What are we?* The identity of this love-gift rests in the tension between divine unifying and human loving. Jesus asks His Father to expand the union of love that they enjoyed since "before the creation of the world" to include His gift. The gift's new identity as an expanded union that reflects the love between the Father and the Son is not left to finite human power where it may be shunned. Rather, Jesus places this expanded union within the scope of divine action, where the Father makes it a reality. Yet, those unified by the Father are not stripped of personhood. They actively exhibit unity in response to the Son's love-imperative. If God exercises Heart Reformation, then this tension is preserved.

3. *Where are we going?* The destiny of this love-gift rests in the tension between divine raising and human remaining. Motivated by infinite love, the Son fulfills His Father's will to safeguard the entire gift, and the Father realizes His Son's will that the gift behold the Son's glory. If members of this love-gift could forfeit their destiny, then both Father and Son would have failed in fulfilling one another's wills. Human power cannot inhibit intratrinitarian love! Yet again, those preserved by the Father and Son are not stripped of personhood. The gift remains qualitatively human as they express obedience in response

to the Son's remain-imperative. If God exercises Heart Reformation, then this tension is preserved.

THE TENSION BEYOND JOHN

Does the broader context of New Testament thought support John's insights on God's ability to actualize love in the human heart? Paul's first letter to the Thessalonians evidences his awareness of two dangerous anti-love trends that threatened to wreak relational havoc in this first-century community. The first anti-love trend took form as mutual sexual exploitation addressed in 1 Thessalonians 4:3–8, and the second as a freeloading idleness addressed in 1 Thessalonians 4:11–12 and 5:12–14 (cf. 2 Thess 3:6–15). The first anti-love trend, sexual immorality, may have been a lingering vice of the Thessalonians' renounced paganism (1 Thess 1:9; cf. 2 Thess 3:6–13), since "pagan moral corruption looked upon fornication either indifferently or favorably."[56] The second anti-love trend, idleness, may be related to a world-disengaging attitude stemming from misappropriating belief in Jesus' immanent return[57] or possibly a vestige of Greek paganism that "held [manual labor] in contempt."[58] Paul handles this "deficiency" (τὰ ὑστερήματα [1 Thess 3:10]) in the Thessalonian church with the Pauline Love Tension:

PLT1: Paul prays to God, requesting divine action to actualize a superabundance of love among the Thessalonians.

PLT2: Paul reiterates the love-imperative to the Thessalonians, holding them responsible to express a superabundance of love.

---

56. *NIV Bible Commentary*, vol. 2: *New Testament*, ed. Kenneth Barker and John Kohlenberger III (Grand Rapids: Zondervan, 1994), 860.

57. Donald Guthrie, *New Testament: Introduction* (Downers Grove, IL: InterVarsity Press, 1970), 566.

58. Robert Gundry, *A Survey of the New Testament*, 3rd ed. (Grand Rapids: Zondervan, 1994), 355.

PLT1. In addition to praying for his personal return to Thessalonica to help "supply what is deficient" (1 Thess 3:10), Paul adopts a tactic that directly reflects how Jesus handles His gift in John 17:20–26. Like Jesus, Paul invokes divine action on behalf of the Thessalonians who were part of the gift for whom Jesus prayed. Like Jesus, Paul prays specifically for God to actualize greater love:

> May the Lord make you increase and abound in love for one another and for all, as we do for you, so that He may establish your hearts blameless in holiness before our God and Father, at the coming of our Lord Jesus with all His saints. (1 Thess 3:12–13)

Paul's pairing of optative aorist verbs, "increase" and "abound" (πλεονάσαι and περισσεύσαι) expresses emphatically the superabundance of love that Paul is asking God to actualize within the Thessalonian community.[59] Having traced the origin of Thessalonian belief and love to God's choice (τὴν ἐκλογὴν [1 Thess 1:4; cf. 1 Thess 1:2–5; 2:13]), Paul now seeks a radical expansion of that love in the same Source. He then stretches the scope of this superabundant love universally to "all" (πάντας). Leon Morris comments,

> While love for each other was "no more than the Gentiles practiced," love for all men was more difficult and "could only come as a gift from God." But the specifically Christian quality of *agape* is never natural to man, and comes only to him who has been transformed by the power of God. Whether it is exercised towards believers or non-believers, *agape* is the gift of God.[60]

Paralleling the eschatological dimensions of Jesus' prayer, Paul's prayer then turns to an expression of confidence that God's love-expanding

---

59. These verbs are "virtual synonyms for Paul to express superabundance (see 2 Cor 4:15 and Rom 5:20)" (E. J. Richard, "First and Second Thessalonians," in *Sacra Pagina*, vol. 11, ed. Daniel Harrington [Collegeville, MN: The Liturgical Press, 1995], 166).

60. Leon Morris, *The Epistles of Paul to the Thessalonians*, Tyndale New Testament Commentaries (Grand Rapids: Eerdmans, 1957), 70.

activity will secure the Thessalonians' moral status at Jesus' return (1 Thess 3:13b; cf. John 17:23–24). Like Jesus' prayer for an expanded love-union, Paul's confident prayer rests on God's ability to "produce the right affections" (Plantinga), "make us lovers" (Aquinas), "infuse supernatural habits" (Turretin), and "form our hearts to obey Him" (Calvin). In Hebrew categories, God's ability to circumcise, transplant, and transcribe hearts forms the theological foundation of the Pauline prayer. In the terminology of the current analysis, Paul's prayer rests on the divine act of Heart Reformation.

PLT2. Paul's emphasis on divine action does not lead him into No Man's Land, where God practices Heart Circumvention. In concert with the ancient Hebrew emphasis on the "heart" (*leb*), God's grace in 1 Thessalonians 3:12 reaches not to machines devoid of will but into the Thessalonians' hearts (καρδίας). E. J. Richard observes, "'Heart' [in v. 13] used in place of 'you' [in v. 12] stands for the inner being or center of volition and director of human activity."[61] The final result[62] of divine action is the reformation of the heart into an "unblameable" (ἀμέμπτους [1 Thess 3:13]) "center of volition" (Richard).

Paul further emphasizes the "human act commanded" with a litany of commands regarding sexual morality (1 Thess 4:1–8). Paul then echoes the language of increasing love from 1 Thessalonians 3:12, but with a new emphasis on human responsibility: "We urge you, brothers, to [love] more and more" (1 Thess 4:10 [περισσεύειν; cf. περισσεῦσαι in 1 Thess 3:12]). Paul closes his call to love by reiterating "the divine act promised":

> Now may the God of peace Himself sanctify you completely, and may your whole spirit and soul and body be kept blameless at the coming of our Lord Jesus Christ. He who calls you is faithful; He will surely do it. (1 Thess 5:23–24)

---

61. Richard, *First and Second Thessalonians*, 166.

62. The εἰς-plus-infinitive structure at the start of 1 Thessalonians 2:13 expresses the result of divine love increasing action.

The closing note of confidence—"He will surely do it"—pushes divine action in Pauline thought beyond Heart Persuasion, Cooperation, and Activation. God's sanctifying and preserving work is not subject to frustration by human willpower. Like John, Paul preserves the tension between the "divine act promised" and the "human act commanded."[63]

Paul reiterates the "divine act commanded" side of the tension in his second Thessalonian letter:

> And we have confidence in the Lord about you, that you are doing and will do the things that we command. May the Lord direct your hearts to the love of God and to the steadfastness of Christ. (2 Thess 3:4–5; cf. 1:11–12; 2:16–17)

In the interim between Paul's letters, God was already active in answering both the prayer for increasing love in the first letter and Jesus' prayer for an expanded union of love:

> We ought always to give thanks to God for you, brothers, as is right, because your faith is growing abundantly, and the love of every one of you for one another is increasing. (2 Thess 1:3; πλεονάζει ἡ ἀγάπη; cf. πλεονάσαι; 1 Thess 3:12).

Paul directs his gratitude for the Thessalonian love to the Father with the Pauline Gratitude Tension:

PGT1: The Father is thanked for the Thessalonians' love.

PGT2: The Thessalonians obey the love-imperative.

---

63. Parallels are detectable between Paul's first and second Thessalonian letters. In 2 Thessalonians 3:4–5, there is an appeal to God as the source of human obedience, in parallel with 1 Thessalonians 3:12 and 5:23a. In parallel with 1 Thessalonians 5:24, there is an expressed confidence in the success of divine action premised on God's faithfulness (2 Thess 3:3–4). In parallel with 1 Thessalonians 3:12 and 5:23b, there is a focus on perseverance (2 Thess 3:5). On the "human act commanded" side of the tension, Paul emphasizes the "heart" (2 Thess 3:5) as the locus of divine activity in parallel with 1 Thessalonians 3:13. In parallel with 1 Thessalonians 4:10, Paul also reiterates moral imperatives (2 Thess 3:4; cf. 2 Thess 2:15). In both letters, the tension remains intact.

If love must originate from a proper exercise of libertarian power, then Paul misplaces gratitude. On the libertarian model, God extends no more than Heart Persuasion, Cooperation, and Activation. God only renders love a possibility. It is the proper human use of libertarian power that moves love from the realm of possibility to the realm of actuality. In this case, the Thessalonians are the proper recipients of Paul's gratitude for the love in their community. If, however, love originates in the divine act of Heart Reformation, then Paul's gratitude to God reaches its proper target.

Paul's belief in God's ability to actualize love without trampling personhood finds further reinforcement in Galatians 5:22–23. The tension takes form as the "Pauline Fruit Tension":

PFT1: Love is a fruit produced by the Spirit.

PFT2: Love is a fruit commanded to and expressed by humans.

Love is a Pauline "fruit of the Spirit." Paul structures the phrase "of the Spirit" (τοῦ πνεύματός) as a genitive of production in which "of" may be translated as "produced by" to get a sharper sense of the intended meaning. Love is a "fruit *produced by* the Spirit." Libertarians object to God's ability to produce love but express no qualms with His ability to produce joy, patience, kindness, goodness, and peace. This *sui generis* treatment of love stands at odds with Paul's inclusion of love with other divinely produced states of the heart. When we attempt to generate peace by our own power, chaos is often the result. Self-powered pursuits of joy lead to chronic dissatisfaction. Just like joy, patience, kindness, goodness, and peace, so the most authentic love emerges not from our power but from His.

This divine production of spiritual fruits does not, for Paul, render the human heart circumvented. In contrast to No Man's Land, humans remain the proper recipients of imperatives to exemplify these qualities throughout the Pauline corpus (cf. Phil 3:1). Immediately prior to identifying love as a fruit of the Spirit, Paul commands the Galatians to "serve one another in love" (Gal 5:13b). Though taking new form as metaphorical fruit, the fundamental tension remains.

We have seen nine forms that the fundamental tension between the "divine act promised" and the "human act commanded" takes through the biblical story:

THE BIBLICAL TENSION BETWEEN "Divine Act Promised" and "Human Act Commanded"	
The Mosaic Circumcision Tension	
MCT1: God promises a heart circumcision, a divine action extended to humans that results in authentic human-to-God love (Deut 30:6).	MCT2: Humans receive the circumcise-imperative, making them morally responsible to circumcise their own hearts and love God (Deut 10:16).
Ezekiel's Transplant Tension	
ETT1: God promises a heart transplant, a divine action extended to humans that results in authentic human-to-God love (Ezek 36:26–27).	ETT2: Humans receive the transplant-imperative, making them morally responsible to get a new heart that loves God (Ezek 18:31).
Jeremiah's Transcription Tension	
JTT1: God promises a heart transcription, a divine action of writing His law on human hearts that results in authentic love for God (Jer 31:33).	JTT2: Humans receive the circumcise-imperative, making them morally responsible to circumcise their own hearts and love God (Jer 4:4).
The Johannine Origin Tension	
JOT1: The Father loves the Son, and "gives" the Son a believing people whose belief follows from divine giving and drawing (John 6:37, 44).	JOT2: The Son issues the believe-imperative, and those given and drawn by the Father do in fact "come" to the Son (John 6:27, 35–38).

The Johannine Identity Tension	
JIT1: The Son prays for His gift, specifically for His Father to bring about unity (John 17:20–26).	JIT2: The Son reveals the love-imperative to His love-gift, commanding unity (John 13:34; 14:15–21, 23–24; 15:9–17).
The Johannine Destiny Tension	
JDT1: The Son and Father fulfill each other's wills for the "raising up" of the love-gift (John 6:38–44; 17:23–24).	JDT2: The Son issues the remain-imperative, commanding ongoing connection to Him (John 15:4, 9).
The Pauline Love Tension	
PLT1: Paul prays to God, requesting divine action to actualize a superabundance of love among the Thessalonians (1 Thess 3:12–13).	PLT2: Paul reiterates the love-imperative to the Thessalonians, holding them responsible to express a superabundance of love (1 Thess 4:1–8, 10).
The Pauline Gratitude Tension	
PGT1: The Father is thanked for the Thessalonians' love (2 Thess 1:3).	PGT2: The Thessalonians obey the love-imperative (2 Thess 1:3).
The Pauline Fruit Tension	
PFT1: Love is a fruit produced by the Spirit (Gal 5:22).	PFT2: Love is a fruit commanded to and expressed by humans (Gal 5:13).

I will offer three conclusions relating this biblical analysis to relevant points of preceding chapters. First, by limiting divine action to Heart Persuasion, Cooperation, and Activation, Pelagia, Cassiana, and Arminia cannot sustain the "divine act promised" side of the biblical tension. No Man's land, by positing Heart Circumvention, cannot do justice to the "human act commanded" side of the tension. Augustinia sustains the tension in all nine forms.

Second, we saw that libertarian free will requires Freedom from the Reformer, i.e., the ability to love or refrain from loving relative to all divine action. The Bible offers at least nine reasons for thinking otherwise (see MCT1–PFT1). The divine act of Heart Reformation does not nullify the authenticity of human love, but ensures the efficacy of intratrinitarian love.

Third, the Relational Vision Argument for libertarian free will requires an absolute reading of its crucial premise, i.e., "relationship requires resistibility" (see 2.3). As humans, we can only remove the risk that others will resist our love-seeking efforts by resorting to Necessity of the Machine and that of the Gunman. Given the biblical argument set forth in this chapter, God is not bound by this limitation. The Creator can bring about love in human agents without trampling our personhood in a way that we, as creatures, cannot. Heart Reformation is a *uniquely* divine ability.

3.3

The Problems of Evil Revisited

Vain is the word of a philosopher which does not heal any suffering of man.

—*Epicurus*, Fragments, No. 54

In this final chapter I will offer what is perhaps the most crucial critique of the Relational Free Will Defense. In answering abstract problems of evil, the Defense rejects God's unique ability to "make us increase and abound in love" (i.e., Heart Reformation), and, thereby, hinders progress against concrete problems of evil.

To develop this final critique, I first address two important objections to the notion of Heart Reformation upon which the critique rests. Vincent Brümmer sets the context for the first objection by drawing an important distinction.

> Sometimes we select the agent's decision as the most important factor and therefore hold the agent responsible for the effect, but this is not necessarily the case. We could hold one of the other factors responsible (including negative or standing

conditions) or even the action of another agent in bringing one or more of these factors about. ... In this way too believers will always give God the credit for their own conversion or spiritual successes: If it were not for the fact that God revealed his will to me and enables me and inspired me to do it, I would never have done it. Therefore to him be all praise and thanksgiving! In thus considering God as "the cause" of their own actions, believers do not, of course, deny that they performed these themselves and of their own free will![1]

Brümmer concludes, "Thus one person's action can be a *contributory* cause, but not a sufficient cause of the action of someone else" (emphasis in original).[2] An actor at the Academy Awards, for example, may credit the Best Actor Oscar that she earned for her riveting performance to a long list of "contributory" causal agents who made her performance possible, e.g., directors, writers, producers, supportive spouses, fans, and even God. From this perspective, the "Divine Contributor Objection" arises: Perhaps God contributes to our expressions of love but is not the sufficient cause of our love expressions. Thus, Heart Reformation overstates God's role in human love, and we may preserve libertarian free will.

A second objection finds poignant expression by the musician, Tom Waits, in a song entitled "Road to Peace." While exposing the escalating mutual destruction of the Israeli-Palestinian conflict, Waits asks, "If God is great and God is good, why can't He change the hearts of men?" The problem takes on even more force if, as I have argued, God *can* change the hearts of men. From this paradigm of Heart Reformation, Waits' question becomes, "If God is great and good enough to change the hearts of men, why doesn't He change more hearts?" Jerry Walls, articulates the objection,

---

1. Vincent Brümmer, *What Are We Doing When We Pray? On Prayer and the Nature of Faith*, 2nd ed. (Farnham: Ashgate Publishing, 2008), 77.

2. Brümmer, *What Are We Doing When We Pray?*, 75.

Arguably, the most damaging strike against compatibilism is its utter inability to explain why God has not predestined everyone to freely choose him if freedom is really compatible with determinism. In our estimation, this is the mortal blow to the compatibilist. If this question cannot be answered convincingly, then compatibilists can hardly expect their position to be taken seriously by those who firmly believe in a profoundly loving and richly relational God.[3]

Walls confronts us with the "Sparsity Objection": If God possesses the ability of Heart Reformation, then why, when we behold the world's gruesome array of anti-loving human actions, does this divine ability seem to be used with such sparsity?

THE DIVINE CONTRIBUTOR OBJECTION

In response to the Divine Contributor Objection to Heart Reformation, I think that Brümmer is fundamentally correct in recognizing a distinction between contributory and sufficient causation. The question is not: Is this distinction is real or artificial? The question is: *Are the biblical motifs that credit God with human love best understood within the framework of God as a contributory cause and libertarian free will as the sufficient cause of human love?* Did Moses, Ezekiel, Jeremiah, John, and Paul understand God's role in human love as contributory in a way that preserves libertarian free will? I offer four points.

1. *Limiting divine action to a "contributory cause" of human love implies that God may also be credited as a "contributory cause" for human anti-love.* Contributory causation is a two-way street. It points not only towards praise in one direction but also toward blame in another.

---

3. Jerry Walls and Scott Burson, *C. S. Lewis & Francis Schaeffer* (Downers Grove, IL: InterVarsity Press, 1998), 266. For repetition of this argument, see Bruce Reichenbach, "Bruce Reichenbach's Response," in *Predestination & Free Will: Four Views of Divine Soveriegnty & Human Freedom*, eds. David Basinger and Randall Basinger (Downers Grove, IL: InterVarsity, 1986), 50.

Brümmer acknowledges such transitivity of blame in the realm of contributory causation with his favorable quotation from Lucas' *Freedom and Grace* (London, 1976):

> The coroner will say that the cause of death was drowning, the unsuccessful rescuer will think the cause was his failure to dive well enough, the teenage chum will know that it was his folly in having dared his friend to swim to the wreck, the mother that it was having let him go out swimming on such a nasty cold day, the father that it was his having failed to instill more sense and more moral courage into his head.[4]

If God merits praise when human agents exercise their power to love, because this power is "bestowed by God," then why would the inverse not hold? Why would God not be culpable when agents use His contribution of free power to actualize anti-love?

2. Limiting divine action to a "contributory cause" of human love requires a transcendent agent foreign to biblical anthropology. For Brümmer, divine contributory causation means that God can "motivate, inspire, and enable" the human agent to love (i.e., Heart Persuasion, Cooperation, and Activation). For the preservation of libertarian two-way power, the agent must be able to resist all of these divine contributions. Says Brümmer, "It is still up to us as human agents to do God's will, and if we decide not to do so (in spite of being enlightened, enabled and motivated) then God's will is not done."[5] In Leibnizian terms, God contributes new "courtiers" to the "royal courtyard": reasons and desires to love Him that were not there before. The queen presides over all of these divine contributory causes from her throne, where she may embrace them and so love or shun them and so frustrate the divine will. From this libertarian perspective, divine action does not touch the queen herself, the innermost choosing agent. Libertarian

---

4. Brümmer, *What Are We Doing When We Pray?*, 77.

5. Brümmer, *What Are We Doing When We Pray?*, 75–76.

free will relegates divine action to the courtyard. The queen must retain the power to plug her ears to these new, divinely appointed courtiers. If God ascends the queen's throne and infuses a new loving *telos* within the innermost choosing agent, then libertarian two-way power is lost.

In addition to philosophical problems with *who* this agent is and *why* she chooses (see 1.3), there is a theological problem with this libertarian agent, namely, how little she resembles the moral agents we meet in the Bible. What in biblical anthropology corresponds to the queen of libertarian anthropology? When God circumcises, transcribes, or transplants the heart, where is the part of the human that transcends the circumcised heart to accept or reject it? When David asks God to create in him a clean heart (Ps 51:10), is he merely asking for the removal of whatever mischievous courtiers voice their immoral opinions to David as he sits on the throne of two-way power? Or is David asking God to create a pure *telos* within his innermost core?

The Bible portrays divine action as affecting the totality of the human person. In the Old Testament, the "heart" (*leb*) that God circumcises, transcribes, transplants, and creates as pure is a "comprehensive term for the personality as a whole, its inner life, its character,"[6] Likewise in the New Testament, "heart" (καρδία) refers comprehensively to the interior human being (cf. 1 Pet 3:4). "Thus, it is the person, the thinking, feeling, willing ego of man, with particular regard to his responsibility to God, that the NT denotes by *kardia*."[7] The biblical semantics of "heart" stand in contrast to primary Greek usages in which the heart "has only one function within the system of spiritual and intellectual processes."[8] When God transforms the heart, He transforms the person. This explains why love (Deut 30:6), walking in God's statutes and rules (Ezek 36:26–27; Jer 32:39–40),

---

6. Walter Eichrodt, *Theology of the Old Testament*, vol. 2, tr. J. A. Baker (Philadelphia: Westminster Press, 1967), 143. See Psalms 22:26; 73:26; and 84:2b.

7. T. Sorg, "Heart," in *The New International Dictionary of New Testament Theology*, vol. 2, ed. Colin Brown (Grand Rapids: Zondervan, 1979), 182.

8. Sorg, "Heart," 181.

faith (Acts 16:14), and increasing and abounding love (1 Thess 3:12–13) occur when divine action reforms the human heart. There is no Leibnizian queen in the Bible.[9] Sorg concludes,

> Because corruption stems from the heart, it is there that God begins his work of renewal. ... Conversion takes place in the heart and is thus a matter of the whole man. God's word does not simply capture the understanding [read: Leibniz's "courtiers"] or the emotions [read: Leibniz's "favourite ladies"], but it pierces the heart. (Acts 2:37; 5:33; 7:54)[10]

3. *Limiting divine action to a "contributory cause" of human love only leads to the libertarian conclusion if we posit a false dichotomy.* Brümmer says,

> God's agency is not coercive but enabling and motivating and therefore does not deny freedom, responsibility and personal integrity of the human agent through whom God realizes his will. ... In this way double agency is a matter of co-operation between two agents and not of one agent using the other as a tool.[11]

Since "God's agency is not coercive," the assumption is that divine agency is limited to "enabling and motivating," thereby preserving libertarian free will. Without "co-operation" between the libertarian and the divine agent, the human being is stripped of humanity and

---

9. God implants a new "heart" (Ezek 36:26). David praises God with "all that is within [him]" (Ps 103:1; cf. Prov 23:16; Rom 2:5). Paul prays that the Father would enlighten the eyes of the Ephesian "hearts" and strengthen them in their "inner being" so that Christ may dwell richly "in [their] hearts" (Eph 3:16–18). Jesus and the Father encourage the Thessalonians' "hearts" (2 Thess 2:16–17). God establishes the Thessalonians' "hearts" in holiness (1 Thess 3:13). The Lord opens Lydia's "heart," resulting in her positive response to the apostolic message (Acts 16:14). The Spirit lives in our "hearts" (Gal 4:6). Paul traces true Judaism to a circumcised "heart" (Rom 2:29). From an uncircumcised "heart" flows continual resistance to the Spirit (Acts 7:51). When the human "heart" is darkened, multiple forms of immorality pour from it (Rom 1:21–32; cf. Matt 13:11–17). All of this biblical heart language, signals deep teleological orientations for or against God at the core of human beings. I repeat: where is the heart-transcending agent required by libertarian free will (see 1.2.4 and 1.3.2) in these biblical motifs?

10. Sorg, "Heart," 183.

11. Brümmer, *What Are We Doing When We Pray?*, 75, 76.

reduced to a mere "tool." This rests on a false dichotomy in which *either* libertarian free will stands *or* responsible human agency falls. There is no acknowledgment of compatibilistic freedom (i.e., Freedom *of* the Heart; see 1.2) as a logical *tertium quid*. There is no recognition of Heart Reformation as a possible mid-point between Heart Activation and Heart Circumvention.

The premise that "God's agency is not coercive" only leads to the libertarian conclusion if it is *presupposed* that libertarian free will is the only game in town. Historically, Augustinia has been a highly developed city in which divine action moves farther than Heart Persuasion, Cooperation, or Activation while stopping short of Heart Circumvention. From Brümmer's analysis, it seems as if Augustine, Gottschalk, Luther, Calvin, Turretin, Jonathan Edwards, and Abraham Kuyper, along with contemporary theologians like D. A. Carson, R. C. Sproul, Michael Horton, and John Piper have contributed nothing to the theological landscape between Arminia and No Man's Land. If God actualizes human love with the "sweet and unfrustratable power" (Turretin) of Heart Reformation, then Brümmer's valuable insight that "God's agency is not coercive" does not warrant the libertarian conclusion.

The salient distinction surrounding the question of divine action in human love is not between contributory causation and sufficient causation. The deeper distinction emerges between contributory causation that is *efficacious* and that which is *thwartable*. Libertarians and compatibilists both reject the claim that God is the sufficient cause of human love. For compatibilists, divine action reforms hearts in such a way that the reformed human heart expresses love with its renovated, uncoerced will intact and active. Heart Reformation is a necessary but not a sufficient cause of authentic human love. If divine action were the sufficient cause of human love, then we have moved beyond Heart Reformation into Heart Circumvention, entering the theological No Man's Land that Brümmer appropriately avoids.

The relevant question is if God's contributions to human love are efficacious or thwartable. Does divine action reach the innermost core of the person, resulting in love without dehumanizing the lover? Or does God reach only the courtiers, leaving an untouched throne of executive human power from where divine contributions may be shunned? The compatibilist may gladly embrace Brümmer's distinction between contributory and sufficient causation without embracing libertarian free will. Brümmer's distinction leads to the libertarian conclusion only if we neglect the deeper distinction between thwartable contributory causation (Heart Persuasion, Cooperation, and Activation) and efficacious contributory causation (Heart Reformation).

4. *Limiting divine action to a thwartable "contributory cause" of human love overlooks biblical contexts in which God's contributory causation is efficacious.* 3.2 explored nine biblical motifs in which divine action is efficacious. When God circumcises, transplants, or transcribes the heart, love results. When Paul asks God to make the Thessalonians increase in love, their love increases. When the Spirit produces fruit, humans express love. When the Father gives, humans come to the Son. When Jesus requests an expanded union of love that includes believers, the Father answers. When the Father and Son mutually desire the raising up of this love-gift, they fulfill one another's will. The Father and Son express their love for one another by initiating, expanding, and perfecting the love of those among the divinely exchanged gift.

In Brümmer's model, the finite human agent can thwart this expression of infinite love between the Father and Son: "If we decide not to do [God's will] (in spite of being enlightened, enabled and motivated) then God's will is not done."[12] Biblically, God's contributory causation, motivated by the vast love within the Trinity, is efficacious. Thwartable causation can go only so far as *the capacity to love* as a divine gift, not to *the love itself* as a divine gift. Moses, Jeremiah, Ezekiel, John, and Paul credit God with both the capacity to love and the love itself.

---

12. Brümmer, *What Are We Doing When We Pray?*, 75–76.

THE SPARSITY OBJECTION

If God has the unique ability to bring about love efficaciously in human agents, then why does this ability seem to be exercised with such sparsity? I offer four points to shed perspective on the Sparsity Objection as raised by Jerry Walls:

1. *The Sparsity Objection is not solved, but merely changes form with the addition of libertarian free will.* Every theological paradigm bears some burden of proof to square its notion of divine action with the reality and extent of anti-love forces in the world. If, for example, we join the majority of libertarian theologians throughout history in affirming that God has exhaustive foreknowledge of the contingent choices of His creatures, then the Sparsity Objection changes shape but persists. If God foreknows the gruesome anti-love choices of certain creatures, then why does He not prevent the massive victimization that results from these choices? A strategically triggered aneurysm could derail the warlord's journey to power. A well-placed lighting bolt could silence a hate speech. A glitch in cyberspace could sever the lines of communication through which murderous schemes flow. On a libertarian framework of divine action, there are a vast number of means to minimize the victimizing power of anti-love choices. Why does such divine action seem to occur with such sparsity?

Simply injecting the power of libertarian free will does not resolve the problems associated with the apparent sparsity of divine action.[13] Furthermore, even if libertarian free will could completely resolve

---

13. Open theism is of little help in this regard. For Boyd, Pinnock, Sanders, and Hasker, God faces an open future but possesses exhaustive knowledge of the past. This vast encyclopedic knowledge of the rise of genocidal warlords throughout history would give the God of open theism a keen ability to anticipate which free creatures are presently strutting down the same path to mass destruction. Boyd, Pinnock, and Sanders' God knew exhaustively the intentions of the yet-to-be-Fuhrer as he sat in prison composing *Mein Kampf*. The God of open theism was privy to the Third Reich's meetings in which they strategized their "final solution." There seems to be a sparsity of divine action exerted to crumble the bridge between Hitler's destructive intentions and destructive actions. Hitler could have exercised his libertarian free will to endorse his agenda, and be held blameworthy for that abuse of free power, without requiring that agenda to become a reality with an eight figure death toll.

the problems associated with sparsity, this notion of freedom still faces the significant philosophical and theological problems raised throughout this work.

2. *The Sparsity Objection is a specific instance of abstract problems of evil, and can thereby be met with the same counterpoints as the abstract problems.* All abstract problems of evil share a twofold structure. The first element of this structure focuses on salient aspects of the divine nature (e.g., a particular theological rendition of divine goodness or power). The second element highlights evil in one form or another, some "unjustified evils" (e.g., moral evil, natural evil, evil as phenomena in general, specific instances of evil). We could insert "the apparent sparsity of divine action in human love" into the second element of abstract problems of evil without altering the logical shape or thrust of the argument.

Viewed in this way, the theist addressing the Sparsity Objection may gain resources from answers to abstract problems of evil. Of particular help in this regard is a theistic strategy articulated in the closing chapters of Job and developed by Alvin Plantinga, William Alston, and Peter van Inwagen.[14] This strategy highlights a vast cognitive gap between the Creator and the creature. According to Plantinga, Alston, and van Inwagen, this cognitive gap jeopardizes the atheologian's case against God's existence. The atheologian's case against God rests on the following notoriously difficult premise:

> **P1:** It is impossible, improbable, or less probable than some nontheistic account that God possesses morally sufficient reasons behind the existence of evil and suffering.

---

14. See Plantinga, "Epistemic Probability and Evil," 69–96; "On Being Evidentially Challenged," 244–61; William Alston, "The Inductive Argument from Evil and the Human Cognitive Condition," 97–125; "Some (Temporarily) Final Thoughts in Evidential Arguments from Evil," 311–32; and Peter van Inwagen, "The Problem of Evil, the Problem of Air, and the Problem of Silence," 151–74. All articles appear in *The Evidential Argument from Evil*, ed. Daniel Howard-Snyder (Bloomington: Indiana University Press, 1996).

Plantinga, Alston, and van Inwagen argue that, given the cognitive gap between Creator and creature, there is no solid ground on which we can stand to establish P1. We are in no cognitive condition relative to God to adjudicate if it is impossible, improbable, or less probable than some rival hypothesis for morally sufficient reasons to exist in the mind of God. Thus, inexplicable evils do not lead to the conclusion of God's non-existence.

The insight of Plantinga, Alston, and van Inwagen applies when approaching the Sparsity Objection. The difference is that it is no longer the atheologian arguing against God's existence, but the libertarian theologian arguing against the existence of one particular view of God, namely, a God with the ability to bring about Heart Reformation. If we seek to justify disbelief in the existence of a Heart Reforming God on the basis of the Sparsity Objection, then we find ourselves, oddly enough, in the same plight as the atheologian. We commit ourselves to a problematic premise that resembles P1:

> **P2:** It is impossible, improbable, or less probable than some libertarian account that a God with Heart Reforming ability possesses morally sufficient reasons behind withholding a more widespread exercise of that ability.

The fatal flaw of P2 is the same as that of P1, namely, how difficult the premise is to establish given the cognitive gap between God and us. Alston argues that the atheologian's induction from "I can see no" to "There is no" is unjustified. Alston's point holds true for the libertarian theologian who attempts to reach the conclusion "There is no [morally sufficient reason for a God with Heart Reforming ability to exercise that ability as sparsely as it may seem]" from the premise "I can see no [morally sufficient reason for a God with Heart Reforming ability to exercise that ability as sparsely as it may seem]."[15] The induction rests on a failure to appreciate the Creator-creature cognitive gap.

---

15. Walls' demand parallels Rowe's demand that a convincing answer must be offered as to why God does or does not do *x*, if a given theistic position is to be taken seriously. Are such demands reasonable? If it was necessary to the theist's position for God to render humanity

3. *The Sparsity Objection does not serve as a defeater of the biblical case for Heart Reformation.* Walls' formulation of the Sparsity Objection bypasses biblical analysis. Even if we face tremendous difficulty in locating convincing answers to why a given divine ability is expressed to this or that extent, such a difficulty is insufficient grounds for rejecting that divine ability *in cases where the Bible ascribes that ability to God.* The Bible credits God with the ability to cause rainfall (Jas 5:17–18). We may have trouble understanding why this ability is not expressed during a drought (particularly if we are residents of a Third World country). Does our inability to grasp why divine rain-causing ability is not expressed in this or that case nullify the biblical insight that God possesses rain-causing ability? If the biblical case set forth in 3.2 represents true insight into God's love-actualizing abilities, then our epistemic limitations do not falsify that insight. If the God who can reform hearts is the same God whose judgments are "unsearchable" and whose ways are "inscrutable" (Rom 11:33b), then it is reasonable to expect a measure of incomprehensibility when seeking to understand the extent to which He exercises His abilities.[16] Neither the Divine Contributor nor Sparsity Objections undermine the unique divine ability of Heart Reformation.

PRAYERS FOR LOVE ACTUALIZATION

It is from this unique divine ability to actualize authentic love that our existential critique of the Relational Free Will Defense proceeds. This final critique takes shape as the Heart Reformation Argument:

---

epistemically privy to the divine rationale for Him either to exist or to exercise Heart Reforming power, then these demands are indeed reasonable. If, however, the God in question is the God of the Bible, whom we behold dimly through a mirror, then such demands are unreasonable. A holocaust survivor, who lost her best friend and many family members to concentration camps, declares, "Who am I to judge God, me this little mortal? That would take some nerve for me to judge Him!" (Madeleine Nussen in a personal interview conducted on April 8, 2011).

16. We may add that the Sparsity Objection rests on a false induction from sparsity to non-existence. For example, wild African dogs are sparse but exist nonetheless. I am indebted to Bram van de Beek for this point.

HRA1: Prayers for love actualization are a biblically endorsed means of answering concrete problems of evil.

HRA2: The Relational Free Will Defense excludes prayers for love actualization as a means of answering concrete problems of evil, since such prayers entail Heart Reformation.

HRA3: A viable attempt to answer abstract problems of evil must be consistent with biblically endorsed answers to concrete problems of evil.

HRA4: Therefore, the Relational Free Will Defense is not a viable attempt to answer abstract problems of evil.

HRA1. There is not simply one problem of evil but a complex tangle of problems. We have distinguished between abstract and concrete problems of evil, each of which mutates into multiple forms (see 1.1). The Bible offers insight into how evil is to be met in its various concrete forms.[17] One crucial aspect of meeting the challenges of concrete evil is the biblical tension between the "divine act promised" and the "human act commanded" (see 3.2). In the biblical narrative, the dual emphasis on divine and human agency is not an abstract tension to be analyzed from the outside by a disinterested Cartesian observer. Rather, it is a tension to be lived existentially in the context of believing communities, so that God's relational kingdom on earth reflects the Trinitarian intimacy of heaven.

How should communities live this tension in response to concrete problems of evil? On the "human act commanded" side of the tension, concrete evil is met with an ongoing and active pursuit of obedience to divine love-imperatives. Interpreting divine action as justification

---

17. Nowhere in the text do we meet the J. L. Mackies of the ancient Near Eastern world putting the intellectual merits of Jewish monotheism to the test with abstract problems of evil. The Bible carries implications for abstract problems of evil, including insights into the infinite scope of God's wisdom, the finitude of human cognition, the impeccable holiness of the divine nature, etc. The Bible speaks *indirectly* (though insightfully) to abstract problems of evil. The opponents of the ancient authors were most often polytheists or inconsistent monotheists, leading to an emphasis on the concrete evils expressed in these worldviews.

for moral passivity, Singer's "waiting quietly for *agape* to descend," fails to sustain the tension. As Singer argues, "Such patience may be admirable, but it hardly counts as love." So Augustine says, "Love cannot be idle. Show me—if you can—a love that is idle and doing nothing!"[18] Reading Augustine's prayer "Grant what Thou commandest" as "I will go morally limp and disengage from all attempts to love until You grant what Thou commandest" is to conflate Augustinia with No Man's Land. A lived response to concrete problems of evil (i.e., existential participation in MCT2-PFT2) entails active human obedience to the divine call to love.

We live the "divine act promised" side of the tension to confront concrete evil through prayers for love actualization. We may view this point through biblical, historical, and contemporary lenses.

In the biblical context, Jesus prays for the Father to bind believers in a visible union of love (John 17:20–26). The threat of concrete evil implicit to this Johannine context is a divisiveness that would mar the accurate reflection of Father-Son oneness. Paul prays that God would realize a superabundance of love in the Thessalonian community facing such concrete evils as sexual exploitation and idleness (1 Thess 3:12–13). Beyond these prayers analyzed in 3.2, prayers for love actualization occur against such concrete evils as David's scandal against Uriah and Bathsheba,[19] inappropriate relations with unbelievers, opposition to apostolic authority, and false teaching in ancient

---

18. Augustine, *On Psalm 31*, 2:5, cited in Hand, *Augustine on Prayer* (New York: Catholic Book Publishing, 1986), 40.

19. Facing this concrete evil, David prays for a clean heart and renewal of a right spirit (Ps 51:10; cf. Ps 119:80, 133). Since a clean heart and renewal of a right spirit entail love, this prayer is a prayer for love actualization. Augustine comments,

> What did [David] long for but to obey God's commandments? But there was no possibility of the weak doing hard things, of a little one doing great things, so he opened his mouth to confess that he could not do them for himself and he drew in power to do them" (*On Psalm 118*, 17:4, cited in Hand, *Augustine on Prayer*, 44).

Corinth,[20] Agrippa's lack of faith,[21] and the infiltration of false teaching both in Colossae[22] and the recipient churches of Jude's letter.[23] In addition, the Lord's Prayer in Matthew 6:10 contains the request for "the Father's will" (τὸ θέλημά σου) to be done on earth. Since the Father's will entails human obedience to the love-imperative (Matt 22:37–40), the Lord's Prayer may be interpreted as a prayer for love actualization against concrete evil (expressed generally as resistance to the Father's will). Given the imperative clause of Matthew 6:9a, "Pray then like this" (Οὕτως οὖν προσεύχεσθε ὑμεῖς), Matthew 6:10 offers not only a *description* of prayers for love actualization but also a *prescription* of such prayers as a commanded means for countering concrete evils.[24]

In the historical context, many have obeyed the biblical command to pray for love actualization. We encounter Augustine's famous prayer—"Grant what thou commandest"—a prayer for God to actualize obedience to the love-imperative. Elsewhere, the Bishop of Hippo expounds: "He to whom is given by God the love of God, and the love of our neighbor for God's sake; he, indeed, ought to pray insistently that this gift may be ... increased in him."[25] In the famous "Prayer of Saint Francis": "Where there is hatred, let me sow love. ... O Divine

---

20. Facing these concrete evils (2 Cor 6:11–7:4; 10:1–18; 11:1–6), Paul prays that the Corinthians will do nothing wrong (2 Cor 13:7a; cf. 9b). Since failure to love clearly meets the criteria of wrongness in Pauline thought, this prayer is a prayer for love actualization.

21. Facing this concrete evil, Paul's prays for Agrippa and his audience to have a positive faith response to the gospel (Acts 26:29). Paul likewise commands the Thessalonians to pray for the rapid expansion of the gospel (2 Thess 3:1). Since wider acceptance of the gospel entails a positive response of love to Jesus, these prayers are prayers for love actualization.

22. Facing this concrete evil, Paul prays for God to fill the Colossians with the knowledge of His will through all spiritual wisdom and understanding so that they may live a worthy life, pleasing Him with good works (Col 1:9–11). Epaphras prays for the Colossians to stand firm in God's will with maturity (Col 4:12). Since a worthy life, good works, standing firm in God's will, and maturity entail love, these prayers are prayers for love actualization.

23. Facing this concrete evil, Jude addresses his benediction to the God who can keep people from falling and present them without fault before his glorious presence (Jude 24). Since not falling and being without fault entail love, this prayer is a prayer for love actualization.

24. This finds reinforcement in Jesus' command to pray that we will not fall into temptation (Luke 22:40; Matt 6:13). If resistance to temptation entails love, then these commanded prayers are also prayers for love actualization.

25. Augustine, *On Psalm 118*, 17th 3:4, cited in Hand, *Augustine on Prayer*, 35.

Master, grant that I may not so much seek ... to be loved, as to love."
Thomas à Kempis prayed:

> My love is yet feeble. ... Therefore, visit me continually, and
> instruct me out of thy law, deliver me from malignant passions
> and sensual desires, that being healed and purified, I may love
> with more ardor. ... Love is born of God. ... Expand my heart
> with love, that I may feel its transforming power, and may
> even be dissolved in its holy fire! Let me be possessed by thy
> love, and ravished from myself! Let me love thee more than
> myself; let me love myself only for thy sake; and in thee love
> all others, as that perfect law requireth.[26]

In his fourteenth "Holy Sonnet," Donne confesses, "I, / Except you
enthrall me, shall never be free, / Nor ever chaste, except you ravish
me."

In the contemporary context, prayers for love actualization
abound. People often pray for the conversion of people who presently lack a relationship of love with God, the healing of friendships
and marriages wounded by anti-love behaviors, victory in some personal moral struggle, divine help in saying the right things with the
right attitude when difficult words must be said, enlarged concern
over social injustices, and so on.[27] These prayers rest on the premise
of God's ability to actualize love and thereby reflect Jesus and Paul's
prayerful approach to concrete evil in the first century.

The tension between the "divine act promised" and the "human
act commanded" is to be lived in response to concrete evil through
ongoing attempts to obey the love-imperative on the one hand and
prayerful reliance on God to actualize obedience on the other (HRA1).
Augustine sustains the tension:

---

26. Thomas à Kempis, *The Imitation of Christ*, tr. John Payne (Boston: Gould and Lincoln,
1856), 175–76, 177.

27. For examples of prayers that involve human choice and pose problems for "free will
theism," see David Ciocchi, "The Religious Adequacy of Free Will Theism," *Religious Studies*
38, no. 1 (2002), 50.

For the man who says ... "Thy will be done on earth as is it in heaven" ... and other prayers of a like purport, which it would take too long to particularize, does in effect offer up a prayer for ability to keep God's commandments. Neither, indeed, on the one hand, would any injunctions be laid on us to keep them, if our own will had nothing to do in the matter; nor, on the other hand, would there be any room for prayer if our will were alone sufficient.[28]

No Man's Land leads to a human passivity incompatible with active obedience, whereas Pelagia, Cassiana, and Arminia undermine prayers for love actualization by granting humans the power to frustrate divine action.

EQUIPROBABILITY, PROBABILISTIC, AND HYBRID MODELS

HRA2. The libertarian may object that prayers for love actualization are not tantamount to prayers for Heart Reformation. Rather, we can harmonize such prayers with libertarian free will. This leads to the second premise of the Heart Reformation Argument (HRA2):

The Relational Free Will Defense excludes prayers for love actualization as a means of answering concrete problems of evil, since such prayers entail Heart Reformation.

Can we harmonize the Defense with prayers for love actualization? In the logic of the Defense, human agents exercising two-way power can resist God's efforts to evoke human love. The Defense requires Freedom from the Reformer, the ability to love or refrain from loving relative to all divine action. It follows that God may positively answer prayers for love actualization, but resistant human willpower prevents the realization of God's positive answers. As

---

28. Augustine, *On Man's Perfection in Righteousness*, 10.21, in *The Nicene and Post-Nicene Fathers*, 5:166.

libertarian David Basinger maintains, "It seems quite probable that there are many prayers for assistance that the God of BFWT [basic freewill theism] would like to answer affirmatively but simply cannot."[29] We may, therefore, narrow our question: *Are prayers for love actualization best understood as requests that may be positively answered by God yet unrealized because of resistant human power?*

We may approach this question by clarifying some basic principles of petitionary prayer. Perhaps on the basis of such passages as Matthew 7:7 ("Ask, and it will be given to you") we could argue for a 100 percent guarantee that God brings petitionary prayers offered in faith into the realm of reality. Let us call this the "Maximal Principle of Petitionary Prayer." We could opt for a softer version in which petitionary prayer raises the probability of the realization of a petitioned outcome to somewhere above 50 percent, though stopping short of 100 percent. Let us call this the "Median Principle of Petitionary Prayer." We may articulate a still more modest principle as follows:

> A petitionary prayer raises the probability of the realization of a petitioned outcome to somewhere above 50% *in cases where God answers a prayer positively.*

Here we have the "Minimal Principle of Petitionary Prayer." If God answers a prayer positively, then the probability of the requested outcome coming about is greater than 50 percent. If we apply this minimal principle to a specific subset of petitionary prayers, namely, prayers for love actualization, then we reach the "Greater than 50 percent Principle of Prayers for Love Actualization":

> A prayer for love actualization helps raise the probability of love being actualized in some petitioned outcome, *x*, to somewhere above 50% *in cases where God answers a prayer positively.*

---

29. David Basinger, *The Case for Freewill Theism: A Philosophical Assessment* (Downers Grove: IL: InterVarsity Press, 1996), 122.

If God may positively answer a given prayer for love actualization without making it any more likely than not that love will be actualized, then the incentive for such prayers is drastically undercut, if not altogether eliminated.

Can libertarian models of divine action accommodate the Greater than 50 Percent Principle? As we have seen, Pelagia, Cassiana, and Arminia stand united in granting human agents the libertarian power to resist all divine action extended to actualize love. Let us move deeper by analyzing three philosophical renditions of libertarian power:

1. *Equiprobability Libertarianism.* We may understand libertarian free will as the Leibnizian queen suspended in a state of indifference above all teleological pushes and pulls (see 1.2–1.3). She has equal ability to go this way or that. Kane writes,

> When undetermined free choices or actions occur, the viable alternatives must be equally probable. Thus, if there are two alternatives, each must have a probability of .5.[30]

Let us call this "equiprobability libertarianism." If humans possess the power of equiprobability libertarianism relative to the cumulative divine efforts to actualize love, then there is a 50 percent probability of the agent accepting divine action and a 50 percent probability of the agent's rejecting it.

On this libertarian model, a significant problem emerges: all divine action extended to answer prayers for love actualization does not raise the probability of love's actualization any higher than 50 percent. Otherwise, a necessary condition of "undetermined free choices" fails to be met. David Ciocchi draws out these implications of libertarian free will,

---

30. Robert Kane, *The Significance of Free Will* (New York: Oxford University Press, 1996), 177.

> As long as conditions allow the agent to make a free choice
> between a particular set of options, there is nothing anyone
> (including God) can do to make it more likely that an agent
> pick one option rather than another.[31]

If the human power to resist is understood in terms of equiprobability libertarianism, and we embrace the modest requirement embodied in the Greater than 50 Percent Principle, then prayers for love actualization are undermined. God may answer positively a believer's petition to actualize love in some agent, Claudia, and set Himself to the task of bringing that love about through Heart Persuasion, Cooperation, and Activation. No matter how extensive these divine efforts, the probability of love being actualized in Claudia does not rise above 50 percent given her two-way power.

This problem compounds the more free agents are involved. A prayer for love actualization offered for a broken marriage in which both partners stand in need of greater love entails two agents capable of "undetermined free choices." The probability of an unblocked positive answer to such a dual agent petition reduces to 25 percent (50 percent x 50 percent). The realization of a positive answer to prayers for a family of five locked in anti-love patterns reduces to a 3.15 percent probability. A realized positive response to prayers for love actualization in a love-deficient church of one hundred members becomes even slimmer.

2. *Probabilistic Libertarianism.* Perhaps prayers for love actualization fare better if we interpret human power in terms of a second philosophical rendition of libertarian free will introduced in 1.2. In the proposals of Timothy O'Conner (as well as Kane, Hasker, and Van Inwagen) we find not an equiprobability account of libertarian free will, but a probabilistic account. Within such "probabilistic libertarianism," the probability of the libertarian agent choosing one

---

31. Ciocchi, "The Religious Adequacy of Free Will Theism," 54.

option over another rises somewhere above 50 percent. "Reasons," in O'Conner's model, "supply relative tendencies to act,"[32] and these tendencies push the probability of a given choice above and beyond 50 percent. To salvage libertarian free will, these "relative tendencies" must not be determinative. Rather, as O'Conner's stipulates, "These are tendencies that it remains entirely up to me to act on or not."[33] The agent in this model may choose an action with a 1 percent probability over and against his 99 percent tendency to act otherwise.

Does such probabilistic libertarianism hold promise for handling the problems associated with prayers for love actualization? Could a higher probability of an agent choosing to cooperate with divine action, given the agent's "relative tendencies to act," enlarge God's ability to realize positive answers to such prayers? In addition to problems endemic to the philosophical merit of O'Conner's probabilistic account,[34] there is a more urgent problem that emerges around prayers for love actualization. Specifically, people frequently offer such prayers on behalf of those whose "relative tendencies to act" are not tilted higher than 50 percent toward love. The lack of loving tendencies, the agent's less than 50 percent orientation toward love, is precisely the motivation for most prayers for love actualization.

God's ability to actualize love on a probabilistic scenario becomes more limited than on equiprobability libertarianism. In the equiprobability model, the probability of God's efforts to actualize love reaching realization is 50 percent. On probabilistic libertarianism, the percentage drops relative to the force of anti-love tendencies in the agent's "nested structure of conative and cognitive factors" (O'Conner). If the human power to resist divine action is understood in terms of probabilistic libertarianism, and we embrace the modest requirement

---

32. Timothy O'Conner, *Persons and Causes: The Metaphysics of Free Will* (Oxford: Oxford University Press, 2000), 95.

33. O'Conner, *Persons and Causes*, 97.

34. These problems include O'Conner's attempt to mix agent causation with a rejection of substance dualism and his attempt to combine a probabilistic account of libertarian free will with a rejection of event causation. See David Ciocchi, review of *Persons and Causes: The Metaphysics of Free Will*, *Philosophia Christi* 2 (2001): 266–70.

embodied in the Greater than 50 Percent Principle, then prayers for love actualization are left without warrant.

3. *Hybrid Libertarianism*. A third libertarian option comes from the proposal by Gregory Boyd analyzed in 2.2. In concert with Boyd, Hasker sets forth a hybrid theory of action that moves beyond probability to "inevitable" choices. Hasker clarifies,

> Choices that are inevitable in view of a person's character and circumstances may still be responsible, and even in a sense free, because it was through her previous libertarian choices that she became that sort of person. ... This facilitates God's ability to elicit from us the response He desires.[35]

Such "hybrid libertarianism"[36] suffers from the same problem as the probabilistic model. People frequently offer prayers for love actualization on behalf of those in some destructive, anti-love state of being. Such prayers are not primarily intended for those who are already probabilistically oriented toward love or those for whom loving choices are "inevitable in view of [their] character and circumstances." We pray for individuals enslaved to anti-loving habits, marriages in which spouses are deeply entrenched in destructive patterns, or social groups in which divisiveness has become the norm. We may offer prayers for love actualization on behalf of a person who "became that sort of person" for whom anti-love choices are "inevitable." The probability of God's bringing about love in such a scenario is more limited than on equiprobability or probabilistic models.

Whether we analyze libertarian power in terms of equiprobability, probabilistic, or hybrid models, significant problems threaten prayers for love actualization. I have formulated these problems with reference to the modest Greater than 50 percent Principle. However, a

---

35. William Hasker, "Is Free-Will Theism Religiously Inadequate: A Reply to Ciocchi," *Religious Studies* 39 (2003): 431–40, 437.

36. I call this position "hybrid libertarianism" because it is a hybrid of libertarian and compatibilistic freedom, combining Freedom *from* and Freedom *of* the Heart.

stronger principle of petitionary prayers is at work within the biblical framework, further intensifying the problems. Jeremiah acknowledges in prayer, "Nothing is too hard for you" (Jer 32:17b). God responds, "Behold, I am the LORD, the God of all flesh. Is anything too hard for me?" (Jer 32:27).

In the context of this general claim that nothing is too hard for God, we find a specific promise:

> I will give them one heart and one way, that they may fear me forever, for their own good and the good of their children after them. I will make with them an everlasting covenant, that I will not turn away from doing good to them. And I will put the fear of me in their hearts, that they may not turn from me. (Jer 32:39–40)

This promise transcends a divine *attempt* to actualize love that may be blocked by a lack of human cooperation. God promises to actualize love, justifying a principle of prayers for love actualization that is stronger than the Greater than 50 Percent Principle above.[37] Jeremiah 32:39–41, like other "divine act promised" passages (see 3.2), entails that God can decisively actualize love in human hearts.[38]

---

37. This biblical insight comports with J. I. Packer's observation,

> You pray for the conversion of others. In what terms, now, do you intercede for them? ... I think that what you do is pray in categorical terms that God will, quite simply and decisively, save them: that He will open the eyes of their understanding, soften their hard hearts, renew their natures, and move their wills to receive the Savior. ... You would not dream of making it a point in your prayer that you are not asking God actually to bring them to faith, because you recognize that that is something He cannot do. ... You entreat Him to do that very thing, and your confidence in asking rests upon the certainty that He is able to do what you ask. ... On our feet we may have arguments about it, but on our knees we are all agreed. (*Evangelism & the Sovereignty of God* [Downers Grove, IL: InterVarsity Press, 1961], 15–17)

38. Hasker contends that such a compatibilistic model of divine action carries its own problems in reconciling petitionary prayer with the religious practices of ordinary believers ("Is Free-Will Theism Religiously Inadequate?," 435–36). This includes why we should bother to pray at all if God has predetermined the course of history, a problem addressed in detail by Jonathan Edwards. See Edwards, *Freedom of the Will*, in *The Works of Jonathan Edwards*, vol. 1 [Peabody, MA: Hendrickson, 2000], IV.5–6, IV.12–13. Moreover, a problem faced by compatibilists does

On libertarian models of divine action, the answer to God's rhetorical question "Is anything too hard for me?" is affirmative. In each case where God answers a prayer for love actualization positively and the libertarian agent refuses to cooperate, the actualization of love has proven "too hard" for God. In Hasker's words,

> No theist who accepts any of the current opinions involving libertarian free will can deny that God could sometimes be prevented from granting a petition by the obdurate wills of creatures.[39]

In contrast to Hasker, Jeremiah answers, "Nothing is too hard for You." If God has the unique ability to reform hearts, then we may echo Jeremiah's confidence when praying for more love.

FREE WILL AND CONCRETE EVIL

HRA3-HRA4. Prayers for love actualization are a biblically endorsed means of counteracting concrete evil (HRA1). The Relational Free Will Defense, particularly its *a priori* rejection of Heart Reformation by making libertarian free will a condition of authentic love, undermines these prayers (HRA2). This leads to a third premise of the Heart Reformation Argument (HRA3):

> A viable Christian response to abstract problems of evil must be consistent with biblically endorsed answers to concrete problems of evil.

The Defense's claim that love requires libertarian free will has been marshaled against abstract problems of evil with little regard for how this idea may alter our approach to concrete problems of evil. Responses to abstract problems must be consistent (though not necessarily identical) with normative methods of engaging concrete

---

not diminish the force of the problems faced by the libertarian but demonstrates (at best) that petitionary prayer calls for deeper analysis from all theological fronts.

39. Hasker, "Is Free-Will Theism Religiously Inadequate?," 439–40.

problems. Since 1.1 already defends this claim, I will not repeat that case here. If we accept that answers to abstract problems should, at a minimum, comport with answers to concrete problems, then it follows that the Relational Free Will Defense is not a viable response to abstract problems of evil (HRA4).

A case study in concrete evil clarifies this conclusion. Let us consider a concrete evil faced by a young man whom we may call Brian. Brian finds himself exhausted in a decade-long war against pornography addiction. He confides this gloomy and alienating struggle with a trusted mentor, Joe. Mirroring Paul's approach to sexual scandal in Thessalonica, Joe prays for Brian to "increase and abound in love." "God," Joe prays, "change Brian's heart to such an extent that the egocentric gratification promised by pornography loses its seductive power, deepening his love for You and your image-bearers." God, moved by Joe's prayer for love actualization, exerts all powers at His disposal toward the requested goal of Brian's transformation.

Given the Defense's claim that "love requires libertarian free will," God must keep Brian's two-way power intact when seeking to answer Joe's prayer. It remains possible for Brian to shun God's every attempt to increase love. For the Defense to stand, God may only exert the powers of Heart Persuasion, Cooperation, and Activation. Suppose Brian uses (or abuses) his God-bestowed free will to propel himself deeper into the downward spiral of pornography addiction. In this scenario, God's answer to Joe's well-intentioned prayer is not "yes," "no," or "not yet," but "I tried my best, but failed." In Ciocchi's terms, God has been "blocked from granting the petition [when] His answer is 'yes.' "[40] In the terms of the present analysis, the Greater than 50 Percent Principle has been violated. In Jeremiah's terms, the actualization of love in Brian's life has proven "too hard" for God.

This case exposes an existential implication of the Defense. If love requires libertarian free will, then for all energies that God may exert to answer a prayer, He may find Himself frustrated by the resistant

---

40. Ciocchi, "The Religious Adequacy of Free Will Theism," 56.

libertarian agent. This entails a significant alteration in our understanding of possible answers we may receive to our prayers. God may not only answer, "yes," "no," or "not yet." Given the executive veto power granted the libertarian agent, the answer may also come, "I tried my best, but failed." Can we tolerate this implication as we seek to make progress against concrete evils? If not, then it seems that the Relational Free Will Defense as a response to abstract evil must go. If so, then it seems that confronting concrete evil through confident prayers for love actualization must go.

Part 3:
Love and the Reformed Heart

Summary and Conclusions

We have distinguished five theological options for understanding the scope of divine action in human love: Heart Persuasion, Cooperation, Activation, Reformation, and Circumvention. We then entered the domain of biblical insight, encountering a fundamental tension between love as a "divine act promised" and a "human act commanded." Envisioning divine action as moving no farther than Heart Persuasion, Cooperation, and Activation fails to sustain the "divine act promised" side of the tension, whereas the Heart Circumvention model of divine action loses the "human act commanded" side.

From the analysis of previous chapters, we can move to a deeper conclusion. Resorting to Necessity of the Gunman undermines the nature of authentic love (see 1.2). Since the God of the Heart Circumvention model resorts to Necessity of the Gunman, his coercive action renders all human love null and void. On this view, all love promised by God throughout the Bible falls short of true love. Therefore, the Heart Circumvention model loses not only the "human act commanded" but also the "divine act promised" side of the biblical tension.

We have also seen that libertarian free will poses problems for meaningful human agency (see 1.3). It requires a transcendent agent devoid of internal desires. This is surely a poor candidate for being a true lover. In addition, libertarian choices of one alternative over another cannot be explained contrastively, rendering them a poor medium for the expression of true love. On this view, all love expressed by human agents throughout the Bible falls short of true love. Therefore, libertarian models of divine action lose not only the "divine act promised" but also the "human act commanded" side of the tension. If God possesses the unique ability of Heart Reformation, then the biblical tension holds.

As finite creatures, we are limited in our capacity to actualize love in other agents. The Creator is not bound to our limitations. The God of the Bible possesses a unique access to and authority over human hearts such that He can successfully reorient our inner *telos* toward love without abolishing our humanity. The Defense's claim that love requires libertarian free will maintains its persuasive power only to the extent that we allow our own ontological, interpersonal limitations to define the contours of divine possibility. A case in point comes from Rob Bell's best-selling book, *Love Wins*, in which he claims,

> For there to be love, there has to be the option, both now and then, to not love. To turn the other way. ... Although God is powerful and mighty, *when it comes to the human heart God has to play by the same rules we do.*[1]

I think that this process of projecting our limitations onto God goes something like this: First, we *encounter the notion that love requires libertarian free will,* whether it comes from scholars, popular publications, pulpits, or movies. Second, we *verify this notion by taking stock of our own experiences* in which humans cannot guarantee another's love without trampling personhood. Perhaps, for example, we

---

1. Rob Bell, *Love Wins: A Book About Heaven, Hell, and the Fate of Every Person Who Ever Lived* (New York: HarperCollins e-books, 2011), 92.

have seen human relationships turn to heartache because one party becomes coercive and controlling. Third, we *impose our limitation on God*, assuming that, just like us, He cannot actualize authentic love in another. It is at this point that we overlook a crucial biblical insight and miss the "divine act promised" side of the tension. Fourth, we *lose something significant in our confrontation of concrete evil* in our lives, families, churches, and cultures.

Through prayers for love actualization, we align ourselves with the "divine act promised," relying on God's unique ability to reform hearts. Since libertarian free will precludes these prayers, we end up confronting concrete evil by focusing only on the "human act commanded," and love *loses*. Deficiencies of love are met with performance-based strategies. When our own power becomes the deciding factor in authentic love, we become entrenched in obsessive rule keeping. We serve others not for their good but for our own validation. We indulge a secret pride when we think that we have made better use of our willpower than others. Our self-powered efforts to love authentically lead to inauthentic "love" in varied, though equally egocentric, forms. In this way, we also lose the "human act commanded" side of the biblical tension.

The more aware we become of the unyielding power of concrete evil in our own hearts, the more precious God's unique ability to reform our hearts becomes. God's ability to change our hearts and actualize authentic love is far more precious than the notion of libertarian free will.

Epilogue

What a Difference
One Word Makes

If the Son sets you free, you will be free indeed.

—*Jesus, in John 8:36*

We have analyzed libertarian free will, with its requirement of non-hypothetical two-way power, as the sum of four relative freedoms:

Freedom from the Machine

Freedom from the Gunman

Freedom from the Heart

Freedom from the Reformer

Together, they capture what Richard Double calls "the [libertarian's] intuition that moral responsibility requires *actual* categorical ability to choose otherwise" (emphasis added).[1] This work has explored philosophical, biblical, and existential problems with 3 and 4.

These problems no longer pose a threat if we alter one word. If we turn "from" in 3 and 4 to "of," then freedom is the sum of:

Freedom from the Machine

Freedom from the Gunman

Freedom *of* the Heart

Freedom *of* the Reformer

As clarified in 1.2, Freedom *of* the Heart means that the heart is free relative to physical and coercive powers to choose in accord with its internal, convergent, and prevailing reasons. This ensures that it is really the agent's heart expressed in the action.

Freedom *of* the Reformer is a concept readily available from the analysis of part 3. It is the freedom of God to actualize love within the heart of a human agent without recalcitrant human power thwarting the process. God is free to extend the grace of Heart Reformation. With this revised set of relative freedoms, i.e., with Freedom from the Machine and the Gunman combined with Freedom *of* the Heart and the Reformer, we move from libertarian freedom to a more significant freedom.

Allow me to illustrate this transition by walking Claudia through successive phases of freedom:

Phase 1. As Claudia comes to transcend her baser physical impulses, making choices that cannot be reduced to natural causation, she expresses a partial though significant freedom, namely, Freedom from the Machine. Such freedom is significant insofar as it raises her power

---

1. Richard Double, "Libertarianism and Rationality," in *Agents, Causes, & Events: Essays on Indeterminism and Free Will*, ed. Timothy O'Conner (Oxford: Oxford University Press, 1995), 65.

above the level of the mechanical world.[2] Nevertheless, such freedom is partial because it is compatible with Claudia being enslaved in other areas. She may no longer be a slave to the Machine but may remain a slave to the Gunman.

Phase 2. Claudia becomes able to resist the manipulative forces exerted by other agents, making choices that are not fundamentally fear-based, choices that engender her character rather than the agendas of coercive persons. With this Freedom from the Gunman and Freedom *of* the Heart, she expresses a partial and yet still more significant freedom. This freedom is significant insofar as Claudia's actions have now become an expression of her own *telos*, rather than that of a coercive agent.[3] This freedom is partial because it is compatible with Claudia still being otherwise enslaved. She may no longer be a slave to the Gunman but may remain a slave to her own heart. She may be free to express her *telos*, while that *telos* remains riddled with anti-love (i.e., "Everyone who sins is a slave to sin" [John 8:34b]). She may choose with Freedom from the Machine and from the Gunman, and even Freedom *of* the Heart and still express nothing more than sheer narcissism.

Phase 3. If the fourth relative freedom intervenes, if the Reformer enters Claudia's heart, instilling a new loving *telos* unimpeded by human two-way power, then her expression of freedom crosses a new threshold. As God, expressing Freedom of the Reformer, continues to alter her *telos*, a new kind of freedom blossoms into existence.

What precisely is this new freedom that supervenes on Freedom from the Machine, Freedom from the Gunman, Freedom *of* the

---

2. Such freedom is indeed significant to college students who want to sustain purposeful action in spite of being taught that their actions are determined by their brain chemistry or physical environment, or anyone else who wants to avoid having their choices reduced to the level of a Pavlovian canine.

3. Such freedom is highly significant to the twenty-seven million victims of human trafficking, or those living under a political totalitarianism whose "choices" reflect less of their own desires and more the desires of coercive masters or tyrants.

Heart, and Freedom *of* the Reformer? It is freedom *from* the burden of self, freedom *from* obsessive rule-keeping, freedom *from* enslaving impulses, freedom *from* the fear of wrath, freedom *from* satanic principalities, *from* condemnation, *from* hopelessness, *from* alienation, *from* meaninglessness, *from* anti-love forces within, in short, Freedom *from* Sin. Wherever God reforms hearts, it is there that true freedom is found.

Such freedom moves us a considerable distance from libertarian free will. Claudia, unlike a Leibnizian queen, does not transcend whatever loving *telos* God has infused into her heart. Freedom *of* the Heart to express its *telos* and Freedom *of* the Reformer to orient that *telos* toward love culminate in the agent's experience of Freedom *from* Sin. With this new freedom we approach not only something like the freedom Jesus experienced, but also move closer to what He perhaps had in mind with the words: "If the Son sets you free, you will be free indeed" (John 8:36). And in this freedom from evil, this freedom to love, we find ourselves most enslaved: "Having been set free from sin [we] also have become slaves to God" (Rom 6:22a). God, may we know this radical slavery that we may know this robust freedom!

Appendix A

Taqdir and *Trinitas*

*Divine Power and Human Responsibility in
Sunni Islam and Reformed Theology*

In Homeric mythology we meet a monster on each side of the Strait of Messina, Scylla and Charybdis. To avoid a fatal encounter with Scylla the sailor would inevitably be swallowed by Charybdis, whereas veering westward away from Charybdis would drive him into the lethal grip of Scylla. In navigating the waters of divine power and human responsibility, the plight of both Christians and Islamic theologians throughout history has not been altogether unlike that of Odysseus seeking safe passage through the Strait of Messina. On the one side, Christians and Muslims face a divine determinism that swallows human responsibility (and therefore, threatens divine justice), and on the other, a human autonomy that threatens to consume divine power.

This essay seeks to draw these two religious traditions into deeper dialogue, surveying significant points of contact and salient points of contrast as they have sought to navigate the waters of divine power and human responsibility. Part 1 explores a significant convergence between the Reformed theological tradition in Christian thought and Sunni orthodoxy, particularly their joint rejection of autonomous human freedom in favor of a predestinarian understanding of divine power. Part 2 approaches points of contrasts through the lenses of John's Gospel, focusing on the deep relational nexus from which Johannine perspectives on divine power emerge. Part 3 focuses on theological contrasts between this relational vision of divine power and the Sunni notion of *taqdir* (predestination), asking how these theological contrasts might alter the existential contours of religious experience within these two religious traditions.[1]

PREDESTINATION:
REFORMED-SUNNI POINTS OF CONTACT

Broadly speaking, both the Bible and the Koran sustain a dual emphasis on divine power and human responsibility. Clarifying the scope of divine power the Bible affirms that God "can do all things, and that no purpose of [His] can be thwarted" (Job 42:2 cf. Dan 4:35; Isa 14:27; 46:8–10; Eph 1:11). The Koran echoes, "He hath power over all things" (Surah 6:17; cf. 2:165). The scope of divine power in both the Bible and Koran encompasses calamity (Amos 3:6; Isa 45:7; cf. Surah 57:22). God's power is also credited for human obedience in both sacred texts (Phil 2:13; cf. Surah 76:29b–30a; 10:100; 74:55–56). Yet in both sources God's obedience-actualizing power over human agents does not imply a heart-nullifying compulsion that might undermine our moral responsibility (Ezek 36:26–27; cf. Surah 2:256; 6:39). Clear affirmations of human responsibility frequent both sacred texts. Humans are significant choice-making agents who are proper objects of imperatives to believe (John 6:29; cf. Surah 18:29). Each individual is morally responsible for his or her choices (Matt 12:36–37; cf. Surah 4:123–24)[2] before a God who

---

1. For a parallel analysis see Derke Bergsma, *The Ideas of Predestination in Sunni Islam and Classical Calvinism Compared* (PhD diss., Northwestern University, 1962).

2. See Muhammad Badiur Rahman, "Implication of Choice," in *The Encyclopaedia of the Holy Qu'ran*, vol. 1, eds. N. K. Singh and A. R. Agwan (New Delhi: Global Vision Publishing House,

'is just' ($\delta i \varkappa \alpha \iota o \nu$—2 Thess 1:6) or in Islamic terms, *Al-Muqsit*, "the observer of Justice" (Surah 21:47–48).

The Bible and Koran, with their shared dual emphasis on divine power and human responsibility, have formed fertile soil for reflection through the histories of both Christianity and Islam, leading to a rich diversity of theological traditions. I limit the scope of the present analysis to the Reformed tradition in Christianity and Sunni Orthodoxy in Islam, traditions defined largely by their shared vision of God's power. How are Reformed and Sunni visions of God's power shared? While many points of convergence can be drawn, the focus of this study is their notions of predestination (Gk. *proorizo*; Ar. *taqdir*).

Both traditions interpret predestination as circumscribing the realm of human action in such a way that humans are neither *autonomous* on the one hand or *automatons* on the other. By *autonomous* I have in mind the notion of *libertarian free will* which credits human agents with an irreducible power to act as first-movers to perform a given action or refrain from performing that action. Relative to forces external to the choice-maker (e.g., God, other agents, physical laws), and forces internal to the choice-maker (reason-states, desires, character), the choice-maker retains two-way power to choose A or refrain from A.[3] Reformed and Sunni theologians jointly reject this account of the human freedom. Their reasons for rejecting libertarian freedom range from the exegetical to the historical (e.g., the origin of autonomy in Greek philosophical speculation rather than divine revelation), as well as philosophical problems surrounding the agent's non-hypothetical two-way power. Yet the core common objection stated from many angles by Reformed and Sunni theologians is that granting the human will an autonomous power to perform A or refrain from A relative to God's predestining power veers

---

2000), 560–71. See also Jacob Neusner, Bruce Chilton, and William Albert Graham, *Three Faiths, One God: The Formative Faith and Practice of Judaism, Christianity, and Islam* (Boston: Brill, 2002), 88, 89.

3. See Alvin Plantinga, *The Nature of Necessity* (Oxford: Oxford University Press, 1978), 170–71.

into a dangerous Scylla where God no longer "hath power over all things" (Surah 6:17).[4]

Reformed and Sunni traditions are also united in their attempt to avoid the Charybdis in which the human agent is reduced to an automaton. By "automaton" I have in mind a *hard determinism* in which man is diminished to a mere pre-programmed machine devoid of what the Hebrew Bible calls "heart" (*leb*—"the seat of feeling, thinking and willing."[5] Reformed and Sunni traditions mutually conceive of predestination as compatible with human beings as morally responsible (though not autonomous) choice-makers. Divine predestination is not tantamount to divine coercion. God does not nullify but *turns* hearts (Prov 21:1; Deut 30:6 cf. "O God, the Turner of hearts, turn our hearts to obedience to You").[6] *That* God exercises power over human hearts without obliterating moral responsibility is a point of contact; *how* this compatibility obtains between divine omnipotence and human responsibility finds diverse accounts, including the al-Ash'ari's notion of "acquisition" (*kasb*),[7] the Westminster Confession's notion of "secondary causes" (*causau secundae*) and the corresponding compatibilistic theory of agency in Reformed thought.

Moral responsibility as an anthropological point of convergence is largely motivated by a deeper point of theological harmony between Reformed and Sunni thinkers in the belief that "Divine Justice is perfect."[8] In John Calvin's words, "none perish without deserving it ... [given God's] most perfect justice" (cf. al-Bukhari 82:3:5). In their joint rejection of man as autonomous and man as an automaton, Reformed and Sunni perspectives on predestination find solidarity

---

4. See Neusner, *Three Faiths, One God: The Formative Faith and Practice of Judaism, Christianity, and Islam,* 87.

5. Sorg. "Heart," 181.

6. Sahih Muslim's *Book of Destiny* (Kitāb al-Qadar), 33, no. 6418, as cited in Jacob Neusner, Bruce Chilton, and William Graham, *Three Faiths, One God: The Formative Faith and Practice of Judaism, Christianity, and Islam* (Boston: Brill, 2002), 87.

7. See Nazif, Muhtaroglu, "An Occassionalist Defence of Free Will," in *Islamic Philosophy and Occidental Phenomenology in Dialogue* 4, no. 2 (2010), 45–62.

8. M. Khadduri, *The Islamic Conception of Justice* (Johns Hopkins University Press, 1984), 41.

in the dual affirmation that God is sovereign over the realm of human choice on the one hand and that humans are morally responsible before a just God on the other.

THE JOHANNINE *ORDO AMORIS*:
THE RELATIONAL ROOTS OF DIVINE POWER

Having introduced basic points of convergence between Sunni and Reformed concepts of God's predestining power, our analysis shifts to points of distinction. I set a context for appreciating distinctions through an exposition of John's Gospel, specifically the way in which John weaves divine power into what may be called an *ordo amoris*, ("order of love"). Below I chart five steps in the Johannine *ordo amoris* (JOA1-JOA5), offering a Reformed interpretation (not to be confused with *the* Reformed interpretation) of how divine power functions within John's unfolding logic of love. This will move us into better position to appreciate some crucial Reformed-Sunni distinctions.

JOA1: *Pre-Cosmic Loving.* The first step of the *ordo amoris* appears in Jesus' prayer in the chapter 17, known as the *precatio summi sacerdotis* or "High Priestly Prayer" (Chyträus). Most salient to the question at hand is the profound emphasis in vv. 20–26 on God's pre-cosmic relational connection. The Father loved the Son "before the world's creation" (v. 26). Before the inception of either the cosmos or personal agents to inhabit that cosmos, the God of the Fourth Gospel was engaged in inter-personal loving relationships.

How is this pre-cosmic love possible from a Johannine perspective? The answer lies in John's Christology in which, in distinction from Islamic Christology, Jesus exists eternally as ὁ λόγος, "the Word" who was both *with* God and *was* God (1:1). 1:3 credits the divine Word with bringing all things into existence, an exclusively divine act (cf. Isa 44:24). The terse Christology of 1:1–3 finds elaboration throughout John's narrative in which Jesus is addressed as the Father's equal (ἴσον ἑαυτὸν ποιῶν τῷ θεῷ—5:18–20), as the "I am" who existed before Abraham (ἐγὼ εἰμί—8:58), and as Thomas' "Lord and God"

with neither refutation nor rebuke ('Ο κύριός μου καὶ ὁ θεός μου—
20:28). The claim of John 17:26 that the Father loved the Son before
the world's creation, therefore, is best interpreted not as the Father's
pre-cosmic love based on prescience of a *mere* human who would
emerge in the continuum of creation, but as the Father's love for His
co-eternal and divine Son.

For John, this pre-cosmic love relation between Father and Son
does not logically exclude a thorough monotheism. There is emphatically only one God for John (John 5:44), in concert with the Koran
(Surah 13:16; 16:51). Contrast emerges as John envisions the single
Deity existing tri-personally as Father, Son, and Holy Spirit. John's
Gospel does not elevate a divine partner *beside* the one true God
(*shirk*), but rather reveals a loving and eternal partnership *within* the
one true God.

What are the implications of this pre-cosmic love for understanding father-son terminology in the Fourth Gospel? We are precluded
from a univocal understanding in which Jesus is the literal biological
progeny of the Father. Christian and Islamic theologies both properly
reject the "literal biological progeny" reading of father-son language
(Surah 6:100–101). Semantically informed by John 17, these terms
express something of a profound relational bond that has existed
between divine persons in the single God prior to the actualization
of the material world in which biological relations are instantiated.

JOA2: *Intra-Trinitarian Giving.* The pre-cosmic love between Father
and Son is neither static nor abstract, but actional and expressive. Pre-
cosmic love between Father and Son finds expression in the giving of a
morally significant love-gift from Father to Son. Jesus refers to all who
would believe in him through the echelons of time (17:24) with a title
unique to the Fourth Gospel—ὃ δέδωκάς, literally, "that which you have
given" (neut. sing.; cf. 6:37). In this love-gift motif, the Father is identified as the giver, the Son as the recipient, and all believers as the gift.

It is here that divine power finds its deepest relational context.
The Father expresses affection for the Son by exercising the active

power necessary to give the Son a people, a living communal love-gift of persons who obediently recognize His divine Sonship (cf. 17:6–8, 20). Thus divine power is cast by John not as egocentric ruling of an arbitrary despot, but as altruistic giving by a loving Father. Ὁ δέδωκάς are a living "I love You" expressed within the one God between Father and Son. I suggest that an accurate understanding of the Johannine perspective on divine power must include this ancient love. God's power expresses itself (in part) as giving, and this giving is an expression of the pre-cosmic relational bond between Father and Son.

JOA3: *Morally Responsible Coming*. John 6 reveals the causal relation between *intra-Trinitarian giving* and the third step in the Johannine *ordo amoris*—*morally responsible coming*. Says Jesus, "All that the Father gives me will come to me" (6:37). To "come" (ἐλθεῖν) to Jesus is tantamount to a positive expression of faith in Jesus and acceptance of His messianic claims (ὁ πιστεύων, 6:35; οὐ πιστεύετε, v. 36).[9] Such a positive faith expression is a moral imperative incumbent on Jesus' listeners. The moral responsibility to believe is underscored with invitation from the lips of Jesus to "believe in Him whom [the Father] has sent" (6:29 cf. 6:35), warranting the conclusion that "Men are not unthinking puppets in the fourth Gospel."[10]

Furthermore, those given by the Father *come* to the Son; they are not dragged kicking and screaming against their wills. It is the given who actively believe in the Son (cf. 1:7; 3:15–18, 36; 7:39; 11:25), not the Father who believes in the Son with ὃ δίδωσιν reduced to passive machinery in the divine exchange. John's theology knows nothing of pantheism in which God remains the only active agent in the universe. Indeed, what value would ὃ δίδωσιν retain as a love gift from Father to Son, if the gift is merely a collection of vacuous robots incapable

9. See Bruce Ware, "The Place of Effectual Calling and Grace in a Calvinist Soteriology," in *The Grace of God the Bondage of the Will*, vol. 2, eds. Thomas Schreiner and Bruce Ware (Grand Rapids: Baker Books, 1995), 349.

10. D. A. Carson, *Divine Sovereignty and Human Responsibility* (Eugene, OR: Wipf and Stock, 1994), 167.

of all meaningful belief and love expression? In concert with both the broader corpus of the Bible and Koran, John envisions humans as the proper objects of divine imperatives to make morally responsible choices (3:36; 12:24–26; 7:37; 13:18; 14:15; 15:10; cf. Deut 30:19; Surah 108:2).

Is the scope of divine power diminished by John's emphasis on human responsibility? On the contrary, John emphasizes the determinative scope of divine power in the origination of the human choice to believe. John predicates the believer's coming on the Father's prior giving, giving the text a "frankly predestinarian."[11] The logic of v. 37 is that the entire group (πᾶν: neuter singular) of the Father-given will be Son-believing. The Father's *giving* (ὃ δίδωσιν) is in the present tense while people's *coming* (ἥξει) appears in the future tense, indicating that being given to the Son by the Father is the basis of coming to the Son by the people. V. 37 is grammatically equivalent to the statement: "All whom the governor *pardons* (pres.), *will enjoy* (fut.) freedom from death row." The governor's pardoning is the basis of the prisoner's enjoyment, just as the Father's giving is the basis of the believer's coming. This present-tense-plus-future-tense-verb grammatical structure occurs in other Johannine contexts with the same implication (John 16:13; cf. 14:15). The foregoing factors warrant the conclusion that people do not believe to *become* love-gifts within the Johannine *ordo amoris*, but believe *because* they are love-gifts, amplifying the predestinarian ring.

JOA4: *Missional Unifying*. Pre-cosmic loving motivates intra-Trinitarian-giving, which in turn leads to the morally responsible coming, ushering us into the fourth stage of the Johannine *ordo amoris*—missional unifying. This forms the crux of Jesus' prayer for His love-gift in John 17:20–23. Jesus' prays for all future believers (v. 20)—specifically, for their "oneness." Recent evidence from the Dead Sea Scrolls has revealed that "oneness" or "the unity" (*yahad*) had been adopted as a

---

11. D. A. Carson, *The Gospel According to John* (Grand Rapids: Eerdmans, 1991), 290.

self-designation by the Qumran community prior to John's composition. The title appears "some 70 times in 1QS alone,"[12] and expresses the Qumran belief in their special communion with angels and allied separation from the corrupt *zeitgeist* of Roman culture.

While there is some conceptual overlap, the unity requested in John 17:22 is of far more profound pedigree than angelic union. The love that existed "before the world's foundation" (v. 26) is the supernatural reality in which the requested unity of believers subsists. This unity is less about Qumranian separation *from* the world and more about Christological mission *to* the world.

What is the precise nature of this unity? Brown observes that "sooner or later most authors say that it is a union of love," and cites Käsemann: "We usually bypass the question at this point with edifying language by reducing unity to what we call love."[13] What more may be said about the "union of love"? The term ἀγάπη and its cognate verb ἀγαπάω are not determinative[14] as John's Gospel occasionally uses φιλέω interchangeably with ἀγαπάω when describing the Father's love for the Son (John 3:35; 5:20; 17:26). The contextual clues inherent to Jesus' prayer itself, therefore, are a more enlightening path toward clarifying the nature of the "union of love" that Jesus requests for His believers. I offer three contextual observations:

1. *The "union of love" requested by Jesus for His love-gifts is itself an extension of the pre-cosmic intimacy between Father and Son.* The prayer of John 17 hinges on a distinction between what may be dubbed "original ἀγάπη," the love expressed between Father and Son *before* the world (i.e., πρὸ καταβολῆς κόσμου—v. 26), and the "expanded ἀγάπη," which Jesus requests for believers. The "original ἀγάπη" of John 17 is defined in terms of the mutual indwelling of the Father in the Son and

---

12. Raymond Brown, *The Gospel According to John XIII-XXI*, The Anchor Bible, vol. 29A (New York: Doubleday, 1970), 777.

13. Brown, *The Gospel According to John*, 776.

14. See Robert Jolly, *Le vocabulaire chretien de l'amour est-il original? Phlein et Agapen dans le grec antique* (Bruxelles: Presses Universitaires, 1968).

Son in the Father (v. 21), with the expanded ἀγάπη defined in terms of the Father-indwelt Son indwelling the believers (v. 23a; cf. v. 26b). This transitive indwelling of Father-in-Son and Son-in-believers ("I in them and you in me"—v. 23a) brings about the miraculous inclusion of believers into the very love union enjoyed before creation within the Trinity. This transitive indwelling generates a bond of such profound intimacy that the original ἀγάπη of the Father for the Son is itself realized "in them," i.e., believers (v. 26b), thereby synthesizing the original and expanded ἀγάπη.

This synthesis casts the moral responsibility of the love-gift in a new light. The *summum bonum* of the believers' moral responsibility throughout the Johannine corpus is captured in the recurrent imperatives to love God and others (13:34; 14:15–21, 23–24; 15:9–17). Obedience to the love imperative forms the litmus test of those who are God-indwelt (1 John 4:12). Thus, the believer's moral responsibility is not "love, because God says so" as if the command is understood along the arbitrary lines of a theological voluntarism. Rather, the moral responsibility of the believer is to love, because obedience to the love imperative expresses the very nature of the Triune God who "is love" (1 John 4:8b), the God who has loved before the creation of the cosmos (17:26), and who expands that love in the love-gift He indwells (17:24). The believers' moral responsibility is therefore best understood from the Johannine perspective as active participation in the divine social nexus, a "union of love" in which they become "so identified with God and dependent upon Him for life and fruitfulness, that they themselves become the locus of the Father's life and work *in them*."[15]

2. *The "union of love" is something actualized by God's power and expressed in the human will.* John does not trace the genesis of the union of love to human willpower but to divine activity pouring forth from the original ἀγάπη. This is evidenced by the fact that Jesus is *praying* for

---

15. D. A. Carson, *The Gospel According to John*, 568.

oneness in John 17, i.e., appealing to His Father's power for the expansion of Triune love into the realm of human expression. The prayer is meaningless unless it lies within the scope of divine power to cause the love eternally enjoyed between Father and Son to become a visible reality within believers, not by trampling the human will, but by effectually reorienting our wills in love. Brown echoes,

> Any approach that places the essence of unity in the solidarity of human endeavor is not really faithful to John's insistence that unity has its origins in divine action. The very fact that Jesus prays to the Father for this unity indicates that the key to it lies within God's power. ... None of this need imply passivity on the part of the believers in the question of unity, but their action is not the primary source of unity.[16]

In line with Brown's insight, we must balance the fact that Jesus' prayer for the extension of intra-Trinitarian love occurs in the farewell discourses of John's Gospel where Jesus has repeatedly confronted His disciples with the imperative to love God and one another (13:34; 14:15–21, 23–24; 15:9–17). Jesus *both* commands love to His disciples, *and* prays to His Father for that commanded love to become a reality in His disciples. There is a profound interface of human responsibility and divine power here: As we seek to obey the love imperative we recognize that all relational success finds its deepest source in the Father's power to answer His beloved Son's request for our oneness.

3. *The "union of love" is to be a missional community in that it converges with Jesus' mission to expose His supernatural identity to the world.* John 17:21 and 17:23 clarify the purpose of the unification of the love-gift with parallel ἵνα clauses: "*In order that* (ἵνα) the world may believe that you sent me" (v. 21) and "*In order that* (ἵνα) the world may come to know that you sent me" (v. 23). As believers share in the oneness between Father and Son (vv. 21a, 22b–23a), they come to echo the

---

16. Brown, *The Gospel According to John*, 776.

challenge that Jesus issued to the world in His claim to be one with the Father—the challenge to recognize messianic identity of the Son (v. 21b) and the tremendous scope of the Father's love (v. 23b). Thus as the "union of love" becomes progressively realized within them, the love-gift is swept into active participation in God's own mission to the world.

JOA5: *Eschatological Raising Up.* The final step in the Johannine *ordo amoris* is eschatological, captured in the mutual will fulfillment between Father and Son for the glorification of the love-gift. John 6:39 clarifies the Father's will: "And this is the will of him who sent me, that I shall lose none of all that he has given me, but raise them up at the last day" (cf. v. 40). That Jesus could fail in the execution of His beloved Father's will lies utterly beyond the scope of possibility in the logic of John's Gospel. If the cumulative sum of the love gift (*pan*—v. 39) does not reach the Father's expressed goal of resurrected glory, then "it would be to the Son's everlasting shame: it would mean either than he was incapable of performing what the Father willed him to do, or that he was flagrantly disobedient to His Father. Both alternatives are unthinkable."[17]

John 6:44 reinforces this point by positing a strong identity relation between being drawn by the Father and raised up by the Son: "No one can come to me unless to Father who sent me draws Him, and I will raise Him up on the last day." "The identity of those raised up on the last day to eternal life *is absolutely co-extensive* with the identity of those who are drawn."[18] Jesus cannot fail in fulfilling His Father's will that the fifth stage of the *ordo amoris* will be realized for all those drawn by the Father. The assurance that the divinely exchanged love gift will be "raised up at the last day" rests on the omnicompetence of the Son to obey His Father's will. Moreover, the Son's obedience

---

17. D. A. Carson, *The Gospel According to John*, 291.

18. James White, *The Potter's Freedom* (Amityville, NY: Calvary Press Publishing, 2000), 160, emphasis in original.

to the Father is, in the Fourth Gospel, a means through which Jesus expresses His love for the Father (14:31; 15:10). The eschatological destiny of the love gift therefore rests on the strength of the Intra-Trinitarian love bond.

This is further supported by Jesus expression of His own will: "Father, I want those you have given me to be with me where I am, and to see my glory" (17:24a). The Father's will (τὸ θέλημα—6:39) and the Son's will (θέλω—17:24) converge in the desire for the glorification of the love-gift. Thus, the believers' destiny is anchored in God's power, which again is expressed in terms of the intra-Trinitarian love bond, specifically in this context, as mutual fulfillment of the will of the divine Other. The Johannine *ordo amoris* culminates with the love gift ushered into eternal future enjoyment (JOA5) of God's relational glory (v. 24), which itself stretches to eternity past (JOA1). Interpersonal love, from John's perspective, is therefore without beginning or end.

In light of the foregoing analysis, I conclude that from the Johannine perspective divine power and human responsibility cannot be properly understood apart from the eternal Father-Son love relationship. The *giving* of a love-gift (JOA2), the inevitability of the love-gift's morally responsible *coming* (JOA3), their *unifying* into a missional community (JOA4), and their being *raising up* on the last day (JOA5), all flow from the love the pre-cosmic love within the one God between Father and Son (JOA1).

A THEOLOGICAL AND EXISTENTIAL POINT OF CONTRAST

At what point then does the picture of divine power in Sunni orthodoxy diverge from a Reformed theology that integrates the Johannine *ordo amoris*? I have argued that divine love within the Trinity underlies divine power (at least insofar as divine power is exercised in the *ordo amoris*). In Sunni thought, by contrast, divine power is not exercised by a Triune God, but by Allah above all multiplicity (*ahad*), a single being in whom no interpersonal distinctions exist.

Both traditions envision predestination as a divine act that precedes the creation of the cosmos (*khalaqa*). In Reformed thinking, predestination originates from one God subsisting in a state of interpersonal love between Father and Son prior to the actualization of all created agents. God predestines as *socium et condilectum* ("an ally and one fellow loved," per Richard of St. Victor). Shedd expounds,

> Here is society within the Essence, and wholly independent of the universe; and communion and blessedness resulting therefrom. But this is impossible to an essence without personal distinctions. Not the singular Unit of the deist, but the plural Unity of the Trinitarian explains this. A subject without an object ... could not love? What is there to be loved?

In Sunni thinking, by contrast, Allah decrees the future (*Al-Lawh Al-Mahfudh*) while existing in a state of *ahad*, above all multiplicity and prior to the actualization of created agents. While a being in *ahad* may express self-love and perhaps even prescience-based love for yet-to-be-actualized creatures, it is not clear how *actual, inter-personal* love could be experienced by a being devoid of interpersonal distinctions while engaging in the divine act of predestination. A non-Triune God seems confined before creation to love-of-self and love-of-the-abstract other. And so a critical (and friendly) question emerges: How could the divine power of predestination (*taqdir*) be a fundamentally *loving* act if it originates from a being who is not engaged in actual, inter-personal love?

I conclude that a fundamental distinction exists between predestination as an act of one God eternally engaged in inter-personal love and *taqdir* as an act of one God without other persons to love before creation. I expand this conclusion with a reflection on how this theological point of departure might alter the ways in which Muslims and Christians seek to fulfill their religious duties. From the account I have sketched in part 2 it was clarified that the eschatological destiny of the love-gift rests on the mutual will-fulfillment of Father and Son for their glorification (JOA5).

From this religious paradigm, the believers' destiny rests on something sturdier than our suspect and profoundly defective ability to obey divine imperatives. Rather the believers' destiny rests on the dual omnicompetence of the Son to carry out His beloved Father's will (John 6:39) and the Father to carry out His beloved Son's will (17:24). This dual omnicompetence ushers believers into and preserves them within a state of obedience to the love imperative. With pre-cosmic love expressed as divine power, and divine power expressed as mutual will-fulfillment for the believers' glorification, the existential contours of religious experience are altered. Believers come to obey divine imperatives less from a fear-based motivation to *become* an object of divine favor (with all the unnerving uncertainty such a religious quest entails), and more from a gratitude-based motivation *because* one is already an object of divine favor secured by the strength of the Intra-Trinitarian love bond (with all the assurance this entails). Thus John could write, "so that you may *know* that you have eternal life" (1 John 5:13; emphasis added).

This "knowing" stands in contrast with streams in Islamic thought in which there is a discernable absence of assurance of one's eschatological destination relative to Allah's judgment. According to the Hadith, "The Prophet said, 'By Allah, even though I am an Apostle of Allah, yet I do not know what Allah will do to me' " (al-Bukhari vol. 5, no. 266; cf. vol. 2, no. 167). Al-Ghazzali expounds in *The Foundations of Islamic Belief,*

> The fear of the end, for no one knows whether or not he will still have belief at the hour of death. If he should end with unbelief all his previous works will come to naught and fail because [the value of these works] depends entirely upon a good ending.

The relational paradigm through which I have analyzed divine power and human responsibility moves beyond "fear" to an obedience that flows from a thankful assurance that: "All those drawn by the Father will be raised up by the Son" (6:44).

Appendix B

Is God Vulnerable?

Evaluating Vincent Brümmer's Notion of Autonomy[1]

THE TWOFOLD STRUCTURE
OF AUTONOMY

As chromosomes are composed of DNA strands, we may ask: What are the "DNA strands" within Brümmer's chromosomal doctrine of autonomy? In *The Model of Love,* Brümmer posits "two-way ability" as a necessary condition of autonomy:

> Since choice is always between alternative courses of action, doing something out of choice entails the two-way ability to do both what one chooses to do and to act otherwise as well. For this reason freedom of choice is incompatible with

---

1. In June 2011 I had the privilege of debating Professor Brümmer on autonomy and divine vulnerability at the Vrije Universiteit of Amsterdam. This essay grew from reflections on that debate and was originally published in *Nederduitse Gereformeerde Teologiese Tydskrif* 53, no. 3 (2012): 228–238.

determinism: one cannot choose to do the unavoidable since the unavoidable leaves no alternative but to do it.[2]

Brümmer clarifies his notion of autonomy as a form of indeterminism, or a "libertarian" view of free will. In the libertarian view of free will as spelled out by Brümmer (along with ancient Greek philosophers and many contemporary theologians[3]), an agent has an irreducible power to act as a first-mover to perform or refrain from performing a given action. If we lose this "two-way ability" (or what has been branded "the ability to do otherwise," "the power of contrary choice," or Harry Frankfurt's technical term, "the Principle of Alternate Possibilities"), then we are no longer "autonomous" in Brümmer's meaning of the term.[4]

To "two-way ability" Brümmer adds a second strand in his doctrine of autonomy. He posits autonomy as a necessary condition of meaningful love relationships. He illustrates this with lyrics from the song "Paper Doll":

I'm goin' to buy a paper doll that I can call my own,
A doll that other fellows cannot steal.
And then those flirty flirty guys
With their flirty flirty eyes
Will have to flirt with dollies that are real.
When I come home at night she will be waiting.
She'll be the truest doll in all the world.
I'd rather have a paper doll to call my own
Than have a fickle-minded real live girl.

---

2. Vincent Brümmer, *The Model of Love: A Study in Philosophical Theology* (Cambridge: Cambridge University Press, 1993), 45.

3. For an extensive bibliography of libertarian free will in Hellenistic thought and contemporary analysis see 1.1 of the current work.

4. Harry Frankfurt, "Alternate Possibilities and Moral Responsibility," *The Journal of Philosophy* 66 (1969), 829. A small handful of contemporary libertarians have broken with the mainstream libertarian view by denying PAP as a necessary condition for freedom. See David Hunt, "Moral Responsibility and Buffered Alternatives" in *Free Will and Moral Responsibility*, eds. Peter French and Howard Wettstein (Blackwell, 2005), 126–45.

Brümmer observes,

> Far from being a love song, this is a lament on the absence of
> love. In the words of Sartre: If the beloved is transformed into
> an automaton, the lover finds himself alone—alone with his
> paper doll. It is clear that a relationship of love can only be
> maintained as long as the personal integrity and free autonomy
> of *both* partners is upheld.[5]

Brümmer defines autonomy as the antithesis of coercion. An agent
is either autonomous or coercively reduced to an "automaton," and
automatons do not make good lovers. While other DNA strands exist
in Brümmer's chromosomal doctrine of autonomy,[6] these two strands—
autonomy as a "two-way ability" that forms a necessary condition
for a "relationship of love"—form the focus of the present analysis.

What shaping effect does this twofold structure of autonomy have
on Brümmer's theology? How might it "color" his understanding of
God as a relationship seeker? Says Brümmer:

> Since love is a reciprocal relation, God is also dependent on
> the freedom and responsibility of human persons in order to
> enter into a loving relation with them. ... Nevertheless, in cre-
> ating human persons in order to love them God necessarily
> assumes vulnerability in relation to them.[7]

There is an inescapable element of risk for *anyone* seeking "a relationship of love" with autonomous agents, the risk that their active "two-
way ability" will choose *against* the relationship. Brümmer is far from
alone in his contention that love requires autonomy and autonomy
requires vulnerability, *even for God*. This contention is behind John

---

5. Brümmer, *The Model of Love*, 161. Emphasis in original.

6. A third DNA strand in Brümmer's notion of autonomy (and one that lies beyond the
scope of this study), is autonomy as a *divine gift* (See *The Model of Love*, 162–63). In viewing
autonomy as a divine gift, Brümmer aligns himself with long-standing traditions in Hellenistic
philosophy (See Williams, *Love, Freedom, and Evil*, 17nn41–42).

7. Brümmer, *The Model of Love*, 162–63.

Sanders' "God Who Risks,"[8] Geddes MacGregor's theory of divine *kenosis* in which God's love "*is* the abdication of power,"[9] and Simone Weil's view of creation as an act of divine "abandonment" to make room for our "free and autonomous existence."[10] Brümmer adds:

> If God did not grant us the ability to sin and cause affliction to him and to one another, we would not have the kind of free and autonomous existence necessary to enter into a relation of love with God and with one another.[11]

Why does autonomy as a chromosomal doctrine manifest so consistently as what may be called the "trait doctrine" of divine vulnerability? An answer can be found by positing a scenario in which autonomy functions chromosomally *without* manifesting the trait doctrine of divine vulnerability. The theologian could simply deny that God seeks "a relationship of love" with his creatures. The relationally disengaged deity of Epicurus, Voltaire, and other deists could remain absolutely *invulnerable* before his autonomous creatures to the extent that he is apathetic about relating with them. Such a blocking mechanism is, of course, not present in any Christian system. Any Christian system must reckon with the reality of a God who *is* love and who uniquely (and even painfully) demonstrates His love in the person and work of Jesus. Once Brümmer's twofold notion of autonomy operates at the chromosomal level of a theology, the theologian *must* embrace some doctrine of divine vulnerability if he seeks to understand God as a God of love.

---

8. See John Sanders, *The God Who Risks: A Theology of Providence* (Downers Grove, IL: InterVarsity Press, 1998).

9. See Geddes MacGregor, *He Who Lets Us Be: A Theology of Love* (New York: The Seabury Press, 1975), 333.

10. Simone Weil, *Gateway to God* (London: Fontana Press, 1974), 80.

11. Brümmer, *The Model of Love*, 163.

THE RELATIVITY OF AUTONOMY

Many biblical passages seem difficult to square with a doctrine of divine vulnerability. The God of Isaiah 46:10 says, "My counsel shall stand, and I will accomplish all my purpose." Job says of God, "I know that you can do all things, and that no purpose of yours can be thwarted" (Job 42:2). The psalmist sings to a God who "does all that he pleases" (Ps 115:3), and Paul worshiped a God who "works all things according to the counsel of his will" (Eph 1:11). Such passages about a seemingly *invulnerable* God ought to open us to ask: Is it possible for humans to be autonomous and God to be loving, without requiring that He "necessarily assumes vulnerability"?[12]

On Brümmer's twofold view of autonomy, no such possibility is open. Since Brümmer's autonomy requires "two-way ability," we must have the power to resist all of God's pursuits for our hearts, and God "*necessarily* assumes vulnerability in relation to [us]" (emphasis added). Are other accounts of "autonomy" available to the Christian theologian that do not lead "necessarily" to divine vulnerability? To approach this question and to further clarify Brümmer's perspective, we must recognize the relativity of the term autonomy (and its synonym "freedom"). "Autonomy" and "freedom" (which I am using interchangeably) are abstract nouns seeking a concrete object bridged by the preposition "from." An agent can have freedom *from* a debilitating disease (often expressed shorthand as "health"), freedom *from* work (expressed shorthand as "vacation"), freedom *from* parental control (expressed shorthand as "college"), or freedom from the luxury of doing things your own way (expressed shorthand as "marriage"). Robust accounts of freedom require us to specify what precisely the agent is free *from*. It is this vast relativity of freedom, an abstract noun that can be linked by the preposition "from" to such a diverse range of objects that gives the notion its perennial and pan-cultural appeal.

---

12. Affirming the invulnerability of God is compatible with a God who genuinely grieves at His creatures' self-destructive choices. See 2.2 of the current work.

"Freedom from x" in the above contexts is synonymous with the first strand of Brümmer's notion of autonomy, namely, "two-way ability." Freedom can be expressed formally as:

> Some agent, Jones, has freedom from some object, X, to do some action, A, if relative to the cumulative causal powers of X, Jones can still choose A or refrain from choosing A.

We can apply this formula to Brümmer's notion of autonomy by stipulating X in four distinct ways:

1. Some agent, Jones, has freedom from [the Machine] to do some action, A, if relative to the cumulative causal powers of *the physical world*, Jones can still choose A or refrain from choosing A.

2. Some agent, Jones, has freedom from [the Gunman] to do some action, A, if relative to the cumulative causal powers of *coercive persons*, Jones can still choose A or refrain from choosing A.

3. Some agent, Jones, has freedom from [the Heart] to do some action, A, if relative to the cumulative causal powers of *his internal character propensities*, Jones can still choose A or refrain from choosing A.

4. Some agent, Jones, has freedom from [the Reformer] to do some action, A, if relative to the cumulative causal powers of *divine action*, Jones can still choose A or refrain from choosing A.

Failing to specify "two-way ability" with these relative clauses may cause us to overlook significant ways in which an agent can be simultaneously free and not free with regard to the same action. Consider a case in which a friend offers Jones a mug of ale. It is *logically possible* for Jones to have Freedom from the Machine, the Gunman, and the Reformer, while lacking Freedom from the Heart. Relative to the physical world, coercive persons, and divine action, Jones can drink or refrain from drinking. He is free insofar as mechanistic physical factors do not determine him to drink. He is free insofar as his friend does not hold him at gunpoint forcing him to drink. He is free insofar as God has not predestined him to drink. It is possible for those three freedoms to be co-exemplified, while simultaneously Jones' internal character propensities are such that he cannot refrain from the mug of ale. Perhaps the beliefs, desires, and aversions that form his "Heart" leave Jones no alternative but to drink.

Would Jones still have "freedom" in such a scenario? Recall Brümmer's claim that "freedom of choice is incompatible with determinism: one cannot choose to do the unavoidable since the unavoidable leaves no alternative but to do it."[13] Jones does not meet Brümmer's libertarian conditions of freedom. However, this conclusion overlooks significant ways in which Jones *is* free with regard to drinking the offered ale. Perhaps Jones has had his head filled at the university with Jacques Monod's *Chance and Necessity* in which "man is a machine."[14] Perhaps he has rationalized hurtful moral patterns in his life with the view that, as a biological robot, he just cannot help it. Jones' Freedom from the Machine is significant to the extent that he can take responsibility for his actions and is no longer reduced to "a digestive tube" (Pierre Cabanis), "a being purely physical" (Paul d'Holbach), "a bulb with thousands of roots" (G. C. Lichtenberg), "a package of tepid, half-rotted viscera" (Louis Ferdinand Celine), or "just an aggregate of trillions of cells" (Jean Ronstand). Such Freedom is highly significant, *even if Jones lacks Freedom from the Heart.*

Or perhaps Jones was raised in an authoritarian, prohibitionist home. Being offered ale where he can express his heart's strongest desires without any Gunmen forcing him to refrain is a significant freedom *regardless of whether or not he can choose contrary to his strongest desires.* Indeed, Freedom from the Gunman is highly significant to

---

13. Brümmer, *The Model of Love*, 45.

14. Jacques Monod, *Chance and Necessity* (New York: Vintage Books, 1972), 180.

slaves or citizens living under tyrants. Such freedom is so significant that many are willing to have their own blood shed in resistance to Gunmen. They do not pay the ultimate price for Freedom from the Heart—two-way ability *relative to their own desires*—but for Freedom from the Gunman—two-way ability to express their own desires *relative to coercive authorities*.

On this relative analysis of freedom, the answer to whether Jones is free is both "yes" and "no." Yes, Jones has Freedom from the Machine, the Gunman, and the Reformer since the causal forces of the physical world, coercive agents, and divine action leave room for Jones to exercise two-way ability. On the other hand, we may consistently answer "no," given Jones' lack of two-way ability relative to his own Heart. On this relative view, it is logically possible for both determinism and indeterminism to hold true in a single agent with regard to the same action. This compatibility can be seen in the fact that the two claims below do not entail a logical contradiction:

C1: Jones *necessarily* drinks the ale *relative to his own heart*.

C2: Jones *freely* drinks the ale *relative to the physical world, coercive agents*, and *divine action*.

The advocate of libertarian free will has two foreseeable moves at this point. First, he could argue that C1 and C2 do entail a logical contradiction. Yet the logical contradiction only emerges if we strip C1 and C2 of their relative clauses. A more promising libertarian response would be to accept C1 and C2 as logically consistent, but deny that, *on the whole*, Jones is significantly free. This response can be seen in the words of libertarian, Clark Pinnock:

> It is not enough to say that a free choice is one which, while not externally compelled, is nonetheless determined by the psychological state of the agent's brain or the nature of the agent's desiring. To say that Harry stole the candy bars because he wanted them is obvious—the question is, could he have

refrained from stealing them in spite of his desire? The idea
of moral responsibility requires us to believe that actions are
not determined either internally or externally.[15]

Pinnock clarifies that a libertarian account of "two-way ability"
requires more than mere Freedom from the Machine, the Gunman,
and the Reformer. It requires the agent to also exercise Freedom
from the Heart. "Harry" only freely steals candy bars if "he could
have refrained from stealing them in spite of his desire." Given these
requirements, we can see why the libertarian would not consider
Jones significantly free when offered ale. Since his heart leaves him
no alternative but to drink, Jones cannot be considered a significantly free agent. A libertarian understanding of "two-way ability"
(the first strand in Brümmer's notion of autonomy) *entails* Freedom
from the Heart.

"TWO-WAY ABILITY" AND
TOO MUCH AUTONOMY

Returning to our genetic metaphor, chromosomes are made up of
DNA strands, which are themselves composed of four base sequences
(a particular arrangement of adenine, guanine, cytosine, and thymi-
nen, or A-G-C-T). We can detect a similar four base sequence in the
"two-way ability" strand of Brümmer's notion of autonomy. Because
"freedom of choice is incompatible with determinism,"[16] Brümmer's
strand of "two-way ability" requires *all four* freedoms above (e.g., if
Jones only has Freedom from the Machine, the Gunman, and the
Reformer, but lacks Freedom from the Heart, then Jones is determined
and, thus, lacks "freedom of choice"). Brümmer's "two-way ability"

15. Clark Pinnock, "God Limits His Knowledge," in *Predestination and Free Will: Four
Views of Divine Sovereignty and Human Responsibility*, eds. David Basinger and Randall Basinger
(Downers Grove, IL: InterVarsity, 1986), 149. For similar libertarian accounts see Robert Kane,
Free Will and Values (Albany: State University of New York Press, 1985), 53; and J. P. Moreland
and Scott Rae, *Body & Soul* (Downers Grove, IL: InterVarsity, 2000), 126.

16. Brümmer, *The Model of Love*, 45.

strand may be pictured as an M-G-H-R sequence (Freedom from the Machine, Gunman, Heart, and Reformer). In the remainder of this analysis, I argue that the Freedom from the Heart and the Reformer (i.e., the H and R in his Brümmer's strand of "two-way ability") carry significant problems. I will argue that a M-G sequence ("two-way ability" understood as Freedom from the Machine and the Gunman, but *not* Freedom from the Heart and Reformer) affords us with an alternative notion of autonomy that does not generate such problems.

I begin with the H-base in Brümmer's sequencing of "two-way ability." Upon closer look, Freedom from the Heart seems to leave the agent autonomous not only from forces *outside himself* but also from those *within himself* in a problematic way. To illustrate the problem let us grant Jones Freedom from the Heart. Jones' friend offers the mug, at which point Jones' "self" (with all of its desires for ale, his aversions to thirst, his propensities for merrymaking, his deliberations about wanting to unwind after a long day at the office) begins to culminate as a pro-ale choice. If these internal factors *determine* Jones to reach for the mug, then he no longer possesses Freedom from the Heart (and cannot be autonomous in Brümmer's sense of the term). Jones must remain autonomous enough from that "self" to resist its pro-ale push.

Suppose that this "deeper self"[17]—the Jones who remains autonomous enough to resist the push of pro-ale Jones—does, in fact, choose to go along with the desires of pro-ale Jones. Did this autonomous Jones himself have desires that were in favor of pro-ale Jones? Was autonomous Jones himself *pro* (in favor of) pro-ale Jones? If not, then why, from such a state of indifference, did autonomous Jones go along with pro-ale Jones? If so, then Freedom from the Heart requires us to posit a still-more-autonomous Jones who can resist the push of this pro pro-ale Jones. Where the story goes from here is predictable. We are left with either a Jones who is truly autonomous from all desires, who is *pro-nothing* and, thereby, profoundly indifferent, or a Jones

---

17. See Susan Wolf, *Freedom within Reason* (New York: Oxford University Press, 1990), 14.

who is pro-pro-pro-pro, *ad infinitum*. Neither agent seems to be a prime candidate for making significantly free choices.[18]

Gottfried Leibniz and Harry Frankfurt clarify this critique of Freedom from the Heart. Leibniz illustrates Freedom from the Heart as follows:

> One will have it that the will alone is active and supreme, and one is wont to imagine it to be like a queen seated on her throne, whose minister of state is the understanding, while the passion are her courtiers or favourite ladies. … [The queen] can vacillate between the arguments of the ministers and the suggestions of her favourites, even rejecting both, making them keep silence or speak, and giving them audience as it seems good to her.[19]

We may add detail to this Leibnizian picture with Frankfurt's distinction between first and higher-order desires,[20] and reach the following scenario: Suppose we place Jones on the throne. A first-order desire—the desire to drink the offered ale—makes a case from King Jones' courtyard. If the King uses his active power to royally endorse this first-order desire, then he either desires to choose the first-order desire or he does not. If not, then King Jones is indifferent toward his courtiers that beckon him to drink. If, on the other hand, he *does* desire to choose this first-order desire, then Brümmer's notion of "two-way ability" demands that this second-order desire is itself resistible. For this second-order desire to be resistible, King Jones must preside over it in such a way that he may royally endorse or reject it. Thus, the second-order desire moves outside of King Jones

---

18. The libertarian may reply that Jones may still choose *for* a desire. However, there is a qualitative difference between *desirously choosing* and *desirelessly choosing for a desire*. In the first case, precluded by libertarianism, the desire is an intrinsic property of the agent. In the second case, the desire does not enter into the agent's innermost nexus of active power, and we are left with an indifferent agent.

19. Leibniz, *Theodicy*, tr. E. M. Huggard (LaSalle, IL: Open Court, [1710] 1985), 421.

20. See Harry Frankfurt, "Freedom of the Will and the Concept of a Person," in *Free Will*, 2nd ed., ed. Gary Watson (Oxford: Oxford University Press, 2003), 81–95.

the choice-maker, and into the courtyard with all other desires. If he chooses in favor of that second-order desire, then he either desires that second-order desire or he does not. If not, then we have slipped back into indifference. If so, then that third-order desire must be resistible (in which case it joins ranks with all other desires in the courtyard).

This tiresome story forces us into a dilemma in which either:

1. King Jones desirelessly (i.e., indifferently) chooses to royally endorse the first-order desire to drink.

Or:

2. King Jones faces the impossible task of royally endorsing an infinite amount of higher-order desires.

Libertarians have opted for the first option. This explains why libertarians throughout history (e.g., Schopenhauer in his *Prize Essay*, Descartes in his *Meditations*, and Melabranche in his *Search After Truth*) have used the term "indifference" to describe their views. Although most contemporary libertarians jettison this term, Brümmer aligns himself with historic libertarians when he affirms that " 'liberty of indifference' ... should be taken as specifying a necessary condition for an adequate concept of moral freedom."[21]

What happens, however, if we remove Freedom from the Heart from our concept of two-way ability? In this case, we can retain the agent's two-way ability relative to the Machine and the Gunman, but are no longer driven to the conclusion of an indifferent agent.[22] The case for removing Freedom from the Heart from our understanding of two-way ability becomes more compelling when seen in relation to Brümmer's second strand of autonomy—autonomy as a condition for "a relationship of love." If autonomy requires Freedom from the

---

21. Brümmer, *The Model of Love*, 45n7.

22. We can add that indifferent agents bear little resemblance to the moral agents we meet in the Bible. See 1.3 of the current work.

Heart, and Freedom from the Heart, in turn, leads to an indifferent agent, then we face a problem in this second strand. Indifference becomes *a necessary condition* of love. Yet, as I argue elsewhere, "being a lover entails a desire for the welfare of the beloved." Brümmer concurs in seeing "a policy of commitment in relation to the beloved" as a distinguishing hallmark of love relations.[23] A lover can no more be indifferent toward his beloved's welfare than a Dodgers fan can be indifferent about the Dodgers' Major League Baseball record. An indifferent agent does not merit the title of "true lover."

To avoid the problem of indifference, let us consider Jones as a father who loves without Freedom of the Heart. If Jones loves his daughters, and yet his heart as a father is such that he cannot refrain from loving his daughters, would we dismiss such love as inauthentic? We cannot easily dismiss such love. Suppose by contrast that Jones' daughters craftily install some Artificial Affection hardware in his brain while he sleeps, a physical mechanism that *forces* him to exhibit love-behavior. The physical necessity and coercion in this scenario strip Jones of autonomy and his love of meaning. To the extent that Jones' daughters remove their father's Freedom from the Machine and Gunman, they find themselves alone with their paper dad.

Freedom from the Machine and the Gunman are essential components of the kind of autonomy that love requires. When we include Freedom from the Heart, however, agents become indifferent in a way that jeopardizes their ability to participate in meaningful love relationships. When we remove Freedom from the Heart, we have agents who can desire the welfare of their beloved while remaining autonomous in precisely the ways we want preserved in meaningful love relationships.

---

23. See 1.3 of the current work.

AUTONOMY AND DIVINE VULNERABILITY

I have offered a case for removing the problematic H-base from the "two-way ability" strand in a chromosomal notion of autonomy. I close with a deeper analysis of the R-base—Freedom from the Reformer as a condition of autonomy. Recall that Freedom from the Reformer expresses the agent's two-way ability *relative to all divine action*. We have seen that Brümmer's chromosomal doctrine of autonomy and his commitment to a God of love lead him to affirm a doctrine of divine vulnerability.

Consider God as He seeks a reciprocal love relationship with Jones. Is it possible for God to act so powerfully in Jones' heart that Jones *cannot* reject a relationship with God *while Jones remains meaningfully autonomous*? This does not represent a real possibility in Brümmer's theology and it is important to see why. For Brümmer, "It is still up to us as human agents to do God's will, and if we decide not to do so (in spite of being enlightened, enabled and motivated) then God's will is not done."[24] To preserve two-way ability in the Brümmer's sense, the agent must be able to resist all divine action.

Brümmer's emphasis on two-way ability relative to divine action can be clearly seen in the way he handles Anders Nygren's concept of divine *agape*. Brümmer argues that Nygren's God

> *causes* us to love him and each other. This seems to turn God into a kind of Heavenly Conquistador. ... Clearly such views take love to be a highly impersonal concept and the relationship of love to be a very impersonal manipulative one.[25]

The way in which Brümmer marshals support for his critique of Nygren's "highly impersonal concept" is revealing. Brümmer appeals to Jean-Paul Sartre's insight that "the man who wants to be loved does

---

24. Brümmer, *What Are We Doing When We Pray? On Prayer and the Nature of Faith*, 2nd ed. (Farnham: Ashgate Publishing, 2008), 77.

25. Brümmer, *The Model of Love*, 159–60. Emphasis in original.

not desire the enslavement of the beloved."[26] Brümmer then cites the lyrics of "Paper Doll" in which a man "laments" the "absence of love." It is revealing that both of these examples occur on the limited plane of human-to-human relations. Sartre, an atheist, is not offering commentary of human-divine relationships, and Johnny Black was not writing "Paper Doll" as a hymn about God's interpersonal abilities. Is it possible that a valid insight on the level of human-to-human relationships becomes fallacious when applied to human-divine relationships?

Jones helps us elaborate on this question. Suppose Jones seeks reciprocal love from a certain available damsel, Jane. Jane's autonomy entails Jones' vulnerability. All of Jones' attempts to woo Jane into a relationship cannot eliminate the risk that Jane will say "no" to the relationship. Jones cannot tolerate that risk. He sets himself to the task *determining* Jane to love him. What means of determination are at Jones' disposal? To guarantee his desired outcome, he can either abolish her Freedom from the Machine or her Freedom from the Gunman (or both). Of course, the moment Jones violates Jane's Freedom from the Machine or the Gunman, he ceases to love her as a person and reduces her to a paper doll. If Jones is unwilling to resort to such deterministic tactics, then he must come to terms with the vulnerability that inevitably follows from her autonomy.

Jones' limitation is our limitation. But is it possible that these limitations do not apply to God as He seeks relationships with His creatures? In approaching this question it is important to see that a God who, unlike us, can bring about love without reducing His lovers to dolls represents not only a possibility, but also an actuality in certain theologies. For Francis Turretin, God draws us into relationship with

strength [so] powerful that it may not be frustrated [yet so] sweet that it may not be forced. ... [God] so sweetly and at

---

26. Brümmer, *The Model of Love*, 160.

the same time powerfully affects the man that he cannot (thus called) help following [Him].[27]

In this theological system we are led not to an affirmation of "divine vulnerability" or to God as a "Heavenly Conquistador," but to a God whom Augustine describes as the "Delightful Conqueror."[28] What if God seeks reciprocal love from Jones in this system? In Turretin and Augustine's view, God is able to guarantee love from Jones in a way that Jones cannot guarantee love from Jane. God can effectively bring Jones to a point of love while sustaining Jones' Freedom from the Machine and the Gunman.

Indeed, for many people such a God is not merely theoretical, but the God who hears and answers their prayers.[29] As J. I. Packer observes,

> You pray for the conversion of others. ... I think that what you do is pray in categorical terms that God will, quite simply and decisively, save them: that He will open the eyes of their under-standing, soften their hard hearts, renew their natures, and move their wills to receive the Savior. ... You would not dream of making it a point in your prayer that you are not asking God actually to bring them to faith, because you recognize that that is something He cannot do. ... You entreat Him to do that very thing, and your confidence in asking rests upon the certainty

---

27. Francis Turretin, *Institutes of Elenctic Theology*, vol. 2, tr. George Musgrave Giger, ed. James Dennison (Phillipsburg, NJ: P&R Publishing, [1696] 1994), 521, 525.

28. Augustine, *On the Forgiveness of Sins and Baptism*, 2.32 (cited in Turretin, *Institutes of Elenctic Theology*, vol. 2, 524).

29. In the famous prayer of Saint Francis: "O Divine Master, grant that I may not so much seek to be loved, as to love." Thomas á Kempis likewise prayed, "Expand my heart with love, that I may feel its transforming power, and may even be dissolved in its holy fire! Let me be possessed by thy love, and ravished from myself" (*The Imitation of Christ*, tr. John Payne [Boston: Gould and Lincoln, 1856], 175–76, 177).

that He is able to do what you ask. ... On our feet we may
have arguments about it, but on our knees we are all agreed.[30]

Such prayers are offered neither on the premise of divine vulnerability
nor of divine coercion, but on the premise that God can effectively
cause us to love without reducing us to paper dolls.

With such prayers we see the need to draw a distinction between
Freedom from the Gunman and the Reformer. When creatures exert
human action to guarantee love from a fellow creature we become
Gunmen. Because we lack the direct access to and definitive authority over our fellow creatures' hearts, we can only eliminate our vulnerability in relation to them by resorting to coercive force. Prayer
assumes that God is not bound by this limitation. We would look
suspiciously at someone petitioning her fellow creatures to do something to guarantee another's love response. We do not share the same
suspicion toward someone who petitions her Creator to do something
that would guarantee another's love response.

This distinction we draw in our practice we must also draw in
our doctrine. It is precisely this distinction that seems missing in
Brümmer's doctrine of "autonomy." This can be seen in Brümmer's
assessment of the "Reformation theology" in which, "human beings
cannot be agents in relation to God [but] merely objects of divine
manipulation."[31] In so caricaturing Reformation theology, Brümmer
sees no middle ground between his theological system and an auton-
omy-abolishing system in which God acts as a divine manipulator.
Brümmer continues:

> God's agency is not coercive but enabling and motivating
> and therefore does not deny freedom, responsibility and per-
> sonal integrity of the human agent. ... [This is] a matter of

---

30. J. I. Packer, *Evangelism & the Sovereignty of God* (Downers Grove, IL: InterVarsity, 1961), 15–17.

31. Brümmer, *The Model of Love*, 189.

co-operation between two agents and not of one agent using the other as a tool.[32]

God is *either* "coercive" and we are mere "tools," *or* divine action is limited to "enabling and motivating" in which case we remain "agents." Brümmer does not see a God who effectively reforms human hearts without trampling our Freedom from the Machine and Gunman as even a *logical possibility*. From Brümmer's analysis it seems as if Augustine, Calvin, Turretin, Jonathan Edwards, and Abraham Kuyper (along with contemporary theologians like D. A. Carson, R. C. Sproul, and Michael Horton) have sought no *via media* between a vulnerable God and a coercive God. From Brümmer's analysis it seems as if there is no biblical evidence for a God who efficaciously draws sinners into love relationships while not obliterating but *enhancing* their freedom.[33]

The foregoing analysis of Brümmer's notion of autonomy helps us to see why he sees no such middle road. On the middle road of Reformation theology, the Creator-creature distinction allows that God can change hearts in ways that we cannot. In seeking to guarantee love from other agents, given our creaturely limitations, we can only become Gunmen, but never the Reformer. Our Creator, by contrast, can draw us irresistibly to love as the Reformer, but never as a Gunman. The salient distinction lies between whether the reciprocated love comes from the agent's heart as *a divinely reformed center of action expressing new supernatural desires now intrinsic to the agent,* or whether it comes from the circumvented heart as *a humanly coerced object expressing not the agent's own desires, but those externally imposed against the agent.* In the second case, the love becomes *less* authentic to the extent that human action coerces the heart. In the first case, the love becomes *more* authentic to the extent that divine action reforms the heart.

---

32. Brümmer, *What Are We Doing When We Pray?*, 75, 76.

33. For exegetical analysis see 3.2 of the current work.

Given the way in which Brümmer has inseparably sequenced Freedom from the Machine, the Gunman, the Heart, and the Reformer, the authenticity of such love cannot be granted. Such love can only be seen as authentic if we modify our chromosomal doctrine of autonomy from M-G-H-R to M-G. We must see agents as meaningfully autonomous when they enjoy Freedom from the Machine and Gunman while loving from an efficaciously Reformed Heart (as saints presumably love in heaven). If, however, we overlook the Creator-creature distinction in how we seek love,[34] then God's gracious and unique ability to reform our hearts without reducing us to dolls can only be seen as an act of "divine manipulation." In this case, the divine Reformer of Reformation theology will continue to be seen by those beyond that system as a Gunman (except, possibly, when they are "on their knees").

---

34. Brümmer does offer three ways that divine love differs from human love (*Atonement, Christology, and the Trinity: Making Sense of Christian Doctrines* [Farnham: Ashgate Publishing, 2005], 29–31). In light of this, my analysis served as a friendly appeal for him to recognize one more difference.

Bibliography

Ackerman, Robert. (1982). "An Alternative Free Will Defense." *Religious Studies* 19: 365–72.

Alston, William. (1996). "The Inductive Argument from Evil and the Human Cognitive Condition." In: Daniel Howard-Snyder (ed.). *The Evidential Argument from Evil*. Bloomington: Indiana University Press. Pp. 97–125.

——— (1996). "Some (Temporarily) Final Thoughts in Evidential Arguments from Evil." In: Daniel Howard-Snyder (ed.). *The Evidential Argument from Evil*. Bloomington: Indiana University Press. Pp. 311–32.

——— (2002). "What Euthyphro Should Have Said." In: William Lane Craig (ed.). *Philosophy of Religion: A Reader and Guide*. New Brunswick, NJ: Rutgers University Press. Pp. 283–98.

Anderson, Susan. (1981). "Plantinga and the Free Will Defense." In: *Pacific Philosophical Quarterly* 62: 274–81.

Anglin, W. S. (1990). *Free Will and the Christian Faith*. Oxford: Oxford University Press.

Aristotle. (1925). *The Works of Aristotle*. Vol. 9. W. D. Ross (ed.). Oxford: Clarendon.

Arminius, James (1986). *The Public Disputations of James Arminius, D. D. The Works of James Arminius: The London Edition*. Vol. 2. Tr. James and Williams Nichols. Grand Rapids: Baker Books.

Arnold, E. V. (1911). *Roman Stoicism*. Cambridge: Cambridge University Press.

Augustine. (1958). *The City of God*. Ed. Vernon Bourke. New York: Doubleday.

——— (1961). *Confessions*. Tr. R. S. Pine-Coffin. New York: Penguin.

——— (1980). *On Grace and Free-Will*. In: *The Nicene and Post-Nicene Fathers*. Vol. 5. Ed. Philip Schaff. Grand Rapids: Eerdmans.

——— (1980). *On Man's Perfection in Righteousness*. In: *The Nicene and Post-Nicene Fathers*. Vol. 5. Ed. Philip Schaff. Grand Rapids: Eerdmans.

——— (1980). *On the Grace of Christ*. In: *The Nicene and Post-Nicene Fathers*. Vol. 5. Ed. Philip Schaff. Grand Rapids: Eerdmans.

——— (1993). *On Free Choice of the Will*. Tr. Thomas Williams. Indianapolis: Hackett.

Bales, Kevin. (2000). *Disposable People: New Slavery in the Global Economy*. Berkeley: University of California Press.

Barker, Kenneth, and John Kohlenberger III (eds). (1994). *NIV Bible Commentary*. Vol. 2: *New Testament*. Grand Rapids: Zondervan.

Barnhart, Joe. (1977). "Theodicy and the Free Will Defense: Response to Plantinga and Flew." *Religious Studies* 13: 439–53.

Barrett, C. K. (1971). *The Gospel According to St. John*. Oxford: Oxford University Press.

——— (1974). *New Testament Essays*. London: SPCK.

Basinger, David. (1996). *The Case for Freewill Theism: A Philosophical Assessment*. Downers Grove: IL: InterVarsity Press.

Bavinck, Herman. (1951). *The Doctrine of God*. Tr. William Hendrickson. Grand Rapids: Eerdmans.

Beasley-Murray, George. (1987). *John*. Word Biblical Commentary. Vol. 36. Waco, TX: Word Publishing.

Bell, Rob. (2011). *Love Wins: A Book About Heaven, Hell, and the Fate of Every Person Who Ever Lived*. New York: HarperCollins e-books.

Berkhof, Louis. (1938). *Systematic Theology*. Grand Rapids: Eerdmans.

Blight, Richard. (1989). *An Exegetical Summary of 1 & 2 Thessalonians*. Dallas: Summer Institute of Linguistics, Inc.

Boyd, Gregory. (2000). *God of the Possible*. Grand Rapids: Baker Books.

———— (2001). *Satan and the Problem of Evil*. Downers Grove, IL: InterVarsity Press.

Brown, Raymond. (1970). *The Gospel According to John: XIII-XXI*. In The Anchor Bible. Vol. 29A. New York: Doubleday.

Bruce, F. F. (1951). *Acts of the Apostles: The Book of Acts.:* New London Commentary. Grand Rapids: Eerdmans.

Brueggemann, Walter. (2001). *Deuteronomy*. Nashville: Abingdon Press.

Brümmer, Vincent. (1993). *The Model of Love: A Study in Philosophical Theology*. Cambridge: Cambridge University Press.

———— (2004). "Ultimate Happiness and the Love of God." In: *Religion and the Good Life*. Marcel Sarot and Wessel Stoker (eds). Assen: Royal Van Gorcum.

———— (2005). *Atonement, Christology, and the Trinity: Making Sense of Christian Doctrines*. Farnham: Ashgate Publishing.

———— (2006). *Brümmer on Meaning and the Christian Faith: Collected Writings of Vincent Brümmer*. Farnham: Ashgate Publishing.

———— (2008). *What Are We Doing When We Pray? On Prayer and the Nature of Faith*. 2nd ed. Farnham: Ashgate Publishing.

Cairns, Ian. (1992). *Word and Presence: A Commentary on the Book of Deuteronomy*. Grand Rapids: Eerdmans.

Calvin, John. (1960). *Institutes of the Christian Religion*. Vol. 20. Tr. Ford Lewis Battles. Ed. John T. McNeill. Louisville: Westminster John Knox Press.

———— (1965). *The Epistles of Paul the Apostle to the Galatians, Ephesians, Philippians and Colossians*. Tr. T. H. L. Parker. Calvin's Commentaries. Ed. David Torrance and Thomas Torrance. Grand Rapids: Eerdmans.

———— (1979). *Commentary on the Gospel According to John*. Vol. 1. Tr. William Pringle. Grand Rapids: Baker Books.

Caneday, A. B. (2003). "Veiled Glory: God's Self-Revelation in Human Likeness—A Biblical Theology of God's Anthropomorphic Self-Disclosure." In: John Piper, Justin Taylor, and Paul Kjoss Helseth (eds). *Beyond the Bounds: Open Theism and the Undermining of Biblical Christianity*. Wheaton, IL: Crossway.

Carson, D. A. (1991). *The Gospel According to John*. Grand Rapids: Eerdmans.

———— (1994). *Divine Sovereignty & Human Responsibility: Biblical Perspectives in Tension*. Eugene, OR: Wipf and Stock.

Chadwick, H. (1981). *Boethius*, Oxford: Oxford University Press.

Charlesworth, J. H., Raymond Brown (1972). *John and Qumran*. London: Geoffrey Chapman Publishers.

Cicero. (1775). *Of the Nature of the Gods*. Tr. Pierre-Joseph Thoulier Olivet. London: T. Davies.

———— (1878) *On Fate*. In: *The Treatises of M. T. Cicero*. London: George Bell and Sons.

Ciocchi, David. (2001). Review: *Persons and Causes: The Metaphysics of Free Will."* In: *Philosophia Christi* 2: 266–70.

———— (2002). "The Religious Adequacy of Free Will Theism." *Religious Studies* 38: 45–61.

Clark, Gordon. (2004). *Religion, Reason, and Revelation*. In: *The Works of Gordon Clark*. Vol. 4. Unicoi, TN: The Trinity Foundation.

Clement of Alexandria. (1885). *The Instructor*. In: *Ante-Nicene Fathers*. Vol. 2. Ed. Alexander Roberts, James Donaldson, and Arthur Cleveland Coxe. Buffalo, NY: Christian Literature Company.

———— (1885). *Miscellanies*. In: *Ante-Nicene Fathers*. Vol. 2. Ed. Alexander Roberts, James Donaldson, and Arthur Cleveland Coxe. Buffalo, NY: Christian Literature Company.

Conzelmann, Hans. (1961). *Theology of St. Luke*. New York: HarperCollins.

———— (1987). *Acts of the Apostles*. Minneapolis: Fortress Press.

Copan, Paul. (2003). "Original Sin and Christian Philosophy," in *Philosophia Christi* 5: 519–41.

Craig, Edward. (ed.). (1998). *Routledge Encyclopedia of Philosophy*. New York: Taylor & Francis.

De Brès, Guido. (1903). "A Personal Letter to His Wife." In: *Bibliotheca Reformatoria Neerlandica* 7: 624–28. Tr. W. L. Bredenhof.

De Condorcet, Marquis. (1998). *Sketch for a Historical Picture of the Progress of the Human Mind*. In: *Readings on Human Nature*. Ed. Peter Loptson. Peterborough: Broadview Press. Pp. 125–28.

De Jong, Peter. (ed.). (1968). *Crisis in the Reformed Churches: Essays in Commemoration of the Great Synod of Dort, 1618–1619*. Grand Rapids: Reformed Fellowship.

DeLillo, Don. (1986). *White Noise*. New York: Penguin Books.

Descartes, Rene (1984). *The Philosophical Writings of Descartes*. Vol. 3. Ed. Anthony Kenny. Cambridge: Cambridge University Press.

De Vries, Peter. (2005). *The Blood of the Lamb*. Chicago: University of Chicago Press.

Dostoyevsky, Fyodor. (2009). *The Brothers Karamazov*. Tr. Constance Garnett. Lawrence, KS: Digireads.com Publishing.

Double, Richard. (1995). "Libertarianism and Rationality." In: Timothy O'Conner (ed.). *Agents, Causes, & Events: Essays on Indeterminism and Free Will*. Oxford: Oxford University Press.

Draper, Paul. (1996). "Pain and Pleasure: An Evidential Problem for Theists." In: Daniel Howard-Snyder (ed.). *The Evidential Argument from Evil*. Bloomington: Indiana University Press. Pp. 12–29.

——— (1996). "The Skeptical Theist." In: Daniel Howard-Snyder (ed.). *The Evidential Argument from Evil*. Bloomington: Indiana University Press. Pp. 175–92.

Dulon, G. (1971). "ὁρίζω." In: Colin Brown (ed.). *The New International Dictionary of New Testament Theology*. Vol. 1. Grand Rapids: Zondervan.

Dunn, James. (1997). *The Acts of the Apostles*. Harrisburg, PA: Trinity Press International.

Edwards, Jonathan. (2000). *A Dissertation Concerning the Nature of True Virtue*. In: *The Works of Jonathan Edwards*. Vol. 1. Peabody, MA: Hendrickson.

——— (2000). *Freedom of the Will*. In: *The Works of Jonathan Edwards*. Vol. 1. Peabody, MA: Hendrickson.

Eichrodt, Walter. (1967). *Theology of the Old Testament*. Vol. 2. Tr. J. A. Baker. Philadelphia: Westminster Press.

Eldredge, John. (2004). *Epic: The Story God Is Telling*. Nashville: Thomas Nelson.

Epictetus. (1866). *The Works of Epictetus*. Tr. T. W. Higginson. Boston: Little and Brown.

Epicurus. (1926). *Epicurus: The Extant Remains*. Tr. Cyril Bailey. Oxford: Clarendon Press.

Evans, Gillian, Alister McGrath, and Alan Galloway. (1986). *The Science of Theology*. Vol. 1. Grand Rapids: Eerdmans.

Feinberg, John. (1997). *Deceived by God? A Journey Through Suffering*. Wheaton, IL: Crossway.

———— (2001). *No One Like Him: The Doctrine of God*. Wheaton, IL: Crossway.

Finney, Charles. (1994). *Finney's Systematic Theology*. 3rd ed. Ed. Dennis Carroll. Minneapolis: Bethany House.

Fischer, John Martin. (1994). *The Metaphysics of Free Will: An Essay on Control*. Aristotelian Society Series. Vol. 15. Oxford: Blackwell Publishers.

Fitzmeyer, Joseph. (1998). *The Acts of the Apostles*. New Haven, CT: Yale University Press.

Flathman, Richard. (1973). *Political Obligation*. New York: Taylor & Francis.

Flew, Anthony. (1955). "Divine Omnipotence and Human Freedom." In: Anthony Flew and Alasdair MacIntyre (eds). *New Essays in Philosophical Theology*. New York: Macmillan. Pp. 144–69.

Flint, Thomas. (1988). "Two Accounts of Providence." In: Thomas V. Morris (ed.). *Divine and Human Action*. Ithaca, NY: Cornell University Press.

Floyd, William. (1971). *Clement of Alexandria's Treatment of the Problem of Evil*. Oxford: Oxford University Press.

Frame, John. (2001). *No Other God: A Response to Open Theism*. Phillipsburg, NJ: P&R Publishing.

Frankfurt, Harry. (2003). "Freedom of the Will and the Concept of a Person." In: Gary Watson (ed.). *Free Will*. 2nd ed. Oxford: Oxford University Press. Pp. 81–95.

Geisler, Norman. (1999). *Chosen But Free*. Minneapolis: Bethany House.

Goshen-Gottstein, M. (1984). "The Theocentric Trend in Ezekiel's Prophecies." *Interpretation* 38: 181–208.

Gould, Josiah B. (1970). *The Philosophy of Chrysippus*. New York: State University of New York Press.

Graham, Gordon. (2001). *Evil and Christian Ethics*. Cambridge: Cambridge University Press.

Greene, W. C. (1994). *Moira: Fate, Good, and Evil in Greek Thought*. Cambridge, MA: Harvard University Press.

Grenz, Stanley. (1994). *Theology for the Community of God*. Nashville: Broadman & Holman.

Grudem, Wayne. (1994). *Systematic Theology*. Grand Rapids: Zondervan.

Gundry, Robert. (1994). *A Survey of the New Testament*. 3rd ed. Grand Rapids: Zondervan.

Günther, W., and H. G. Link. (1971). "Love." In: Colin Brown (ed.). *The New International Dictionary of New Testament Theology*. Vol. 2. Grand Rapids: Zondervan.

Guthrie, Donald. (1970). *New Testament: Introduction*. Downers Grove, IL: InterVarsity Press.

Haenchen, Ernst. (1966). "The Book of Acts as Source Material for the History of Earliest Christianity." In: Leander E. Keck and J. Louis Martyn (eds). *Studies in Luke-Acts*. Nashville: Abingdon. Pp. 258–78.

——— (1971). *The Acts of the Apostles: A Commentary*. Louisville: Westminster/John Knox Press.

Haji, Ishtiyaque. (1998). *Moral Appraisability: Puzzles, Proposals and Perplexities*. New York: Oxford University Press.

Hand, Thomas. (1986). *Augustine on Prayer*. New York: Catholic Book Publishing.

Hare, John. (2000). "Naturalism and Morality." In: William Lane Craig and J. P. Moreland (eds). *Naturalism: A Critical Analysis*. London: Routledge.

Harnack, Adolph. (1961). *History of Dogma*. Tr. James Millar. New York: Dover.

Harrison, Everett. (1976). *Romans-Galatians.* The Expositor's Bible Commentary. Vol. 10. Ed. Frank E. Gaebeleien. Grand Rapids: Zondervan.

Harrison, Jonathan. (1999). *God, Freedom and Immortality.* Avebury Series in Philosophy. Burlington, VT: Ashgate Publishing.

Harrison, Simon. (1999). "Do We Have a Will?" In: Gareth Matthews (ed.). *The Augustinian Tradition: Philosophical Traditions, 8.* Berkeley: University of California Press, 1999. Pp. 195–205.

Hasker, William. (1999). *The Emerging Self.* Ithaca, NY: Cornell University Press.

———— (2003). "Is Free-Will Theism Religiously Inadequate: A Reply to Ciocchi." *Religious Studies* 39: 431–40.

Hatch, James Edwin. (1892). *The Influence of Greek Ideas and Their Usages Upon the Christian Church.* 4th ed. London: Williams and Norgate.

Hayes, Zachary. (1989). *Vision of a Future: A Study of Christian Eschatology.* Collegeville, MN: The Liturgical Press.

Helm, Paul. (1974). "God and Free Will." *Sophia* 13: 16–19.

Hendricks, M. Elton. (1983). "John Wesley and Natural Theology." *Wesley Theological Journal* 18: 7–17.

Henry, Margaret Y. (1927). "Cicero's Treatment of the Free Will Problem." In: *Transactions and Proceedings of the American Philological Association* 58: 32–42.

Hofius, O. (1977). "Erwählung und Bewahrung. Zur Auslegung von Joh. 6, 37." *Theologische Beiträge* 8: 24–29.

Hallie, Philip. (2004). "From Cruelty to Goodness." In: Christina Sommers and Fred Sommers (eds). *Vice & Virtue in Everyday Life: Introductory Readings in Ethics.* 6th ed. Belmont, CA: Wadsworth. Pp. 4–16.

Hume, David. (1980). *Dialogues Concerning Natural Religion.* Ed. Norman Kemp Smith. Indianapolis: Bobbs-Merril.

Hunt, Dave. (2002). *What Love Is This? Calvinism's Misrepresentation of God.* Sisters, OR: Loyal Publishing.

Irwin, T. (1992). "Who Discovered the Will?" *Philosophical Perspectives* 6: 453–73.

Johnstone, Patrick. (1993). *Operation World*. Grand Rapids: Zondervan.

Joly, Robert. (1968). *Le vocabulaire chretien de l'amour est-il original? Phlein et Agapen dans le grec antique*. Brussels: Presses Universitaires.

Josephus. (1981). *Antiquities of the Jews*. In: *Josephus: Complete Works*. Tr. William Whiston. Grand Rapids: Kregel.

Joyce, Paul. (1989). "Divine Initiative and Human Response in Ezekiel." In: *Journal for the Study of the Old Testament Supplemental Series*. Sheffield: Academic Press.

Kahn, Charles. (1988). "Discovering the Will: From Aristotle to Augustine." In: C. Dillon (ed.). *Eclecticism: Studies in Later Greek Philosophy*. Berkeley: University of California Press.

Kaiser, Walter C. (1995). *The Messiah in the Old Testament*. Studies in Old Testament Biblical Theology. Grand Rapids: Zondervan.

Kane, Robert. (1985). *Free Will and Values*. Albany: SUNY Press.

——— (1995). "Two Kinds of Incompatibilism." In: Timothy O'Conner (ed.). *Agents, Causes, and Events: Essays on Indeterminism and Free Will*. Oxford: Oxford University Press. Pp. 115–50.

——— (1996). *The Significance of Free Will*. New York: Oxford University Press.

Kant, Immanuel. (1953). *Critique of Pure Reason*. Tr. Norman Kemp Smith. London: Macmillan.

——— (1960). *Religion within the Limits of Reason Alone*. Tr. Theodore Greene and Hoyt Hudson. New York: Harper and Row.

Kekes, John. (1990). *Facing Evil*. Princeton, NJ: Princeton University Press.

——— (1998). "The Reflexivity of Evil." *Social Philosophy and Policy: Virtue and Vice* 15: 222–32.

Kempis, Thomas à. (1856). *The Imitation of Christ*. Tr. John Payne. Boston: Gould and Lincoln.

Kistemaker, Simon. (1991). *Acts*. New Testament Commentary. Grand Rapids: Baker Books.

Kripke, Saul. (1980). *Naming and Necessity*. Cambridge, MA: Harvard University Press.

Larkin, William J. (1995). *Acts*. The IVP New Testament Commentary
     Series. Ed. Grant Osborne. Downers Grove, IL: InterVarsity Press.

Larrimore, Mark. (2004). "Autonomy and the Invention of Theodicy."
     In: Natalie Brealer (ed.). *New Essays on the History of Autonomy:
     A Collection Honoring J. B. Shneewind*. Cambridge: Cambridge
     University Press. Pp. 61–91.

Leibniz, Gottfried. (1985). *Theodicy*. Tr. E. M. Huggard. LaSalle, IL: Open
     Court.

Lewis, C. S. (1952). *Mere Christianity*. New York: MacMillan.

——— (2000). *A Grief Observed*. San Francisco: HarperCollins.

Lüdemann, Gerd. (1989). *Early Christianity According to the Traditions in
     Acts: A Commentary*. London: SCM Press.

Lundin, Roger, A. C. Thiselton, and C. Walhout. (1985). *The Responsibility
     of Hermeneutics*. Grand Rapids: Eerdmans.

——— (1991). "Hermeneutics." In: *Contemporary Literary Theory: A
     Christian Appraisal*. Grand Rapids: Eerdmans.

Luther, Martin. (1957). *Bondage of the Will*. Tr. J. I. Packer and O. R.
     Johnston. Weswood, NJ: Revell.

——— (1961). *Bondage of the Will*. In: *Martin Luther: Selections from His
     Writings*. Ed. John Dillenberger. Garden City, NY: Anchor Books.

MacArthur, John. (1994). *Acts 1–12*. The MacArthur New Testament
     Commentary. Chicago: Moody.

MacGregor, Geddes. (1975). *He Who Lets Us Be: A Theology of Love*. New
     York: The Seabury Press.

Mackie, J. L. (1955). "Evil and Omnipotence." *Mind* 64: 200–12.

Marsden, George. (2003). *Jonathan Edwards: A Life*. New Haven, CT: Yale
     University Press.

Marshall, I. Howard. (1975). "Predestination in the New Testament."
     In: Clark Pinnock (ed.). *Grace Unlimited*. Minneapolis: Bethany
     House.

——— (1980). *Acts*. Grand Rapids: Eerdmans.

Martin, Michael. (1990). *Atheism: A Philosophical Justification*.
     Philadelphia: Temple University Press.

McGrath, Alister. (1998). *Historical Theology: An Introduction to the History of Christian Thought.* Oxford: Wiley-Blackwell.

——— (2010). *Christian Theology.* Hoboken, NJ: John Wiley & Sons.

Michalson, Gordon. (1999). *Kant and the Problem of God.* Oxford: Blackwell.

Miethe, Terry. (1989). "The Universal Power of the Atonement." In: Clark Pinnock (ed). *The Grace of God, the Will of Man: A Case for Arminianism.* Grand Rapids: Zondervan.

Millar, J. Gary. (1998). *Now Choose Life: Theology and Ethics in Deuteronomy.* New Studies in Biblical Theology. Grand Rapids: Eerdmans.

Miller, Patrick. (1990). *Deuteronomy.* Philadelphia: Westminster Press.

Missler, Chuck. (1995). *The Sovereignty of Man: Supplemental Notes.* Coeur d'Alene, ID: Koinonia House.

Moltmann, Jürgen. (1990). *The Crucified God.* San Francisco: HarperSanFransisco.

Monod, Jacques. (1972). *Chance and Necessity.* New York: Vintage Books.

Moreland, J. P., and Scott Rae. (2000). *Body & Soul: Human Nature & Crisis in Ethics.* Downers Grove, IL: InterVarsity.

Moreland, J. P. (2002). "Miracles, Agency, and Theistic Science: A Reply to Steven B. Cowan." In: *Philosophia Christi*, 4: 139–60.

Morris, Leon. (1957). *The Epistles of Paul to the Thessalonians.* Tyndale New Testament Commentaries. Grand Rapids: Eerdmans.

Mulholland, Leslie. (1991). "Freedom and Providence in Kant's Account of Religion: The Problem of Expiation." In: Philip Rossi and Michael Wreen (eds). *Kant's Philosophy of Religion Reconsidered.* Bloomington: Indiana University Press. Pp. 77–102.

Muller, Richard. (1985). *Dictionary of Latin and Greek Theological Terms Drawn Principally from Protestant Scholastic Theology.* Grand Rapids: Baker Books.

Nygren, Anders. (1953). *Agape and Eros.* Tr. Philip Watson. Philadelphia: Westminster.

O'Conner, Timothy. (2000). *Persons and Causes: The Metaphysics of Free Will.* Oxford: Oxford University Press.

O'Keefe, Timothy. (2005). *Epicurus on Freedom*. Cambridge: Cambridge University Press.

Osborn, Eric (1981). *The Beginning of Christian Philosophy*. Cambridge: Cambridge University Press.

Owen, John. (1989). *A Display of Arminianism*. Edmonton: Still Water Revival Books.

———— (2004). *The Mortification of Sin*. Edinburgh: Banner of Truth.

Packer, J. I. (1961). *Evangelism & the Sovereignty of God*. Downers Grove, IL: InterVarsity Press.

Petrik, James. (2000). *Evil Beyond Belief*. Armonk, NY: M. E. Sharp.

Pinnock, Clark. (1986). "God Limits His Knowledge." In: David Basinger and Randall Basinger (eds). *Predestination and Free Will: Four Views of Divine Sovereignty and Human Responsibility*. Downers Grove, IL: InterVarsity.

———— (1989). "From Augustine to Arminius: A Pilgrimage in Theology." In: Clark Pinnock (ed.). *The Grace of God, the Will of Man: A Case for Arminianism* Grand Rapids: Zondervan.

Piper, John. (2000). "Are There Two Wills in God?" In: Thomas Schreiner and Bruce Ware (eds). *Still Sovereign: Contemporary Perspectives on Election, Foreknowledge, and Grace*. Grand Rapids: Baker Books.

———— (2011). *Desiring God: Meditations of a Christian Hedonist*. 25th Anniversary Reference Edition. Colorado Springs, CO: Multnomah.

Plantinga, Alvin. (1974). *God, Freedom and Evil*. New York: Harper and Row.

———— (1978). *The Nature of Necessity*. Oxford: Oxford University Press.

———— (1990). *God and Other Minds: A Study of the Rational Justification of Belief in God*. Ithaca, NY: Cornell University Press.

———— (1996). "Epistemic Probability and Evil." In: Daniel Howard-Snyder (ed.). *The Evidential Argument from Evil*. Bloomington: Indiana University Press. Pp. 69–96.

———— (1996). "On Being Evidentially Challenged." In: Daniel Howard-Snyder (ed.). *The Evidential Argument from Evil*. Bloomington: Indiana University Press. Pp. 244–61.

———— (2000). *Warranted Christian Belief*. Oxford: Oxford University Press.

Pohlenz, Max. (1966). *Freedom in Greek Life and Thought: The History of an Ideal*. Tr. C. Lofmark. Dordrecht: D. Reidel.

Polhill, John B. (1992). *Acts*. The New American Commentary. Vol. 26. Nashville: Broadman & Holman.

Rakestraw, Robert. (1984). "John Wesley as a Theologian of Grace." *Journal of the Evangelical Theological Society* 27: 196–99.

Reichenbach, Bruce. (1986). "Bruce Reichenbach's Response." In: David Basinger and Randall Basinger (eds). *Predestination & Free Will: Four Views of Divine Soveriegnty & Human Freedom*. Downers Grove, IL: InterVarsity.

Richard, E. J. (1995). "First and Second Thessalonians." In: Daniel Harrington (ed.). *Sacra Pagina*. Vol. 11. Collegeville, MN: The Liturgical Press.

Ricoeur, Paul. (1985). "Evil: A Challenge to Philosophy and Theology." *Journal of the American Academy of Religion* LIII: 633–48.

Rossi, Philip. (2004). "Kant's Philosophy of Religion." In: Edward Zalta (ed.). *The Stanford Encyclopedia of Philosophy*. Stanford: Stanford University Press.

Rossi, Philip, and Michael Wreen. (eds). (1991). *Kant's Philosophy of Religion Reconsidered*. Bloomington: Indiana University Press.

Rowe, William. (1996). "The Evidential Argument from Evil: A Second Look." In: Daniel Howard-Snyder (ed.). *The Evidential Argument from Evil*. Bloomington: Indiana University Press. Pp. 262–84.

———— (1996). 'The Problem of Evil and Some Varieties of Atheism.' In: Daniel Howard-Snyder (ed.). *The Evidential Argument from Evil*. Bloomington: Indiana University Press. Pp. 1–11.

Ruble, Richard. (1976). "Determinism vs. Free Will." *Journal of the American Scientific Affiliation* 28: 70–76.

Ruse, Michael. (2002). "Darwinism and Christianity Redux: A Response to My Critics." In: *Philosophia Christi* 4: 189–94.

Ruse, Michael, and E. O. Wilson. (1993). "The Evolution of Ethics." In: J. E. Huchingson (ed.). *Religion and the Natural Sciences*. Orlando: Harcourt Brace. Pp. 308–11.

Sanders, John. (1998). *The God Who Risks: A Theology of Providence*. Downers Grove, IL: InterVarsity Press.

———— (2008). "Divine Providence and the Openness of God." In: Bruce Ware (ed.). *Perspectives on the Doctrine of God: Four Views*. Nashville: B&H.

Sarna, Nahum (ed.). (1996). *Deuteronomy*. The JPS Torah Commentary. Philadelphia: The Jewish Publication Society.

Savage, Denis. (1991). "Kant's Rejection of Divine Revelation and His Theory of Radical Evil." In: Philip Rossi and Michael Wreen (eds). *Kant's Philosophy of Religion Reconsidered*. Bloomington: Indiana University Press. Pp. 54–76.

Schaeffer, Francis. (1983). *How Shall We Then Live? The Rise and Decline of Western Culture*. Wheaton, IL: Crossway.

Schaff, Philip. (1848). "The Pelagian Controversy—A Historical Essay." *Bibliotecha Sacra and Theological Review* 5, no. 18: 205–43.

———— (1985). *History of the Christian Church*. Vol. 3. Grand Rapids: Eerdmans.

Schaffer, Harry. (1965). *The Soviet System on Theory and Practice*. New York: Appleton-Century-Crofts.

Schlatter, Adolf. (1948). *Der Evangelist Johannes: Wie er spricht, denkt und glaubt. Ein Kommentar*. Stuttgart: Calwer.

Schlesinger, George. (1988). *New Perspectives on Old-Time Religion*. Oxford: Oxford University Press.

Shmaltz, Tad. (2006). "The Science of Mind." In: Donald Rutherford (ed.). *The Cambridge Companion to early Modern Philosophy*. Cambridge: Cambridge University Press.

Schnackenberg, R. (1976). *Das Johannesevangelium*. Vol. 1. Freiburg: Herder.

Schopenhauer, Arthur. (1999). *Prize Essay on the Freedom of the Will*. Tr. Eric Payne. Ed. Günter Zöller. Cambridge: Cambridge University Press.

Schreiner, Thomas. (1995). "Does Scripture teach Prevenient Grace in the Wesleyan Sense." In: Thomas Schreiner and Bruce Ware (eds). *The Grace of God, the Bondage of the Will*. Vol. 2. Grand Rapids: Baker Books. Pp. 365–82.

Schwartz, Baruch. (2000). "Ezekiel's Dim View of Israel's Restoration." In: Margaret Odell and John Strong (eds). *The Book of Ezekiel: Theological and Anthropological Perspectives*. Atlanta: Society of Biblical Literature. Pp. 43–67.

Seeberg, Reinhold. (1977). *History of Doctrines in the Ancient Church*. Vol. 1. Tr. Charles Hay. Grand Rapids: Baker Books.

Seneca. (1887). *On Benefits*. Tr. Aubrey Stewart. London: George Bell and Sons.

Singer, Irving. (2009). *The Nature of Love: Plato to Luther*. Vol. 1. 2nd ed. Cambridge, MA: MIT Press.

Smilansky, Saul. (2000). *Free Will and Illusion*. Oxford: Oxford University Press.

Smith III, J. Weldon. (1964–1965). "Some Notes on Wesley's Doctrine of Prevenient Grace." *Religion and Life* 34: 70–75.

Sorg, T. (1979). "Heart." In: Colin Brown (ed.). *The New International Dictionary of New Testament Theology*. Vol. 2. Grand Rapids: Zondervan.

Sproul, R. C. (1998). *Willing to Believe: The Controversy over Free Will*. Grand Rapids: Baker Books.

——— (2001). "The Pelagian Captivity of the Church." *Modern Reformation* 10: 22–29.

Stott, John. (1994). *The Message of Acts: The Spirit, the Church, and the World*. Downers Grove, IL: InterVarsity Press.

Strobel, Lee. (2000). *The Case for Faith*. Grand Rapids: Zondervan.

Sterba, James. (2002). "Liberalism and the Challenge of Communitarianism." In: Robert Simon (ed.). *The Blackwell Guide to Social and Political Philosophy*. Oxford: Wiley-Blackwell.

Swinburne, Richard. (1991). "Necessary A Posteriori Truth." *American Philosophical Quarterly* 28: 113–23.

——— (1994). *The Christian God*. Oxford: Oxford University Press.

Taylor, Richard. (1974). *Metaphysics*. Englewood Cliffs, NJ: Prentice Hall.

Teggart, Frederick. (2009). *The Processes of History*. Charleston, NC: BiblioLife.

Tertullian. (1885). *Exhortation to Chastity*. In: *Ante-Nicene Fathers*. Pt. 4. Ed. Ernest Cushing Richardson, Bernhard Pick. New York: The Christian Literature Publishing Company.

———— (2004). *Tertullianus Against Marcion: Ante Nicene Christian Library Translations of the Writings of the Fathers Down To AD 325*. Part 7. Tr. Alexander Roberts. Whitefish, MT: Kessinger Publishing.

Thielman, Frank. (1994). *Paul & the Law: A Contextual Approach*. Downers Grove, IL: InterVarsity Press.

Turretin, Francis. (1994). *Institutes of Elenctic Theology*. Vol. 2. Tr. George Musgrave Giger, James Dennison (ed.). Phillipsburg, NJ: P&R Publishing.

Van De Beek, Bram. (1990). *Why? On Suffering, Guilt, and God*. Grand Rapids: Eerdmans.

Van Inwagen, Peter. (1996). "The Problem of Evil, the Problem of Air, and the Problem of Silence." In: Daniel Howard-Snyder (ed.). *The Evidential Argument from Evil*. Bloomington: Indiana University Press. Pp. 151–74.

Van Til, Cornelius. (1947). "The Nature of Scripture." In: *The Infallible Word*. N. B. Stonehouse and Paul Woolley (eds). Philadelphia: Presbyterian & Reformed.

Vroom, Hendrik. (2007). "Sin and a Decent Society: A Few Untimely Thoughts." *International Journal of Public Theology* 1: 471–88.

Walls, Jerry, and Scott Burson. (1998). *C. S. Lewis & Francis Schaeffer: Lessons for the New Century from the Most Influential Apologists of Our Time*. Downers Grove, IL: InterVarsity.

Ware, Bruce. (1995). "The Place of Effectual Calling and Grace in a Calvinist Soteriology." In: Thomas Schreiner and Bruce Ware (eds). *The Grace of God the Bondage of the Will*. Vol. 2. Grand Rapids: Baker Books. Pp. 339–63.

Weaver, Rebecca Harden. (1998). *Divine Grace and Human Agency: A Study of the Semi-Pelagian Controversy.* Mercer, GA: Mercer University Press.

Wesley, John. (1979). *The Works of John Wesley.* Vol. 10. Ed. T. Jackson . Grand Rapids: Baker Books.

White, James. (2000). *The Potter's Freedom: A Defense of the Reformation and Rebuttal of Norman Geisler's Chosen But Free.* Amityville, NY: Calvary Press Publishing.

Whitney, Barry. (1998). *Theodicy: An Annotated Bibliography on the Problem of Evil, 1960–1991.* Bowling Green: Bowling Green State University Press.

Wierenga, Edward. (1989). *The Nature of God.* Ithaca, NY: Cornell.

Wiggins, David. (1970). "Freedom, Knowledge, Belief and Causality." In: G. Vesey (ed). *Knowledge and Necessity.* Royal Institute of Philosophy Lectures 3. London: Macmillan.

Wiley, H. Orton. (1952). *Christian Theology.* Vol. 2. Kansas City: Beacon Hill.

Witherington, Ben. (1994). *Paul's Narrative Thought World: The Tapestry of Tragedy and Triumph.* Louisville: Westminster/John Knox Press.

——— (1998). *The Acts of the Apostles: A Socio-Rhetorical Commentary.* Grand Rapids: Eerdmans.

Wolf, Susan. (1990). *Freedom within Reason.* New York: Oxford University Press.

Wolterstorff, Nicolas. (1991). "Conundrums in Kant's Rational Religion," In: Philip Rossi and Michael Wreen (eds). *Kant's Philosophy of Religion Reconsidered.* Bloomington: Indiana University Press. Pp. 40–53.

Wright, R. K. McGregor. (1996). *No Place for Sovereignty: What's Wrong with Free Will Theism.* Downers Grove, IL: InterVarsity Press.

Yancey, Philip. (2000). *Reaching for the Invisible God.* Grand Rapids: Zondervan.

Acknowledgements

In the words of Albert Schweitzer,

> Nothing that is done for you is a matter of course. Everything originates in a will for the good, which is directed at you. Train yourself never to put off the word or action for the expression of gratitude.

In that spirit, I would like to express gratitude to the many who directed "a will for the good" at me, making this work possible.

Dr. Hendrik Vroom of the Vrije Universiteit of Amsterdam supervised this work from a sketchy blueprint to the final product with patience, support, and insight. His constant encouragement to "go deeper," while recognizing that we always perceive "through a mirror dimly," was immensely helpful. This encouragement not only helped to move this text beyond much of the superficiality and hubris of early drafts, but also helped to move me beyond much of the superficiality and hubris in my own life and theology. I look forward to our reunion one day in the new heavens and new earth.

I would also like to thank:

Dr. Bram van de Beek, for his enthusiastic support of this work, his valuable critiques, and his willingness to take on a "co-debater" of far lesser knowledge.

Taylor Landry, for his diligence, editorial insight, and generous time investment without which this would be an entirely different (and almost entirely unreadable) book.

Joseph Mellema, Esq., for his willingness to "be in" the arguments and his editorial assistance that fundamentally altered the DNA of this work.

Aron Mckay, not only for his editorial input, but also for his conversations thirteen years ago (along with Jason Pfeiffer) that sowed the seeds of doubt about free will that have blossomed into this book.

Dr. J. P. Moreland, for modeling clear thinking as my mentor and now colleague at Talbot School of Theology, and for many patient dialogues about free will that powerfully shaped my thinking on the topic.

Milan Yerkovich, for his mentorship that helped to bridge the divide between my head and heart as I developed the "relational theology" of this work.

Henry Jansen, for his keen attention to detail and vast editorial expertise.

Zonneweelde, for their generous support that helped to make this publication a reality.

I am also indebted to my parents, Russell and Judy Williams, Dr. Jon Marshall, Dr. Michael Horton, Dr. James White, Sean Maroney, Fox Clark, Israel Gomez, John Reed, Henk Reitsema, Bobbie Clement, UNITE, and my dear students at Biola University.

Lastly, I thank my beautiful wife, Jocelyn, and our children, Gracelyn, Holland, Harlow, and Hendrik, who have taught me more about authentic love than all of the profound theological volumes combined. To my family, I most affectionately dedicate this work.

Thaddeus Williams
Talbot School of Theology
Biola University
La Mirada, CA

Index